911 208

SEXUAL COUNSELING

911 208

THE CONTINUUM COUNSELING SERIES

SEXUAL COUNSELING
New Expanded Edition

A Practical Guide for Those Who Help Others

EUGENE KENNEDY

CONTINUUM • NEW YORK

1989

The Continuum Publishing Company
370 Lexington Avenue
New York, NY 10017

Copyright © 1977 by Eugene Kennedy
New material Copyright © 1989 by Eugene Kennedy

All rights reserved. No part of this book may be reproduced,
stored in a retrieval system, or transmitted, in any form
or by any means, electronic, mechanical, photocopying,
recording, or otherwise, without the written permission of
The Continuum Publishing Company.

Printed in the United States of America

Library of Congress Cataloging-in-Publication Data
Kennedy, Eugene C.
  Sexual counseling : a practical guide for those who help others /
Eugene Kennedy — New expanded ed.
    p.   cm. — (The Continuum counseling series)
  Bibliography: p.
  ISBN 0-8264-0502-9
  1. Sex therapy. 2. Sex counseling. I. Title. II. Series.
RC557.K46 1989
616.85'83—dc19   88-38322
                                                              CIP

Portions of this book appeared first in *Insights*, copyright
© 1974 by the Thomas More Association, 180 N. Wabash,
Chicago, Illinois 60601. Used by permission.

For Sara—with thanks to Maggie

Contents

Introduction

THIS book has not been written for some grand purpose of persuasion nor, indeed, for any of the various political reasons to which writing on sexuality has been recently addressed. Neither is this a guide for sexual happiness nor a manual to justify every would-be counselor's transformation into the role of sex therapist. It has been prepared not for those who ambition the destiny of supervising or re-shaping the sexual lives of others but for persons, various in their main occupations, who meet and must respond in some fashion as counselors to men and women with sexual conflicts and symptomatic complaints. It is a book conceived during the preparation of a more general book on counseling principles for non-professional counselors.* It complements that volume as an introduction to understanding and responding to sexual problems as they are encountered by educators, clergy, general physicians, and even lawyers in their everyday work.

To this end I have treated a number of specific sexual difficulties and related psychological variables, such as the question of transference, because these represent realities with which so many helpers must deal on a regular basis. This is not a how-to-do-it book for the perennial menace to American well-being, the amateur therapists who cannot balance their almost passionate need to help others with the actual needs of those seeking help. One hopes that this book will even discourage these psychological marauders from forcing their attentions and their philosophies on unsuspecting clients. The fact remains, however, that most of the black-and-blue trauma of ordinary living is revealed first to non-professional counselors; this includes the minister of religion, the counselor at law, the boss on the

*See Eugene Kennedy, *On Becoming a Counselor* (New York: Continuum, 1976).

job, and the coach in the locker room. People want to tell others the story of their lives and something of the special agonies they suffer in trying to understand or to express their sexuality. They want to tell of the problems they have in just being human. They are not sure to whom they should turn and, for fear that they might imprudently invite unnecessary dread by speaking to a highly trained expert in psychology, they turn to someone they trust even when that person does not have the full technical qualifications to assist them.

The trust thus invested is the main therapeutic strength of these troubled individuals, it is the best of the energies they need to deal constructively with their problem. It is never easy for these persons to talk about themselves because they usually lack language that is specific enough to describe their sexual distress except in simple or, at times, symbolic form. What counts is their willingness to talk about themselves in general and their readiness to travel the furthest route of truth in describing themselves. In general, people want to tell the truth about themselves, even though they do this in confusing and contradictory ways. Helpers must be able to catch at least the broad outlines of their clients' life stories, incorporating the sexual uncertainty or conflict in their overall understanding of them, in order to be of some help. There is enormous benefit for the troubled individual—even when there is no immediate solution to the specific difficulty— in being heard, in that mysterious and transcendent experience of being received with respect and compassion by another human being. And the people who first hear these clouded tales of life are almost always non-professionals who need assistance in order to ground themselves in the sometimes obscure or at least unfamiliar ways in which these stories are narrated. With just a little more insight, technical information, and self-confidence, these non-professional counselors can respond in ways that are almost sure to be beneficial even when they may not be finally curative.

The first step is the accurate reception of the story; that is as simple and unsophisticated as getting its point, being able to grasp the essential purpose of its telling instead of becoming absorbed or distracted by its details which, especially in sexual problems, can so easily overcome the restraints on our curiosity. This ability to get the main idea of the other's life may be a special strength of those who have not had much professional training. Theories and preconceptions do not clutter their consciousness nor clog the pores of their understanding. Undergraduate students in counseling often make better and more natural responses to troubled people than do more advanced graduate students. The latter carry a greater burden of trying to make a clinically correct or approved response, to prove their competence. The more naive, however, merely try to understand people and their responses are generally to the point of what is happening rather than to some subtler distorting need. Ordinary persons reach across acres of theoretical psychological complications to make successful human contact all the time and, like great natural athletes or actors, they do not necessarily understand the inner workings of their own technique. They are free of self-consciousness and their impact is greater for that. They may not be able to get far beyond catching the core of the other person's central conflict, but that is more than a minor accomplishment. Free of politicizing, innocent of theoretical insistence, they retain the bright primal powers of health and spontaneity as the chief ingredients in their gift of profound human understanding.

Perhaps only non-professional counselors can preserve something which some experts—awash in data, techniques, and a greening-of-America optimism about sexual experience—have clearly lost. That is the sense of the tragic in our existence which does not exclude the sexual dimension and does not promise it as an earthly paradise just waiting to be regained. Americans, it has been observed, have tried to solve too many problems through sex and, when this fails to deliver them from loneliness or alienation, their last state is more desperate than their first. Enthusiasm for personal redemption through more successful sex abounds; one need not downplay sex to understand that it cannot of itself provide complete and unending happiness. That is why persons with a broader view—and with less commitment to the eventual triumph of the therapeutic—may supply a sense of life and its complexities that sex therapy in itself cannot.

Educators, physicians, and members of the clergy may be able to season this newest of American dreams with an appreciation of the faulted landscape of the human condition, of the compromises that are our daily lot, and of the way things sometimes—most of the time—do not work out even for the most energetic and successful among us. Human sexuality must be seen in human perspective and, if it is no longer spoken of against the background of an original sin, it can at least be talked about as something less than the Utopia of the human potential movement. The new romantic perfectionism eclipses a feeling for the way people actually are and the way they live. Only counselors with a vision of our flawed situation can assist troubled persons to come to better terms with themselves and their sexuality.

The problem for most professionals who are not trained in psychology is, however, that they are trained in something else; they have a language and a vocabulary sometimes more dense than that of the mental health specialist. It becomes their native professional tongue, the source of the substance and shading of their construction and percepts of the world. Often enough, it is their own specialty that robs them of their single best strength, that of hearing another person with simple clarity. The minister, the priest, or the rabbi, for example, may structure his working environment with the concepts of sin and morality, the categories that are presumably his specialty, the themes of his training and perhaps even the language of his dreams. The greatest temptation for the clergyman is to interpret everything he hears in terms of these moral categories—to see a harlot or an angel on every streetcorner. And lawyers, twice literate, may cast everything in words that curl lifelessly when they find themselves anywhere but in writs and subpoenas. The visitor to the cleric's office may inquire about whether a certain sexual activity is "all right" or not, but this search for moral judgment may be the least of the threads of the story the person wishes to tell. The sexual conflict may be quickly labelled a serious sin—is there anything we feel more confident in judging?—but it may have the remotest relationship to sin and a larger significance in what it tells about the client's overall personality and struggles with life. Clerics who can withhold moral judgment can hear much more, and in the long run will understand more about the nature of good and evil, if they listen to whole persons whose sexual acting-out is merely one of their voices of protest, the faintest echo of the inner wounds that need to be recognized and healed.

Of course, not every clergymember proceeds immediately to judgment nor does every lawyer draw up an instant brief, but these are the responses they have been highly trained to give and, in the absence of other specialized knowledge about the language of sexual conflict, they may not know what else to do except to fall back on the still-lively old wives' tales and rumors that float like polluted ectoplasm above the ruins of history. Ill-informed advice is still given despite the explosion of knowledge about sexuality in recent years. Data have not been enough to lift the grey cloud of our unknowing about sexuality. This book is written to provide non-professional counselors with a key to the translation of the meaning of sexual conflict in some of its more pervasive forms and to enable them to respond more sensitively and helpfully to those who consult them. They are on the front lines of the human condition and they are frequently the only ones to whom the great secrets and small shames of life are disclosed. Their capacity to respond with human understanding rather than moral, legal, or educational judgment at these moments furthers the insight of their clients and, indeed makes more clear the limits and possibilities of the professional service they may otherwise render to them. The sexual problems of the people who seek out religious, legal, or other help are often the tender points of their personalities, the most available focus for other conflicts and rumbling dynamics. These problems may resolve much more smoothly if nonprofessional counselors do not focus too sharply on them, if they try instead to see them in the larger context of these people's lives.

The reflections on counseling sexual problems in this book are rooted in a dynamic understanding of the human person. We are, all of us, filled with wonder and contradiction, moved by forces of the unconscious that are not dead files but the living fibers of our personalities. That adds to our fascination and our mystery and suggests that we can never understand ourselves if we remain only at the surface of our behavior. Non-professional counselors who are able to develop a feeling for the complexity of the person, for the unique and inter-connected nature of human existence, immediately better their chances to comprehend the meaning of the sexual problems whose roots run so deep in the psyche. This is not to dismiss completely the behavioral treatment of sexual dysfunction which is described in this book. Genuine benefit can come from certain simple treatments of sexual complaints that are bothersome but rooted only superficially in personality. This is true even when there is no effort to provide insight into the underlying emotional causes of these complaints. But this treatment is likely to have difficulties even in those situations in which it is applicable if the counselors do not have a clear appreciation of the psychological factors that are significant in all treatment relationships. In any case, I do not suggest that non-professionals who use this book should engage in attempting to modify the sexual behavior of those who seek their assistance. They do need to understand its worth and appreciate responsible sources of referral for such therapy, but they should not attempt to offer it.

There are already too many self-defined sex-therapists offering a questionable blend of such services. It is an embarrassment to genuine professionals and a scandal that there are no better ways as yet to regulate the kinds of persons who may freely use therapeutic-sounding titles. Non-professional counselors need some sense of human dynamics both to grasp the potential significance of the sexual problems that are brought to their attention as well as some understanding of the legitimate resources, including symptomatic behavioral treatment, to which they may wish to refer troubled people. All of that requires good judgment, that distillate of maturity for which no prescriptions exist. There is little doubt, however, that a deeper sense of personality dynamics improves our judgment, if only because it makes us hesitate about making our usual mistakes.

Indeed, this book is written not to make ministers, lawyers, managers and teachers into experts on sex education and therapy, but to assist them in maintaining and deepening their own professional identities. It is a serious error to try to transform the judge into the surgeon or to make the special-education teacher into a member of the clergy. More information about human sexuality and the way it manifests itself in lives that may already be painful should help non-professional counselors to understand better what is actually going on inside those who seek their assistance, to sort out the underlying emotional stresses, to avoid making mistakes in judgment or action, and to make better decisions about the moral, legal, or educational needs of these seekers of advice. In other words, non-professional counselors can provide sensible responses to the specific sexual problems that come to their attention and also understand more clearly how they can best render their own professional services. They can also avoid entangling themselves in issues and styles of relationships that may only impede or compromise their best professional responses.

It is particularly important, for example, for non-professional counselors to develop some feeling for the nature of transference and counter-transference in helping relationships. Only the totally innocent or the insupportably self-confident get themselves involved in sexual counseling without some sense of the complex interplay of emotions, of the enormous relevant and powerful communication, intense and sudden sometimes, that takes place between patient and therapist. Many of the painfully involved relationships that at times envelop amateur counselors are seeded by a basic ignorance of the manner in which human beings affect each other at close range. Non-professionals who can operationally understand that a client comes with a psychological history that, in edited fashion, will be transferred to them right from the start will have a much better grasp of what is taking place, will maintain a better sense of themselves, and will avoid misinterpreting the transferred feelings as directed personally toward them. A large porportion of the conflicts that counselors themselves experience about the sexual attractiveness of their clients can be traced, not to something genuinely reciprocal in the relationship, but to the dynamics of transference and counter-transference that cause the eroticizing of the responses. When non-professionals can expect such things to occur and keep enough perspective about them not to feel either excessively threatened or enormously flattered, they maintain their own adjustment and are able, in the long run, to be more helpful to others. Half the office affairs of the world are not the stuff of romance but the erotic products, ground as fine as a powdered aphrodisiac, of the mills of transference.

And all of this is not without its relationship to our contemporary general mood about sexuality and human relationships. This is not a mood filled with sunlight or the bracing air of a fresh spring morning; it is one more of foreboding and ambiguity, of threats piled high as thunderheads at the end of a sluggish summer afternoon. Uneasiness outweighs peace and anxiety rages like the fire in a hearth furnace in the innards of the race. There is a growing feeling that this sexual revolution, like so many uprisings before, has left scattered bodies and shattered villages but nothing that could be called victory. The mood is one of disappointment that the liberalization of sexuality has produced little more than open pornography and grinding frustration. Human sexuality, human beings, deserve more than that and non-professionals may constitute our greatest resource in clearing the air and in assisting persons to come to better terms with the still shadowed mystery of their own sexuality. We need better informed people at all levels who can look at human sexual experience with an effort to understand it more patiently and without making grandiose promises that a new and totally untroubled day is dawning.

We are still very much at the beginning of understanding human sexuality and of speaking with greater wisdom about its moral and legal complications. Still less, even with the help of poets and novelists, have we been able to trace the manner in which it enervates personality or reflects and expresses so much of our longing and our loss. Non-professional counselors need not be complete experts in human sexual functioning—how few there are anyway!—to respond more effectively at every level on which they must face sexual problems in their clients. It is to assist in this larger purpose, as well as in the multiplied purposes of all the unnumbered counseling sessions of the sexually troubled, that this book is written.

SEXUAL COUNSELING

ONE

Basic Attitudes

HUMAN sexuality has been celebrated as a mystery. But it is also a puzzle both perennially and personally fascinating; one in which we are all involved. In order to be helpful we need accurate, up-to-date information about human sexuality. But, more important than this, we need to be sure of our attitudes and objectives in trying to help people with sexual problems. We need a philosophy or theology of human personality for this work, not in order to be moralistic, but in order to be realistic. Sexuality is a profoundly human function; we can only be helpful, then, if we have a thorough and practical understanding of the total personality.

There is a current mode of speaking about "sexual behavior"—which implies that what we do sexually has a life of its own. Such a term suggests that we can restrict our analysis to the behavioral level and not worry about the roots of our actions which are deep within our personalities. There is, of course, a sensible way of understanding such an analysis of human behavior—a helpful way, in fact, of using such information. However, people engaged in counseling—and by that I mean primarily para-professional counselors, such as teachers, clergy, doctors, nurses, lawyers, and even supervisors and managers—never deal only with behavior. They deal with human beings in whose lives sex is a significant dimension. This is why what counselors believe about human personality—the model of the person they use—is so significant in their work with individual sexual difficulties. We deal with persons caught up in a specific culture of a certain time in history, each with a separate set of experiences more complicated and interwoven than telephone circuitry. We must relate to people in all of their complexity, and be always ready to hear what is unique to them as they explore their confusions about or problems with human sexuality. The steady response of personalistic counselors is not to bodies or parts of bodies but to total human beings. To respond otherwise is to contribute to the segregation of sexuality from human personality.

In the same way, counselors must be ready to face their own blocks and difficulties so that they can take these into account or factor them out lest they interfere in a marked way with their assistance to others. Helpers need to listen as carefully to themselves as they do to individuals with sexual difficulties. Otherwise their own needs to solve or stabilize some personal problem may subtly become the dominant motive in their work. Counselors have to listen to all the messages from inside themselves so that they will not be deceived by the distortions that their own unrecognized needs can slowly build into their counseling work. They have to be prepared to deal openly with their own uneasiness or discomfort in the area of sexuality.

Despite all the talk over the last decade about the so-called sexual revolution, many persons, including counselors, still experience marked anxiety when something sexual is mentioned in conversation. This is why people make so many lame jokes about it. The uneasiness can't be willed away. We have to explore it to rid ourselves of it.

It is difficult to know which is more harmful in sexual counseling: embarrassed silence or misinformation. A bored or falsely blasé attitude is worse than either of these. We cannot expect to have all the answers about either our own sexuality or that of others, but we can develop a mature learning stance so that we are open to a steady discovery of deeper truths about ourselves and others in the course of this work. We are all on the same human journey together.

Another important concern for counselors is a frank and honest estimation of what they think they can do for persons with sexual problems. It is possible that some counselors, eager to solve sexual difficulties, may overcome the tyrannical old wives' tales of a previous generation only to commit themselves to new and uncertain notions about sexual functioning that are faddish in nature and, in the long run, no more helpful than the old distortions. Sexual counseling is one of the areas in which we need humane wisdom about the possibilities and limits of working with other persons. Such wisdom knows the attractiveness of fads and always seeks deeper and more lasting levels of human understanding. It does not settle for superficiality.

Our basic capacity to help others depends on the character of our own human presence in their lives; it is far more dependent on this than on the amount of scientific information we may have. One of the benefits of being well-informed about sexual matters is, of course, that it builds in counselors the self-confidence they need to enter into relationships easily and deeply. Nothing makes us more awkward than being only approximately sure of what we are talking about. Scientific information is as helpful to us as counselors as it is to our clients because it solidifies the human presence that is the core of our helping energy.

We help others with their problems when we possess our persons in such a way that we can enter into peaceable and understanding contact with them. If we offer only information but withhold ourselves, we diminish our capacity to assist other persons. Even the most sophisticated information can still be used as a shield to cover our own uneasinesses or our own preoccupations. Sexual information must be a blend, something integrated into our own way of making ourselves available to others. The self remains our most essential resource in assisting persons in distress of any kind.

American culture harbors an ambivalence toward authority. It dislikes it, tests it constantly, and yet, at certain levels, longs for its support and consolation. Counselors—especially those who also serve as clergy or educators or doctors—are, whether they like it or not, persons in authority. People expect them to know what they are talking about. People in general may have some hesitancy about authority figures, but are also ready to follow their advice and do what they say. Sometimes this is complicated by the fact that some people who come for help are more profoundly dependent than they seem on the surface. They are always ready to shift responsibility for their decisions and their lives to the counselor. This is a classic position, especially for educators and clergy who symbolize a certain tradition of belief and values as they stand ready to assist persons with sexual problems.

It is impossible for counselors to disown their authority. They must, instead, be ready to deal with the complicated issue of the attitudes people have toward authority, especially the need for dependence which many people may express in a disguised way when they come for assistance. Indeed, so central is the client's perception of the counselor as an authority that we must be carefully attuned to whatever issues may flow from this in counseling. Dependence, especially in sexual problems, may be a core difficulty that affects the counseling relationship directly but also reflects a basic problem such persons experience in their own life situation.

Counselors who deal with individuals with sexual difficulties must be *transference-sensitive.* They must, in other words, be ready to hear, right from the start, the sometimes faint signals about the psychological factors that lie beneath the surface. These shape the character of the counseling relationship while at the same time they convey something about the character of all other relationships in troubled persons' lives. To sort out their way of presenting themselves to us when we are in the role of authority, to judge accurately, for example, the possible conflict that others experience over dependence-independence, becomes the first order of business for the counselor.

This is merely one reaction that is possible in the context of a counseling relationship. Such interpersonal factors constitute the setting for the sexual difficulty, however, and if we are not sensitive to them we can miss the realities that stand behind the symptom that is presented to us. We enter a relationship and we recall that what people do to us in the course of the relationship is generally a fair sample of what they do to everybody. Because conflicts about independence-dependence can clearly be a factor in sexual dysfunction, we must carefully appraise the role which this possible difficulty may play in any relationship of which we are a part.

We do not help an individual, for example, by reinforcing dependency that is already at the root of their sexual difficulties. We do not unnecessarily amplify what they already perceive as a position of authority on our part. We cannot be blind to the impact of our position, the symbolic weight of our title, or of any of the many other factors that clearly affect helping relationships. This is merely a way of saying that we must be *person-sensitive* by being sensitive to the fact that being experts in some sense shapes the initial reaction of clients to us, whether we like it or not.

It is not possible to disown our authority. Neither clergymen nor educators can successfully deny that they stand for certain sets of values. These cannot be negated; they are associated with their professions and part of the reason that people come to them for assistance in the first place. Many persons, for example, come to clergymen because clergy represent the values of the culture in which they grew up and which they still respect. They feel they can depend on the clergy for an understanding of their life situation. People come to the clergy because they are already in a relationship through the habits and experiences of a lifetime. These things cannot be dissolved by clergymen asking people to call them by their first names, by changing their costumes or the design of their offices. The reality of the clergyman's position is always a factor; the more strenuous his efforts to deny it, the more clearly he may reveal his own conflicts about the situation —and all of this applies to a greater or lesser degree to other counselors who may be traditional authority figures.

Standing for values does not mean that the counselor has to impose them in an authoritarian way on other persons. Others do expect the counselor to be influenced by personal beliefs, however, just as they expect the counselor to defend the substance of the philosophy or theology to which he or she is committed. Counselors do not help anybody in any situation, sexual or otherwise, by uncertainty, passivity, or vagueness about the symbol system by which they lead their own lives. Counselors need not be moralistic to realize that they are almost always involved, to one degree or another, in moral issues with persons.

Most people not only want a better life through clearing up whatever problems may be troubling them most at the moment; they also want to do the right thing with their lives. They not only want a pleasurable life, but they are generally searching for the good life. They come to clergymen, teachers and other counselors because they expect them to be reliable guides in relationship to the decisions they make about their own existence.

Counselors cannot ignore the realities of this situation. Nobody can do our theological or ethical reflection for us. That is something we must carry out for ourselves. It will be part of our presence, however, and we always communicate what we believe whether we put it into words or not. If we have not formulated a clear position—if we are not sure of what we believe about the important issues of sexuality—then correcting this becomes our first business in preparing to counsel persons with sexual difficulties.

Perhaps most essential for the counselor preparing for this work is the realization that we deal fundamentally with a human problem when we deal with sexual difficulties. Any attitude that either excessively exalts or trivializes sexuality diminishes its human content and potential meaning. Counselors assisting persons with sexual conflicts are not preoccupied with solving only a few pieces in the puzzle of human nature. The counselor's whole personality, his or her entire life history, is in relationship with another highly complex individual or pair of individuals who cannot achieve wholeness by merely presenting symptoms. The achievement of a genuine wholeness of personality works to improve all individual human functions. The more we understand and prize human personality, the more effective we can be in our interactions even when people are talking about highly specific sexual difficulties. This is not just sexual "behavior." It is a special form of human communication, a statement about a person's own identity made by someone in distress. We are on the right track when we try to hear the whole person who makes that statement.

The best general instruction that can be given to counselors in the field of sexuality is not to be surprised at anything they encounter or anything they hear. Counselors may think, at some time or other, that they have heard everything. This is a false assumption; there is always something new to be heard, not only about sexual behavior, but about almost everything to which human persons can turn their attention. This is particularly true in the area of sexuality because this becomes the avenue of expression for a great many other essentially nonsexual conflicts and situations. A number of these will be discussed in succeeding chapters of this book.

As we listen carefully we begin to understand the complex language of sexuality. We can see more deeply into human personality, appreciate the pervasiveness of sexuality, and never seem either shocked or overcurious about the kinds of things that human beings can think about or get themselves into. Counseling persons with sexual difficulties is not for the naive or the easily shocked. Neither is it a very good field for those who rush to judgment about the moral good or evil of what people sometimes do sexually. Sexual problems are so often symbols of something deeper that it is unfortunate when helpers move too swiftly out of moral outrage to get people to change or modify behavior that they really don't understand. Taking our time prevents us from moving in too quickly with solutions which may be inappropriate and, therefore, unhelpful. We are always on a voyage with the other person toward self-discovery. It is a trip that requires our constant alertness and sensitivity far more than a panicked readiness to jump overboard at the first sign of heavy weather.

We commit ourselves to total persons, trying to grasp what they say about their whole selves when they struggle to tell us about their sexual difficulties. But we can't hear them if we listen only to their problems. Our question to ourself becomes: What are these persons trying to tell us not just about their problems but also about their lives? This question helps us to be *person-sensitive* as well as *transference-sensitive*—both indispensable aspects of our counseling work. Our effort to understand brings us ever more deeply into the existence of others so that we can gradually understand the meaning of an individual's difficulty in the context of his or her overall life. This is an objective toward which we must always strive.

We must understand the total person rather than just fix on a certain aspect of personality. We might well recall the words of novelist John Cheever in his resolution not to write steamy descriptions of sexual activity: "Out with this and all other explicit descriptions of sexual commerce, for how can we describe the most exalted experience of our physical lives, as if—jack, wrench, hubcap . . . we were describing the changing of a flat tire?" ("A Miscellany of Characters That Will Not Appear")

On the other hand, it is sometimes possible to respond to the sexual problem directly, without trying to go too deeply into underlying personality factors. In fact, this is precisely the attitude that many qualified sex therapists have, especially those who emphasize learning techniques in resolving symptomatic difficulties. These approaches are derived largely from the work of Dr. William Masters and Virginia Johnson and, to oversimplify they focus on assisting partners with sexual difficulties to "learn by doing" through a series of appropriate and graduated "learning" exercises. They emphasize the need for people to develop some skill in sexual relations comparable to the level of skill required in any other human activity. Sex does not take care of itself, in their judgment, and troubled persons can be helped enormously through techniques that are fairly basic and fairly simple. If sexual behavior is learned, then it can be taught. Faulty learning—

and persisting in maladaptive patterns—can explain many problems.

Such training for sexuality is generally carried out by very competent professional persons who also possess an understanding of deeper psychological dynamics. Indeed they use this understanding in trying to develop settings in which people can re-learn sexual behavior without the fear of failure or the pressure of other anxieties that may have previously inhibited them. The use of such techniques depends on a deep sensitivity to human beings as well as an appreciation of the role of learning in their sexual activity. Used by competent and ethically concerned persons, such techniques have proved extremely helpful to many troubled couples.

Two cautions are in order, however. First, most of the readers of this book do not work at this level with their clients and should not, of course, attempt to employ such techniques without proper training and evidence of qualification. Secondly, there are practitioners who set themselves up as sex therapists who do not have the competence or sensitivity to carry out such work. While there is presently the beginning of a nationwide effort to certify sex therapists, this is far from accomplished and counselors should employ prudence in making referrals for this kind of assistance.

The proper use of such procedures is very helpful. As Dr. Raul Schiavi, psychiatrist and director of the Human Sexuality Program at New York's Mt. Sinai Hospital, notes: "The main objective is a rapid resolution of the sexual problem. We employ basic behavior techniques that the couple can use in the privacy of their homes."

This direct resolution of a presenting problem does not disavow the presence of underlying psychological difficulties. Those who follow this approach believe that much can be accomplished by giving people the opportunity to learn or re-learn aspects of their sexual responsiveness without necessarily going deeply into other problems right away. While there is an emphasis on learning, there is a respect for the wholeness of persons implicit in the proper use of these techniques. Indeed, the basic premise is that we learn best when we don't have to prove anything and when we are free from crippling psychological expectations.

References

Bruch, Hilde. *Learning Psychotherapy.* Cambridge: Harvard University Press, 1974.

Cohn, Frederick. *Understanding Human Sexuality.* Englewood Cliffs, N.J.: Prentice-Hall, 1974.

DeMartino, Manfred. *Sexual Behavior and Personality Characteristics.* New York: Citadel Press, 1968.

Duyckaerts, Francois. *The Sexual Bond.* New York: Delacorte Press, 1968.

————. *Encyclopedia of Sexual Behavior.* New York: Hawthorn Books, Inc., 1961.

Engel, George. *Psychological Development in Health and Disease.* Philadelphia: W. B. Saunders Co., 1962.

Gagnon, John H. and Simon, William. *The Challenge to Man.* National Conference of the American Social Health Association.

Greeley, Andrew. *Sexual Intimacy.* Chicago: Thomas More Press, 1973.

Kaplan, Helen. *The New Sex Therapy: Active Treatment of Sexual Dysfunction.* New York: Brunner, Mazel, 1974.

Katchadourian, Herant A. *Human Sexuality: Sense and Nonsense.* San Francisco: W. H. Freeman, 1974.

Kennedy, Eugene. *The New Sexuality.* New York: Doubleday, Inc., 1972.

Kogan, Benjamin A. *Human Sexual Expression.* New York: Harcourt, Brace & Co., 1973.

Lederer, Wolfgang. *The Fear of Women.* New York: Grune & Stratton, 1968.

MacKinnon, R. A. and Michels, R. *The Psychiatric Interview in Clinical Practice.* Philadelphia: W. B. Saunders Co., 1972.

Maddock, James W. and Dickman, Deborah L. *Human Sexuality: A Research Book.* University of Minnesota Medical School, 1972.

Masters, William and Johnson, Virginia. *Human Sexual Inadequacy.* Boston: Little, Brown & Co., 1969.

————. *Human Sexual Response.* Boston: Little, Brown & Co., 1966.

————. *The Pleasure Bond.* Boston: Little, Brown & Co., 1975.

May, Rollo. *Love and Will.* New York: W. W. Norton & Co., Inc., 1969.

————. *Sexuality and Man.* Compiled by the Sex Education and Information Council of the United States. New York: Charles Scribner's Sons, 1970.

TWO

Sexuality: Faces and Masks

ALL that is genital, psychiatrist Judd Marmor once commented, is not sexual. Sex only seems simple. Nothing connected with human beings lacks complexity and sexual activity bears the weight of all that is unresolved and uncertain as well as everything that is rich and sure about human personality. Counselors must, then, avoid giving simple answers when the questions, even when they seem straightforward, are fairly complex. Neither can sexual difficulties be held in too fine a focus as "the problem." While the behavioral treatment of sexual difficulties has had promising results, the surface phenomena all too often reveal the mask rather than the true face of human sexual exchange.

Counselors need to work continually at understanding the many meanings of sexual transactions. Sensitive helpers place specific sexual complaints in the context of the personality and relationships of those who seek help. As they listen they detect problems that contain, in codified form, the deeper significance of the sexual symptom. Many people do not really understand the multiple strands of motivation that affect their sexual activity. Sometimes they sense its surprisingly driven quality and at other times they realize that sexual expression does something for them—expresses something—in a way that no other activity can. A mysterious, multilayered language, human sexuality; but few persons have a deep or clear picture of the way sex speaks for them. As counselors widen the focus of their attention from individual sexual activities to broader motivations, they begin to understand the person better. They appreciate better the human psychological style and they see sexual activity as an important aspect of this. Sexuality is not merely biological behavior without roots in human need. It is always a reflection, sometimes clean and sometimes shadowed, of overall personality functioning.

9

The understanding of sex and its many dimensions makes counselors or other advisors hesitate to recommend specific sexual practices as some kind of panacea for anxiety, lack of interpersonal communication, or for the relief of one's tensions. Sex has been advised for all of these reasons; such advice is still given by self-assured and supposedly experienced persons. They suggest, for example, that the hysterical woman needs "a man to make a woman of her." So too, others have advocated breaking through sexual repression as a way toward maturity and a full exercise of personal freedom. Others have emphasized the cultivation of sexual pleasure and its pursuit as the added ingredient that improves marriage and other relationships in contemporary America. Indeed, many of the books supposedly on human sexuality are addressed to persons who have larger problems with life but who turn to sex in an effort to improve their self-esteem and to work through many of their other difficulties in living. Sex as human deliverance is not a minor subject.

It is not the business of counselors to get into philosophical discussions with their patients about the role of pleasure in life. They can, however, help persons to hear their own almost secret distress, the conflicts that they do not quite understand but which are greatly involved in their sexual lives. One thing people do not need is more tension surrounding their sexual lives. Anxiety regarding the expectations of others and the need to perform well sexually is already widespread enough to be classified as epidemic. Neither do people need their sexuality transformed, as it often is these days, into a political weapon in the cause of others. There are those who know just how to manipulate the secret needs of people that get expressed through sexuality; they do this quite regularly, much to the confusion of the persons involved. What most people need in this difficult area is not excessive direction or supervision but rather some time and space in which they can begin to consolidate their sense of themselves and perhaps sort out the motivations that are caught up in their sexual activity. This is precisely the atmosphere which the para-professional counselor can provide. They need not have answers to every sexual question in order to be understanding of the total person who comes to them to search out the truth about his or her own life. Even relatively healthy people need the opportunity to do this. They do not need to be preached to again. They need rather the atmosphere in which to look more deeply at themselves to be able to possess their own lives more surely within a gradually deepened and consolidated sense of their own personalities. Para-professionals can be a great help to them without knowing everything about sex. Many of the complex motivations for sexual activity can be understood, not by directly digging into them, but by helping persons to grow in a more general understanding of themselves.

As they develop a better sense of their own identity, as they become more maturely free, they can drop the masks and live out their sexual lives with far less tension and conflict. They are at peace with who they are and therefore are more at peace in everything, including sex.

Sexuality is a special language and it speaks about more than biological behavior. It is a constantly informative human voice. Sexuality reflects what we are like, indicating what is strong and what is as yet unresolved about us. Even when counselors do not have all the specific answers for sexual difficulties they can listen carefully to the language and pick up the cues which tell so much about the person with whom they are working. Even when a counselor sees a person a few times, the nature of the sexual complaint in the way he or she speaks about it—the emotion that they express or discuss—is indicative of their lifestyle. Recognizing this pattern and listening for the echoes from the unconscious that are expressed through sexual conflicts enables counselors to avoid making mistakes and to assist persons to move, not just toward solving concrete symptomatic complaints, but toward a better understanding of their total personality.

What are some of the ways in which this language is spoken? Many people are currently frustrated because sexuality does not provide automatic happiness or successful human intimacy. Sex by itself does not deliver what they hoped it would. Perhaps all that they can present are the symptoms of dissatisfaction that arise when their sexuality does not seem to be integrated in their lives. This is not a place for counselors to be moralistic. They should not be interested, for example, in stopping people from performing certain sexual practices as much as understanding what factor leads them to these practices in the first place. A truly moral outlook does not stop short at the surface but tries to understand the inner motivations that lead people to do things which prove to be painful in their quest for happiness. Sexuality is a language that leads us deeper into people.

A superficial moral outlook is psychologically defensive. It protects people from looking directly at their conflicts, an experience that would produce excessive anxiety, while at the same time it tends to maintain or enhance their self-esteem. Self-esteem is often beneath a symptomatic sexual complaint. Some people use their sexuality to secure or bolster their sense of themselves. The sexual difficulty is not at all the problem that needs attention. People are struggling for something that is far more basic, something that can be achieved only through a healthier relationship with themselves and better inter-relationships with other persons. The use of sex in a defensive manner only retards the resolution of inner conflicts and leads to greater personal frustration. However, it is not enough just to tell people these things, because the problem is not just an intellectual one. They can agree to everything that is written here and at the same time find it impossible to make their way out of the confusing maze of their own unconscious motivations. They cannot understand their own sexual language. That is why they need counselors.

One of the most frequently observed uses of genital behavior for nonsexual reasons is in the effort to ward off or deal in some way with the fear of rejection. This, closely linked to self-esteem, is a pervasive and disturbing problem that affects a great many people, even those who on the surface may seem self-assured and sophisticated. They use their sexuality to get some reassurance that they are truly loved. Sexuality is not, in these cases, used for sexual expression or release but to deal directly with the crippling fears of rejection that affect so many people. This is particularly true for teenage girls who have a great need to be loved and wanted and, in pursuit of this, they may use their sexuality in a promiscuous manner. They do not enjoy it much and they do not achieve the kind of relationships they are seeking. The problem is not merely to stop them from being promiscuous —frequently that which is demanded by the pastors or the educator to whom these people may be referred—but to help them to understand their own needs for affection and the faulty manner in which they are attempting to meet them. Long-term counseling aims at more basic human problems than the symptomatic nonsexual use of sexual activity. Counselors who understand this difficulty not only help persons struggling with this problem but also assist their families and others connected with them to understand more subtly the nature of the problem. They are better equipped to assist these searching young people when they can appreciate and, through effective counseling, help the others to begin to appreciate what they are really looking for and why there is so much frustration for them when they cannot find it through the use of their sexuality.

Closely related to this, as Dr. Judd Marmor has observed (*Medical Aspects of Human Sexuality,* June 1969), is the use of sexuality as a defense against loneliness. This is not so much the fear of rejection as the fear of isolation and being cut off, ending up out of relationship and out of contact with others. Sex is often perceived as a cure for loneliness, but frequently ends up as a cry that is a symptom of emotional isolation.

One of the mistakes of, for example, self-consciously moral preachers is their misunderstanding of how people are motivated by the search for self-esteem and the staving off of loneliness in the use of their sexuality. The moralist condemns sexual promiscuity, branding it as evil or bad, and showing little capacity to understand how emotionally deprived people use sex in quite another way; to get out of it what they can only get out of a deeper kind of life.

Moralists would be far more effective by displaying an appreciation for the complexities of the human situation and of the way people can mistakenly attempt to use sex in their search for a happier life. The positive task of moral education depends on more than controlling sexual behavior; it rests on helping people to hear and understand the nonsexual uses of sexuality. Counselors who have any responsibility for a sex education program or for teaching courses connected with the values of human sexuality, cannot neglect this very central point. Too many human beings are deceived and hurt for life because they have not been helped to see these issues in better perspective. They cannot deal with loneliness through their sexuality alone. The problem is that such persons find that, although they have been intimate sexually, they remain strangers to each other. It is obvious that sexual activity may be momentarily satisfying, but that is not enough to provide the armor against isolation that they are really looking for. This, as I have said, is especially difficult for young women who are looking for a lasting relationship and who are sometimes persuaded to use their sexuality as a short cut.

Sexuality can, oddly enough, destroy rather than enrich human communication. If sex dominates the early stages of a friendship, for example, it undercuts the possibility of people getting to know each other more deeply. In a real sense, it keeps them strangers, relieving them of all the difficulties that are involved in developing a genuine relationship with somebody else.

Marmor also points out how sexuality is employed in an attempt to overcome feelings of inferiority. This is a problem for males in our culture and, despite the liberation of recent years, the situation seems not to have improved very much. If anything, more expectations have been made on men through developments like the women's liberation movement and the widespread interest and speculation about male sexuality. Many men still use their sexuality to reassure themselves of their virility. Although it has been pointed out endlessly that this use of sexuality is ultimately self-defeating, men do not always hear this quite clearly, especially when they are uneasy about themselves and lack confidence in their own judgment and human capacities. They often identify sexually with the conqueror role. *Don Juan* has reappeared many times in history, moving always from one woman to another, losing interest in each as soon as she has been conquered, and starting all over again in the quest for assured masculinity. Now that there are even greater expectations on male performance, his sexual anxiety has increased even more.

Men who are shaky about their own masculinity invest everything in sexual performance. Many observers suggest that it is this underlying anxiety and self-doubt that is related to many men's complaints of their impotence, premature ejaculation, or frigidity in their partner. When men fail in the test in which they have invested so much of their self-esteem, they become more anxious about future sexual performance. A vicious cycle develops that gives rise to additional anxiety which produces failure which, in turn, increases anxiety. Men caught up in this are actually caught up in themselves. They try to satisfy narcissistic needs and they frequently only defeat themselves. That is why there is still so much emphasis on the physical endowments and capacities of a man, even though it is widely understood that these, in themselves, have little to do with mature masculinity and sexual fulfillment. This difficulty haunts many immature men throughout their lives.

It may be a part of the motivation in their choice of immature girls as sexual partners. They do not have to prove themselves nearly so much when they have unsophisticated and naive partners and so they can feel at least temporarily reassured. The manipulation of other persons that goes into the maintenance of their self-esteem is enormous. It is a measure of the narcissism of such individuals that they can perceive the rights of other persons so dimly and can use them merely as objects to gratify needs that are basically nonsexual. Immaturity is clearly a basic problem here.

Obviously the problem is not just in their sexual behavior; it is deep inside themselves. There is no way to assist them merely by trying to change their surface habits. They need to deal with more basic issues about their own maturity. It is very difficult for such men to talk directly about their problems because this causes them the kind of anxiety they are trying to overcome. Outward appearance means a great deal to them. Counselors, therefore, need a subtle kind of understanding and acceptance that does not further threaten their masculinity.

Sex can also be used to express a person's power over others. This need to assert strength or dominance imprints a distinctive character on the sexual activity of those who, without much insight, employ their sexuality to express their unconscious striving for power rather than any true tenderness or concern for another person. Sexuality as an expression of power is obviously rooted in interior difficulties and conflicts which need psychological attention. The imbalance indicated in this misuse of sex for power can only be dealt with through more intensive personal counseling; hence the need for counselors to recognize what is really going on beneath the behavioral surface.

Closely related is the use of sexuality to express hostility or contempt for others. These conflicting feelings are expressed in sexuality that is used to punish others or to punish the self. The roots of sex used in this manner are very convoluted and, again, a more intensive kind of counseling assistance is required.

Society has, strangely enough, come to accept or at least to begin to look indifferently on much of the hostility that has been incorporated into contemporary sexual behavior. Many observers feel that we are caught up in a period of fascination with sado-masochistic sexuality that reflects some of the deep fears and difficulties that seem to be shared by a wide range of people. The primitive and undeveloped connection of eroticism with bondage, suffering, and violence is apparent in much contemporary entertainment as well as in a style of chic sexual kinkiness. For example, many young people have recently turned to so-called kinky fantasies about each other in order to arouse themselves sexually. This kind of distorted use of sexuality points back to unresolved personal and cultural issues. Such employment of sexuality is neither sophisticated nor sinful; it is first class evidence of major unresolved human problems. Counselors need some perspective on these issues—and on the people who may come to them with conflicts related to sex as an expression of hostility—if they are to respond wisely on a cultural as well as an individual level.

It has become almost unfashionable for people to examine the quality of sexuality that prevails between consenting adults. However, those charged with understanding and helping culture to mature must try to learn from the sexual styles of the day about the more basic conflicts that require attention in society. This does not call for a crusade as much as it does for both counseling sensitivity on an individual level and a more informed discharge of other professional obligations in the churches and schools on a public level. It is obvious that human sexuality cannot be taught as a behavioral subject isolated from the rest of human personality. Neither, however, can moral theology be taught or preached in the same isolated way. The more comprehensive approach to human personality requires a measured understanding of the symptoms that are presented regularly in the nonsexual uses of human sexuality. Every professional who counsels must take some responsibility in promoting positive sex education and in strengthening those institutions which seem crucial in helping people to develop more fully as sexual human beings. If we can strengthen, even a little bit, the maturity in each generation we will contribute much to the resolution of the difficulties that are manifested in the various ways that have just been discussed. This is a long and difficult process and one that does not take care of itself. It needs the balanced participation of a wide range of professionals—educators, lawyers, physicians, and members of the clergy—who help shape society and its values.

In this regard it is prudent to observe that these distortions of sexuality are spread along a continuum; at one end they are very intense and at the other only fleeting, if present at all. Most persons caught up in the use of sexuality for nonsexual reasons do not quite understand what they are doing. Everybody may occasionally have fantasies that are frightening or disturbing. Everyone's erotic interest may be piqued at times by things which they consider shameful or outrageous. It is only when these impulses and fantasies are acted out without much insight that we witness the frustrating and destructive effect of misunderstood human sexuality.

There are two major concerns which para-professional counselors need to reflect upon. The first is their ability to recognize what is healthy and what is unhealthy in human sexuality. We are not without the capacity to recognize this even though human sexual activity has been morally blurred in an age which has justified erotic turn-ons of almost any description. Educators and others do not have to apologize for defending healthy sexuality as a manifestation of genuine human development. When sexuality is part of a relationship that expresses genuine liking and responsible love between persons, then it potently reinforces, by its own depth, an already deep reality. When sex is used to express interpersonal guilt, hate, or some other form of hostility, when it expresses boiling emotions in one person that are not related to the good of the other, then the whole action suggests a lack of personal development. As Marmor notes (*Journal of The American Medical Association,* July 12, 1971, Vol. 217, no. 2), "Healthy sexuality seeks erotic pleasure in the context of tenderness and affection; pathologic sexuality is motivated by needs for reassurance or relief from non-sexual sources of tension. Healthy sexuality seems both to give and receive pleasure; neurotic forms are unbalanced towards excessive giving or taking. Healthy sexuality is discriminating as to partners; neurotic patterns often tend to be non-discriminating. The periodicity of healthy sexuality is determined primarily by recurrent erotic tensions in the context of affection. Neurotic sexual drives, on the other hand, are triggered less by the erotic needs than by the non-erotic tensions and therefore more apt to be compulsive in the patterns of occurrence."

One does not have to be rigid, authoritarian, or insensitive to maintain that there are some reference points that are vital in our understanding of human sexuality and the way that it expresses something deep about personality. One of the most important ways in which para-professional counselors assist culture in general and individuals in particular is through offering persons a deeper understanding of their sexuality as a source of personal revelation.

Counselors who are usually involved in other major responsibilities in the community can participate in the positive building of human relationships in a wide variety of ways. They can help all those movements which solidify the institution of the family or which help younger people to sort out and appreciate the kind of values that ultimately provide meaning, in a lasting sense, in their lives. While there is something to criticize in almost any movement that tries to support these vital institutions, it is far better for counselors to give their endorsement to activities such as marriage encounter movements or marriage enrichment programs which reflect, even in separate religious traditions, the purpose of integrating human values in a mature fashion. There will be a certain amount of faddishness connected with all such movements, but counselors cannot wait for the perfect organization to come along when the situation is so desperate and requires the cooperation of all healthy and balanced resources in the community. While educators cannot expect to see great successes in a short time, they can do much on an individual level to relieve the unhappiness and anxiety of people by helping them to understand better the true nature of their problems and by helping them to avoid the mistakes, especially in the area of sexuality, which merely compound their already painful difficulties.

References

Adams, W. J. "How Hidden Feelings Spoil the Sex Act." *Sexology* 35 (1968): 220–222.

Bell, R. R. and Gordon, M. *The Social Dimension of Human Sexuality.* Boston: Little, Brown, 1972.

Ellis, Albert. *Sex Without Guilt.* New York: Grove Press, 1961.

Demartino, Manfred F. (Ed.). *Sexual Behavior and Personality Characteristics.* New York: Grove Press, 1966.

Marmor, Judd, in *Medical Aspects of Human Sexuality* (June, 1969).

————, in *Journal of the American Medical Association* (July 12, 1971), p.217.

Stoller, R. *Perversion: The Erotic Form of Hatred.* New York: Pantheon Books, 1975.

THREE

Common Problems, Common Approaches

WHAT kinds of sexual concerns do people regularly bring to doctors, counselors, and clergy? It is helpful for all those called upon for help to identify these and to study the various issues involved with the particular problems or constellations of problems. Counselors can be prepared, for example, with accurate information, as well as a more finely tuned understanding of the potential dynamics that may be involved in any situation. With an informed anticipation of these common problems and the usual way in which people raise them, counselors are ready to respond in a truly human and helpful way.

Even in this sophisticated era people still approach sexual problems indirectly. They may say that they want to talk about a problem that "a certain friend of theirs" has or they may speak only in vague terms or in highly qualified suppositions. They may have a persistent physical or psychological complaint about which—despite efforts to deal with them over a long period of time—they seem to do little but move laterally in their conversations. It is still difficult, in other words, for most persons to talk about their own personal sexual difficulties. It has been observed that it is easier for some people to admit a crime than it is for them to admit possible sexual inadequacy or abnormality. Counselors must be prepared, then, to overhear the difficulty, to catch the outlines in the recurrent patterns of conversation, or in the protracted uneasiness about certain areas in clients' lives.

Counselors can gently sense the potential conflict, realize quite clearly that it is sexual, and still not force people to confront it until they are more comfortable with it. People are hesitant to talk because their sexual problems seem to be so threatening to their ego. Counselors should remain unhurried and make responses that identify the partially hidden areas of concern and acknowledge their clients' uneasiness in even beginning to talk about these. In this way they set the stage for clients to approach such difficulties at their own pace and from their own angle of vision.

Counselors may well ask themselves what the nature of the presenting symptom is. It may be a physical symptom that hints of a persistent problem in a marital relationship. There are few, if any, sexual problems that are experienced by only one of the partners in a marital relationship. But most people symbolize their difficulties because they cannot fully understand their unconscious roots and because it makes them too anxious to get too close to these areas. Physical symptoms that interfere with normal sexual functioning strongly suggest the possibilities of internal conflict about sex. Patients may also experience moral concerns that are difficult for them to verbalize. They may feel that whatever it is that they experience sexually makes them perverted, sinful, or estranged from most other people. It is very hard for them to bring such information out into the open.

When the vague complaints persist, counselors have a clue to the threatening quality of a possible sexual difficulty. There are other quite obvious indications of this at times. Occasionally, for example, a patient will seem to be quite seductive, acting out a sexual conflict so that counselors can hardly miss it. The issues involved even in this behavior, as I shall point out in a later chapter, are complex; counselors, far from becoming immediately defensive, must read this behavior accurately in order to understand and respond humanly to it.

As in other aspects of counseling, it is unfortunate if counselors respond as though they understood a problem when they really do not. If patients say, "Well, you know how it is . . ." and we respond because we do not wish to increase their embarrassment or engender any of our own, we are caught in a trap from which it is difficult to escape. This does not mean that we should ask direct or embarrassing questions about sex. Many experts believe that the technique of asking direct questions about sexual matters has been vastly overrated as a source of reliable information. People tend to defend themselves in this area quite carefully in order to preserve their self-esteem. It is far better to be sensitive and to let the issues emerge slowly. Sexual issues will become clear enough if we have the patience and subtlety of understanding to allow it to happen.

Counselors should not immediately consider sexual problems as either medical, moral, or informational challenges. The temptation to find easy answers to complex human difficulties is very real, especially when counselors are pressed for time or when their own uneasiness prompts them to deal with the patient as quickly as possible. Counselors do well to remember that every sexual problem includes medical, moral and informational aspects. It is all of these because it is, first of all, a human problem. It needs a response on a fully human level.

What are some of the questions and concerns people bring? They include the following: Am I Normal? This may be the concern that is most pervasive in the questions brought to counselors by men and women who are troubled by sexual difficulties. For a variety of reasons they are anxious about whether they compare favorably to other persons in the culture. This kind of anxiety has far reaching implications for their sense of identity and for the way they present themselves in relationship to others in life. A healthy resolution of such doubts is an enormously helpful contribution to the overall well-being of persons troubled by this concern.

Questions may center, for example, on aspects of a person's image of his or her body. People wonder if their sexual organs are like those of other persons or whether they are, by comparison, too small or otherwise inadequate; they wonder whether they are sufficiently attractive according to current standards of sexual development. Despite the fact that the myth about everybody being required to have sexual organs of a certain dimension has been challenged by science and found to have no substance, people continue to suffer from anxiety in this regard. Men worry about penis size, regardless of the fact their concern has very little scientific basis. They need reassurance in this regard just as women need reassurance about the size of their breasts or attractiveness of their own sexual organs. Sometimes people, driven by the pressures of the culture, suffer terribly through many years because of what they perceive as their own physical sexual shortcomings.

To have accurate scientific information at hand is, of course, important; but it is more important to be able to respond to the deeper areas of concern that are evident when these anxieties are mentioned. These concerns reflect a general feeling of inadequacy or an inability to meet what they feel their environment demands of a real man or real woman. A sensitive exploration of these concerns is far more important than reassurance, helpful though that may be. It is well known that people can be reassured, can even inspect the evidence that should dispel their fears, and because they are still not satisfied with themselves, continue to find reasons to raise doubts about themselves.

When a man wonders whether he is man enough, he doesn't need encouragement or a sermon as much as he needs someone sensitive enough to help him explore the reasons for doubting the adequacy of his masculinity. Such empathy is vital in counseling persons with sexual uneasiness. What are the roots of the fears they express? Only when these roots are revealed can these persons find lasting answers to nagging inner questions about their manliness.

Another way in which this doubt is frequently phrased centers on men's concern about whether they can satisfy a woman sexually. This is aggravated in an era in which cultural forces have overemphasized male sexual performance. Man is expected to be potent and to be able to produce an orgasm in a woman. This is one of the stereotypes that has emerged from the sexual revolution. There is a tyranny to it that intimidates many men who do not feel that they are as sexually vigorous as society expects. This is a clear case of a person whose chief problem centers on his self-image and self-confidence; these must be explored at a deeper level than that of reassurance or encouragement.

A further way in which this anxiety may be expressed, especially by women, centers on their fear of losing control of themselves if they freely experience their sexuality. What will happen if they let themselves go? Will they be overcome by this experience that receives so much discussion and about which such a persistent mystique exists in our culture? People wonder whether they can trust their sexual feelings or whether the very strength these feelings sometimes seem to exert on them is not terrifying in its insistent psychological and physical demands. Again, the important issue is whether these persons are really like other persons or whether they are different in a way that is destructive of their self-image.

Adequate information coupled with counseling sensitivity and understanding are essential because, despite the public explosion of information about sexuality, many people, especially young ones, still reach their adult years with a pitiful lack of understanding of basic sexual knowledge. As sex researcher Virginia Johnson noted a few years ago: "With all the freedom to discuss the subject of sex, we still don't find that much increase in knowledge. It is still a society that lives by illusions." Her colleague, Dr. William Masters, adds that "the greatest cause of sexual problems is misinformation, misconception, and taboo." This means that counselors should be well prepared with up-to-date information concerning the possible questions that might arise. Guessing won't do. Counselors need to continue to study and to keep up with the body of research connected with human sexuality.

Ordinarily, well-informed mature counselors do exactly this and are well prepared when they encounter people who misunderstand basic sexual information. The fact that contemporary culture seems obsessed with sex does not mean that it has been able to absorb correct information about it. This is partially explained by the many unconscious emotional blocks to understanding that still exist. Counselors must be aware of the fact that to tell people is hardly ever enough. The factors that interfere with their hearing and being able to learn must first be explored and dissolved.

Seeking advice about contraception is very common, especially among young people. Counselors must interpret the real meaning of these requests in terms of the way that they feel they, as professionals, are perceived by those who come to see them. A physician may well be perceived differently than a member of the clergy by a young woman seeking contraceptive advice. Physicians, therefore, may feel far freer to dispense contraceptive advice and may fail to appreciate the subtler issues which may still be involved in these inquiries even in a so-called liberated society. So, too, clergymen who may feel that they are being asked about the moral aspects of such a request must be aware of the other issues that may also be involved.

Some counselors have practically narrowed all advice on this question to the practical details of what pill or what other method of contraception is best for the individual involved. They perceive this situation as though the main question always centers on how to obtain sufficient protection to prevent conception. This narrowing of vision is true even of some clergymen and other educators who are convinced that the woman must be protected because she is going to have sexual experience anyway.

What are some other possible issues that may be present when people come for contraceptive advice? Frequently young persons perceive counselors, physicians or educators as authority figures and ask not only for information, but also for permission or approbation. Guides who are unaware of being drawn into the decision process itself may fail to respond sensitively because they are focused in another direction. Counselors must listen to more than the words of the questions asked by young people.

Counselors must be ready to let people explore what they really feel about their own participation in sexual intercourse, especially if this is before marriage. Frequently, young people have serious doubts which they suppress because of peer pressure. They get caught up in contemporary philosophies which make them feel, to give but one example, that they can never refuse what a friend asks of them. They may be in conflict and searching for someone to recognize it in a culture which no longer seems to feel there is any conflict connected with birth control. They may also feel in conflict with their own value system or their religious tradition. This is quite often the hidden issue when they come for advice to a member of the clergy.

Some liberated clergy may feel that it is old fashioned for people to have such concerns. Sensitive counselors recognize that these concerns do indeed exist and that young people must be given time to explore them in order to make up their own minds about how they are going to lead their lives. Frequently, young people consult clergy precisely because they want help in what amounts to forming their own conscience about these issues. They sometimes want someone else to present contrasting arguments to the ones which they hear from their peers all the time. The clergyman or woman who fails to sense this may miss the real issue at stake in the counseling; they may miss helping the person make some meaning out of his or her sexual experience.

Counselors may also find that the conflict is really one of *dependence* versus *independence.* Sometimes young people act out sexually in order to establish their independence from their parents or their cultural background. Counselors are failing their clients if they do not appreciate the nature of the concern. Counselors should be alerted to a conflict about independence if the person seems insistent on having the counselor take responsibility for his or her decision. To follow up on this difficulty with dependence is far more important than a quick endorsement of birth control or premarital sex.

The basic issue, which transcends the explicitly sexual dimensions of the person's problem, may well center on the individual's developing sense of personal identity. This is a difficult achievement as it involves all the complex psychological maneuvers that are involved in learning how to stand free from one's family of origin and to establish a new base for relationship with one's peers. While people want to be independent they may also experience feelings of wanting to be dependent on somebody else at the same time. These may be somewhat conscious feelings or they may operate out of the individual's awareness.

Growing persons, in other words, may be working steadily toward a healthy independence or they may be acting out an inner, unresolved conflict on the same issue. The roots and emotional surroundings of this conflict may be largely unconscious as they are, for example, with the obsessive person caught in the psychological dilemma of rebellion-conformity. The psychological conflicts with elements of dependence-independence are numerous, of course, so we should not be surprised to find evidence of this type of conflict in patients with sexual problems. Such strains are almost certain to manifest themselves in this intimate area. All the more reason, then, to listen carefully and not to presume that we know what the problem is in advance.

The resolution of dependence-independence may be common in the lives of relatively conflict-free persons as well. Sexuality requires persons to let themselves go with each other in ways that are healthily dependent. Persons who cannot let go, who refuse to open themselves to dependent experience in their sexual lives, have more basic conflicts with which to deal.

The very notion of coming to an authority figure—an educator or a member of the clergy—carries with it the possibilities of an independence-dependence conflict built into the relationship. When this is linked with a need for approval, it is obviously a psychological reality which must be taken seriously by counselors because of its implication for the course of treatment.

References

Allport, Gordon, *Personality: A Psychological Interpretation.* New York: H. Holt and Co., 1960.

Erikson, Erik H. *Childhood and Society.* New York: W.W. Norton & Co., 1963.

Eysenck, Hans Jurgen. *The Structure of Human Personality.* London: Methuen, 1970.

Gardner, Riley and Moriarty, Alice. *Personality Development at Preadolescence: Explorations of Structure Formation.* Seattle: University of Washington Press, 1968.

Hall, Calvin and Lindzey, Gardner. *Theories of Personality.* New York: Wiley, 1970.

Kelly, George. *The Psychology of Personal Constructs.* New York: W. W. Norton & Co., 1955.

Krech, David (Ed.). *Theoretical Models and Personality Theory.* New York: Greenwood Press, 1968.

Lidz, Theodore. *Person: His Development Throughout the Life Cycle.* New York: Basic Books, 1968.

Maslow, Abraham. *Toward a Psychology of Being.* Princeton, N.J.: Van Nostrand, Reinhold, 1968.

Masters, William H. and Johnson, Virginia, E. *Human Sexual Response.* Boston: Little, Brown & Co., 1966.

Murphy, Gardner. *Personality: A Biosocial Approach to Origins and Structure.* New York, Basic Books, 1966.

Mussen, Paul H., et al. *Child Development and Personality.* New York: Harper and Row, 1974.

Sullivan, Harry Stack. *Interpersonal Theory of Psychiatry.* New York: W. W. Norton & Co., 1963.

Trevett, Reginald. *The Tree of Life: Sexuality and the Growth of Personality.* New York: Kennedy & Sons, 1963.

Zubin, Joseph and Money, John. *Critical Issues in Contemporary Sexual Behavior.* Baltimore: Johns Hopkins University Press, 1973.

FOUR

Feelings About Sex

FEELINGS about sex need to be distinguished from sexual feelings. The former refers to our attitudes, some of them unconscious, about the experience of sexuality itself; frequently these are the stuff of counseling. People are sometimes more concerned about their feelings about sex than they are about their sexual experiences. These feelings about sex can be occasioned by fantasy or daydreaming; they may have long histories and they may be related to very important aspects of people's ideas about themselves. Often enough people do not understand their feelings about sex and they find it difficult to know even how to begin to talk about the subject. It is painful for them to bring up these feelings. Indeed, they may express these feelings only in a disguised and defensive fashion.

It is clear that there are many ways to feel about sexuality besides guilty. Guilt, however, is quite pervasive and continues to be strong in cultures in which very strict moral and religious principles exist. Feelings of guilt about sex are frequently related to the overall self-esteem of persons. Sex is only one area about which people are uneasy. They may feel excessively guilty about many other aspects of their personalities as well. Yet their more basic problem of overall self-esteem needs response before any lasting help can be given them.

It is helpful to remember that not all guilt feelings are neurotic; it is possible for people to experience valid feelings of guilt about their behavior, sexual and otherwise. A genuine experience of guilt over some personal failing may center on an episode in which sex has played a part. However, rarely is the issue exclusively sex; many other values and circumstances are bound to be involved. These latter include a person's general attitude toward others, whether he or she uses persons selfishly or tries to reach out to them in a free and respectful way. This can also include persons' evalua-

25

tions of their own behavior in the light of their religious convictions and their own estimate of their self-awareness and freedom at the time of their behavioral difficulties.

A person, for example, may well feel guilty for seducing another person. The guilt feelings involved, however, will be more extensive than those which might quite specifically surround the sexual dimensions of the event. Focusing exclusively on feelings about sex in this regard would unnecessarily underscore one part of a totally personal choice whose impact and significance can only be appreciated if the action is seen as a whole.

Feelings about sex that concern us here are of a different order. Moral guilt about sexual behavior cannot be ignored nor treated as if it were of no consequence. Such a massively reassuring approach does not help resolve feelings of any kind. Telling people to forget about their sexual feelings or not to worry about them does not help much even when the feelings seem so neurotic or commonplace that objectively they should not cause worry. The response that perceives and acknowledges the total person of the other is appropriate for all feelings about sex.

Some of the common feelings about sex spring from the general cultural surrounding or from the folklore of a particular segment within it. Others seem to originate from inner conflicts that have not been resolved, from personally traumatic events, or from basic existential experiences which the individual cannot name or define very accurately. At times they are as simple as a person who, frowning at a persistent worry, raises an issue to the counselor like this: "Say, I've been meaning to ask you about this. . . ." Or, "I'm a little worried about whether I'm normal or not. . . ." Whatever follows requires sensitivity as well as a knowledge of an infinitely wide range of possible feelings about human sexual experience. Whatever counselors may think of these feelings objectively, they deserve to be respected subjectively so that the person experiencing them can place them in better perspective within a better integrated sense of self.

Some people report bewilderment or feelings of intimidation at the state of sexual discussion in the country today. They feel that enormous expectations about attitude and performance have been built up in and through the culture in which they live. These feelings of intimidation are reinforced through the media, especially in popular magazines and on television discussion programs. Something pervades the American air demanding sexual awareness and participation as *the* signs of healthy maleness or femaleness. The sensate contemporary culture exaggerates these expectations so that quite normal people feel uneasy because their own sexual feelings do not seem to match this vague public expectation. They are uneasy because they feel that they may somehow be falling short or missing something, or that there is some secret about sex that all their neighbors know but which has been kept from them.

Such people generally respond very well to an open discussion which reveals that healthy people are not always thinking about sex nor are they always prepared to engage in it. Intimidated persons are reassured through the validation of their own reactions; validation that can come from counselors who have a common-sense understanding of human nature and who can, perhaps with some wry humor, put things into a better perspective for them. Enormous relief comes to many people when they are released from the tension created by these cultural moods. They feel better when they can accept their own lack of perfection both personally and sexually. They are reassured and gain great support from authority figures, such as counselors, who allow them to explore their concerns and their bewilderment without judging them to be ignorant or naive. Such persons feel better about themselves in general when they realize they are not the only ones who feel the way they do.

Young people are sometimes convinced that sexual experience transforms them to such an extent that they appear different in the eyes of their friends; they feel that other people can "tell." It is not a sign of guilt as much as it is a residue of awe about an experience that still holds a measure of wonder about it. It is a human reaction that is quite understandable at a period of fuller awakening to maturity in men and women. Sometimes the significance of sexual experience is trivialized because it has been made to appear so casual in the attitudes that have become popular in our culture.

The cultural trivialization of sexual experience may diminish the depth or significance of sexuality in many people's lives. A recent book, for example, chronicles in first person stories the initial sexual experience of a number of so-called "personalities." Despite the book's general hollowness, it makes a strange kind of tribute to the kind of definition that sexuality can give to the lives of persons growing into a greater sense of their individuality.

A whole array of feelings and expectations are associated with a person's first sexual experience. That is why an experience which is hurried or lacking in tenderness can diminish sexual fulfillment so sharply and leave people feeling cheated or disappointed. There will be enough complications to sexuality without unnecessarily adding these.

When, however, relatively healthy people engage in sexual relations in a loving way they may well feel that they look different because in some profound personal way they are different. They have had, as psychiatrist Warren Gadpaille has noted, validated their maleness and femaleness in a way that is not possible through fantasy or through daydreams. Gadpaille

(*Medical Aspects of Human Sexuality*, June, 1975) suggests that the feeling of being different is a residue of the magical thinking of childhood which does not entirely disappear even in adults. This is not an unusual experience, then, and in the presence of a sensitive counselor persons may be able to understand these feelings about an experience that is not just trivial or totally casual. Counselors should let people explore these reactions without turning them off or making little of them.

There are a number of popular notions, some real and some highly imaginative, about the kinds of feelings that men and women experience after they have had sexual relations. It is a fact, for example, that men are sometimes reported to become more cold and distant after intercourse, while a woman becomes more affectionate. This does not hold true in every situation but it is an area with which counselors should be familiar if they are going to be able to respond to the small but still disturbing questions that people bring to them. Distinctions are, however, in order.

Freud commented on what he described as the "almost universal tendency of men to separate the two currents of affection and sensuality" (cf. Freud, Standard Edition, London, Hogarth Press, Volume II, pp. 165, 179). He describes the situation in which a man pursues a woman ardently as long as she refuses intercourse. Once he has experienced sexual relations with her he loses respect for her. This is sometimes called the "prostitute-madonna" syndrome. The man has a very strong idea about what constitutes a "good" woman and in this fantasy she is desexualized.

Psychiatrist Mark Schoenberg of New York's Roosevelt Hospital has observed that this behavior is classically explained in terms of the male resolution of the Oedipus complex in which the mother must be rejected as a possible sex object. This becomes generalized to the notion that all good women reject sex and the man ends up really in love with "his own unrealistic projected fantasy" of a good woman. Schoenberg contends that these feelings of turning away from the woman represent an inhibition of sexuality rather than a loss of affection. What is needed is some deeper resolution of this inner precipitating conflict through more extended counseling. There is no simple way of dealing with this through reassurance or simple intellectual interpretation. The motives are at an unconscious level and can be very powerful.

Schoenberg also describes the way some men react to sex by suddenly feeling depressed, hostile, angry or rejecting. These feelings are also generally related to specific conflicts about sexual intercourse that lie within the individual. There is abundant folklore about the way a woman gains power over a man through sexual intercourse. These old tales of men being bewitched by women through sex are still powerful in certain parts of the culture. So too are the notions of sexual intercourse as a dangerous situation in which a man loses power to a woman and may possibly be destroyed by her. The feelings that surface are the remote end products of these conflicts. Only through a resolution of the basic feeling can we expect some moderation in men's willingness to believe these other notions (*Medical Aspects of Human Sexuality,* June, 1975).

Dr. Charles William Wahl, professor of Clinical Psychiatry at the U.C.-L.A. School of Medicine, feels that the crucial variable "is whether one's parents have been warm, affectionate, and tactile to one during childhood and were themselves able in their own lives to fuse passion and tenderness." In other words, people may act out later on what they have inherited psychologically from the style of the relationship of their parents and the parents' attitudes toward their children. It is helpful for counselors to recall the way in which these present complaints were forged in the early life history of the people who come to them. Informed counselors will be wary of offering simple solutions, sermons, or reassurances that do not respect the deep history of these experiences (*Medical Aspects of Human Sexuality,* May, 1975).

Psychiatrist Nathan Roth of the N.Y.U. School of Medicine discusses the experience of anger in men after sexual relationships noting that, no matter what the woman feels, a man may report that he is "quite unsatisfied and still charged with much tension" after sexual relationships. Roth feels that some men really do not know what good sex relations are until they have dealt with the defenses and conflicts which inhibit their experience of sexuality.

Dr. Roth's general conclusion, however, is that "an unhappy post-coital state means unsatisfactory sex relations." He suggests that these experiences in the man may indicate that "he fears involvement. Happy sex relations require at least a moderately good relationship between the partners and tend to make the relationship more durable." If the man, according to Roth, is uneasy about committing himself to his partner, then "he gets angry just because the sex relation binds him more firmly to the woman." Dependency seems to loom up as his fate, dependency on the woman and her dependency on him. This triggers an angry rejection because he is not ready for the responsibilities involved in a lasting relationship. Anger after sex can then be a key to far more complex problems.

If the person uses sex relations with the woman as a defense against his own homosexuality then, according to Dr. Roth, he becomes angry because sex with the woman blocks him from the sexual gratification that he really desires. So, too, for some men a sexual relationship represents the possibility that a woman will drain him of all his resources. There is complicated symbolic interplay involved in reactions of this kind and sensitive counselors must allow persons the time to explore these feelings carefully so that they can at least come close to discovering the edge of their source inside themselves.

Psychiatrist Joost Meerloo of Amsterdam observes that the feelings involved in human relationships are sometimes difficult to symbolize except in and through sexual relations. He writes of intercourse as the occasion for the "release of sadomasochistic impulses" and other phenomena of a deep and seemingly psychologically lost sort, the mood of which "remains hovering during and after the sexual activity." People can be bewildered because they do not quite understand all the things that have stirred within them. They do not have the names for them, nor, sadly enough in our culture, a framework within which to view sexuality as an existential mystery rather than as a merely erotic or pleasurable event. While sex has been over-mystified at times, so that people had naive expectations that it would deliver more than it possibly could, it has now been demeaned to such an extent that its human significance is frequently difficult to grasp.

There are echoes of humanity's long history that can still be heard in the unconscious of persons having sexual relations; signals of man's biological role being finished and woman's just beginning; reminders of conquests and new hunts to be started. All these intimations can be present even in half-formed ways and they give their own special emotional cast to the feelings of these moments. That is why one cannot tell people that they should or should not feel one way or the other about sexuality. It is too profound a human experience to be treated as incidental or casual without diminishing it even further. One recalls Norman Mailer's argument in favor of some guilt being attached to sexuality instead of having it the victim of what he calls the "super-hygiene" that impregnates "the air with medicated vaseline." "For guilt," he continues "was the existential urge of sex. Without guilt, sex was meaningless. One advanced into sex against one's sense of guilt, and each time guilt was successfully defined, one had learned a little more about the contractual relation of one's own existence to the unheard thunders of the deep—each time guilt herded one back with its authority, some primitive awe—and some creative clue to the rages of the deep—was left to brood about" (*The Armies of the Night,* New York: The New American Library, 1968, pp. 33–34).

Headaches have been used for a long time as excuses for not having sexual relations. But recently there has been identified the "benign sexual headache," a reality that afflicts a small group of persons during and after sexual activity. Sexual headaches, according to physician George Paulson of Ohio State College of Medicine, "are intense, severe, and incapacitating, occurring abruptly in an otherwise enthusiastic sexual participant." Those who suffer from them can be of any age or gender but in the cases that have been reported in the literature they seem to affect men in early middle life more than others. Instead of wanting to lie down, these persons report "restlessness, irritability, or a need to keep walking during the pain." Although they sometimes only last an hour or two some of those who have experienced them report a dull "ache of the neck or scalp for several days after the acute, intense headache." Research has not proceeded very far, especially in terms of the possible emotional basis for this difficulty, but it seems to be related to the intensity of the sexual activity itself. Masters and Johnson reported on muscle tension in certain of the subjects of their study who experienced pain when the sexual experience was intense, hurried, or very strenuous.

Paulson suggests that counselors who hear this complaint should recommend a careful neurological examination because headaches are frequently the first signs of serious underlying problems in the central nervous system. In most cases, however, he suggests that a great deal of help can come from "emphasizing good general health plus treatment of any mild hypertension and allaying of anxiety." In other words, the reduction of a person's anxiety over this experience is in itself therapeutic. It seems that one's general physical tone may have a relationship to the experience of this difficulty and so regular exercise is prescribed. If the headaches occur in persons who seem to be obsessive, then some help in dealing with their underlying psychological conflict is indicated. The benign sexual headache is not a common difficulty but it should not be casually dismissed as a reaction to or defense against sexual relationships.

One of the most crippling feelings that comes upon a woman is that of the fear of sexual relationships or the experience of orgasm. As psychiatrist John C. Sonne of the Hahnemann Medical College in Philadelphia has noted, such fear is seldom the chief complaint presented to counselors. Women with this difficulty are "usually unaware of their fear of orgasm because they have displaced it on to something else." Examples of displacement may be found in a fear of having an accident or in something even less symbolic such as overeating or depression. These women may also complain, according to Dr. Sonne, "about feeling used and abandoned by 'animal' men, whom they unaccountably attract but don't enjoy."

Psychiatrists generally relate these fears to sexuality perceived as a loss of control and a demand for a total surrender of the self. These aspects of experience are present in sexual relations and are elements of its power and wonder. The roots of crippling fear may lie in the anxieties associated with frustration and bodily harm that have seeped into adult life from childhood. Add to this the actual fear of death and mutilation and one begins to appreciate how complex and commanding this fear can be. Sexual relation-ships, far from being casual, tap the unconscious levels of human personal-ity and therefore can trip off fears from primitive or long forgotten sources.

A woman's hostility toward her mother, according to Dr. Sonne, may emerge without being recognized as the hidden motive for an adult fear of sexuality. Sexual relationships mark a step toward fuller maturation. They involve individuals in the powerful and moving experience of separation and individuation that is necessary for independent adult life. Even for women who have grown past these fears, according to Sonne, "orgasm will proba-bly always be somewhat frightening," and he adds, "as it should be."

Sonne, moreover, catches some of the existential content that is impor-tant to appreciate if counselors are to understand the presence of unresolved fears in the heart of sexual intimacy. "It is in the nature of the orgasm that one surrenders to one's own involuntary self and gives up control. Can she trust the mate with whom she dares let this happen? And with what depth of one's ontogeny and phylogeny does one come into contact in the brief regression, progression, and near dissolution of one's ego that one experi-ences?

"If one were ever a part of history, it is at the moment of orgasm. Is it not perhaps a reminder of death to come or of a time before life began? And what of the happiness-sadness one experiences? Is not such acute happiness a reminder in itself of how precious it is to be alive? Yes with this is a quickly suppressed but frightening awareness of how short life actually is. And consider the growth that can occur through orgasm. Is this not existentially frightening as well as exhilarating? . . . In long-term, meaningful male-female relationships, the shared orgasm is the epitome of trust and chance taking" (*Medical Aspects of Human Sexuality.* October, 1973, p.132).

It is clear that counselors cannot come with ready made answers, exer-cises, or diagrams to solve the problems that may be involved in situations in which a woman is afraid of orgasm. Patience, understanding, and some grasp of the psychodynamics that are involved beneath the surface are indispensable for counselors who wish, even in a preliminary way, to assist persons to define and understand the fear that interferes so much with their sexual functioning. It may be necessary to refer such persons for more intensive psychotherapy, but the preliminary attitudes and sensitivity of the counselor remain significant keys to opening up for persons the unknown but resonating territory of their own inner lives.

References

Adams, W. J. "How Hidden Feelings Spoil the Sex Act." *Sexology.* 35 (Nov., 1968), pp. 220–22.

Bell, R. R. and Gordon, M. *The Social Dimension of Human Sexuality.* Boston: Little, Brown & Co., 1972.

Bell, R. R. "Some Emerging Sexual Expectations Among Women." *Medical Aspects of Human Sexuality* (Oct., 1967), 72:65–67.

Brenton, Myron. *The American Male.* New York: Coward-McCann, 1966.

Broderick, C. B. and Bernard, J. (Eds.). *The Individual, Sex and Society.* Baltimore: Johns Hopkins Press, 1969.

DeMartino, M. F. (Ed.). *Sexual Behavior and Personality Characteristics.* New York: Grove Press, 1966.

Ellis, A. *The American Sexual Tragedy.* New York: Grove Press, 1962.

———. *Sex Without Guilt.* New York: Grove Press, 1961.

Fletcher, Joseph. *Moral Responsibility.* Philadelphia: Westminster Press, 1967.

———. *Situation Ethics.* Philadelphia: Westminster Press, 1966.

Grummond, D.L. and Barclay, A.M. *Sexuality: A Search for Perspective.* New York: Van Nostrand Reinhold, 1971.

Grunwald, Henry A. (Ed.). *Sex in America.* New York: Bantam Books, 1964.

Kasterberger, J. S. "Outside and Inside, Male and Female." *The Journal of the American Psychoanalytic Association* (1968), 16:457.

FIVE

Translating Sexual Communication

IT is an axiom of the day that most relationships can be improved by the betterment of communication. But what is communication? Some individuals define it through the amount of information which they give to their partner about their daily activities. People can, however, keep date pads, schedules and notes tacked on the refrigerator that account for every minute of their day but still fail to reveal very much about themselves in the process. They have all the outer data but that does not necessarily reveal much of the inner person. So too, some marriage contracts contain specifications aimed at improving communication through anticipating certain traditional marital difficulties before they happen. These are inserted "to avoid possible misunderstandings." And yet the drawing up of such contracts already communicates potential misunderstandings, worried hopes that the written word somehow guarantees a less risk-filled relationship.

Communication is not just keeping in touch, although this is obviously part of it. It is fundamentally the capacity we have to reveal the truth about ourselves to others. Effective communication depends on whether we make ourselves present as we really are or whether we use masks or play roles for those around us. The communication problems that surface with sexual difficulties are not amenable to solution by superficial efforts to improve communication. People need to get in touch with each other's personalities at a deep level. This is a traditional function of counseling. Sexual counseling isn't just knowing all the facts about the subject and handing them on to another. It is simply to know the other and to assist the other in communicating his or her truth more fully.

The counselor is not involved in anything less than this deeper challenge of communication. To assist persons in achieving mutual communication with their real selves, counselors must hear what people are trying to say about themselves through their descriptions of their sexual conflicts. What are some of the messages people give to each other in the language of sexuality? They frequently come for counseling only with the surface outlines of the communication and with no idea of what it actually means. If counselors cannot hear the real message, it will be very difficult to help two people understand what they are really trying to get across to each other.

The sexual problems that people bring to counselors frequently offer many clues about their overall personal relationships. People speak sexually to each other about their deepest feelings toward each other. They communicate their real appraisal of each other. They do this even when they are not aware of everything they are trying to get across. Husband and wife do this in the way they greet each other, in the way they may neglect to smile at each other from across the room at a party. They do it in the way they give reasons for postponing sexual intercourse or through their self-absorbed style in trying to promote it. This is an extremely complex field and counselors can begin to pick up the messages almost immediately if they are listening carefully enough.

It is possible, for example, for a man to carry out what he perceives to be his sexual role very dutifully. He may even boast about the frequency with which he has intercourse, fancying that he is fulfilling the role of the good husband while he is actually only bolstering his own self-image rather than communicating deep affection to his spouse. It isn't the *what;* it is clearly the *why* that is the key to understanding a relationship in which a dutiful but self-concerned man can be preoccupied more with his self-esteem than with communicating his real self to his wife. The wife gets the message, however, and, although their sexual life is very active, she feels that he is essentially a dutiful child who is far more concerned with sexual performance than anything else. Such attitudes resemble those that go into keeping a perfect attendance record in school. Such a couple can be miles apart, communicating their separate worlds in the very intimacy of sexuality itself.

It is also possible to see the reverse of this communication in a woman who perceives herself as the perfect wife, fully emancipated sexually, and quite free in her behavior. She may be so overwhelming, however, in her display of independence and self-sufficiency that she diminishes her husband's sense of himself. She cannot understand it, then, when her marriage suffers serious tensions. She, after all, is the "perfect wife" in many ways. What more could a man want? Only as counselors get to the level of what such transactions are all about can they be effective in assisting persons to understand these difficulties.

Counselors must be ready to search out with couples the answers to the questions or statements they constantly make to each other through their sexual lives. What are they saying about each other and about their relationship? What are, as communications theorists call them, the *meta-messages?* The refusal of sexual relations is one of the clear areas in which this communication takes place. As psychiatrist John Schimel observes, a wife's refusal to have sexual relationships with her husband may be a way of responding to what she feels to be his rudeness earlier in the evening. She punishes him, righting a wrong and, as Schimel notes, "educating and training a man she considers her social and human inferior." As to the husband, the psychiatrist notes that the "inference was that he wasn't loved or, in another vernacular, that he was being castrated." This enormous and powerful symbolic transaction cannot be appreciated unless the counselor helps the people involved to explore this exchange of communication. This is not to say, of course, that difficulty over the timing or frequency of sexual relationships always carries such complicated messages. Such reactions, however, do carry some messages and only the discovery of their true nature can help persons work through their sexually expressed difficulties with each other.

There are many other areas of life in which sexual behavior contains messages that counselors must understand with sensitivity. It is not unusual, for example, for persons to find themselves troubled by a previously unknown sexual difficulty after they have suffered some loss in life. Such occurrences are not signals that these people are becoming dissolute or hopelessly preoccupied with sex. These manifestations are signals of the unconscious processes taking place inside them. The sexual activity in these cases cannot be treated as though it were a problem in and of itself. It must be linked to whatever other disturbance or loss has occurred in the life of the person involved.

The counselor's objectives may be limited by the amount of time he or she is able to spend with the person or couple who come for assistance. No matter how limited the time, however, it is always possible to make persons feel more comfortable with themselves and less guilty and obsessed with their sexual difficulty. This is the kind of gift we give to persons when we make ourselves present as competent, mature, and understanding persons who are in no rush to condemn them or in any other way judge their sexual difficulties.

Some counselors may want to make a good referral. This may be a wise course of action, especially when there is a clearly pronounced sexual difficulty that is amenable to further specific treatment. There need be no rush to do this, however. It is better to allow persons to get their messages across to us and for us to show that we can receive them without panicking.

There will be plenty of time to decide, in collaboration with the counselee, whether another referral is needed. Counselors should become aware of local sexual therapy clinics to which they can refer couples with confidence about the clinic's medical, psychological and ethical standards.

In dealing with a sexual conflict it is important for religious figures, particularly Roman Catholic priests, to separate their function as ministers of forgiveness, for example, from their function as counselors. Sometimes persons want to get absolution and psychological advice at the same time. It is ordinarily wise for a confessor or clergyman in a comparable role to deal straightforwardly with the person's sometimes insistent desire to confess his or her sins. Better always to separate this from counseling itself. To scramble sin and its forgiveness with a search for the roots of a psychological entity confuses both the counselor and the person seeking help. It is also clear that confessors, even while they are restricted in this role, may be able to assist persons a great deal through an understanding response to their sexual difficulties. Religious ministers should not attempt any long range counseling or therapy, however, in the context of an official religious function.

Clergy and other people discharging pastoral or educational responsibilities are not really responsible for stopping people from doing certain things; neither are they supposed to get people to follow what they consider their ideal of sexual relations. There is a large aspect of human sexual behavior which, in its details, must be left to people themselves. One may try to help people develop a better understanding of their own identity, but one must leave them free to make their own decisions about their individual activities.

Counselors are not engaged, as some experts are, in trying to make everybody function sexually in the same way. There is no liberated lifestyle that can be applied to all men and women in the United States at the present time. Such an attempt would be unfair, clumsy and most certainly harmful in the long run.

Neither is it wise to try to help everyone perform sexually the same way all the time. It is impossible to introduce machine-like precision into the sexual life of persons, no matter what good intentions may be involved in this. Counselors remember that they are dealing fundamentally with a human activity that is subject to all the variations and imperfections that are found in every other human activity of any worth. They become wise as counselors when they understand and implement this simple fact.

Counseling can be understood as an effort to translate the emotional communications of clients so that they can finally hear what they are saying to themselves and to other persons about themselves. Helpers need some of the grace and judgment of good translators in any field. The art of translation lies not in getting every single word into a new language, but in capturing the point and mood, the rhythm and style of the original material. So it is with the work of counselors in dealing with persons with sexual complaints. Over-literalness or the over-employment of Freudian or other interpretations is not called for. Catching the pattern of the troubling sexual communication in reference to two persons' relationship to each other is far more helpful than imposing a studied theoretical explanation on persons.

In order to do this, counselors may wish to widen their focus to include other areas of the person's life. What is going on, from physical illness to new ambition to the puzzlements of a middle-age crisis? Only as counselors see the entire scope of a couple's life together can they be confident about their understanding of a specific sexual complaint. Simply put, human beings only say things to each other sexually that they are already expressing to each other in a dozen different ways. When they cannot hear or respond to each other in varied ways in their life together it is not surprising that their basic conflict should also be revealed in the language of sexuality.

Couples also bring their previous experiences to their sexual relationships, sometimes expecting and often being disappointed that marriage does not remove earlier unresolved conflicts. The communication in sexuality may reflect difficulties that were not seen or appreciated in earlier stages of the couple's relationship. The lingering problem of dependence on one partner that may have seemed charming before marriage may emerge as a far more serious problem in the sexual aspect of marriage. A number of similar problems may only be discovered in the regular intimacy of marriage and counselors need all their sensitivity to trace these difficulties to their true place of origin.

Expectation may also distort the language of sexuality and counselors should not be surprised, even in this day and age, at encountering a host of general adjustment problems that express themselves sexually. Obviously, listening to the whole person rather than just to sexual problems is necessary.

References

Brammer, L. and Shostrom, E. *Therapeutic Psychology.* Englewood Cliffs, N.J.: Prentice-Hall, 1968.

Carkhuff, R. R. *Helping and Human Relations,* 2 Vols. New York: Holt, Rinehart & Winston, 1969.

Cuber, John F. and Harroff, Peggy B. *Sex and the Significant American.* Baltimore: Penguin, 1966.

Egan, Gerald. *The Skilled Helper.* Monterey, California: Brooks/Cole Publishing Co., 1975.

Erikson, Erik. *Childhood and Society.* New York: W. W. Norton & Co., Inc., 1963.

Grummon, Donald L. and Barclay, Andrew. *Sexuality: A Search for Perspective.* New York: Van Nostrand Reinhold Co., 1971.

Journal of Marriage and the Family. National Council of Family Relations. 1219 University Avenue, S.E., Minneapolis, Minnesota 55414.

Sexology Magazine. 154 West 14th Street, New York, New York 10011.

Shiloh, Ailon (Ed). *Studies in Human Sexual Behavior: The American Scene.* Springfield, Ill.: Charles B. Thomas, 1970.

Shope, David F. *Interpersonal Sexuality.* Philadelphia: W. B. Saunders, Co., 1975.

SIX

Sex Drive: Too Much, Too Little

OUR environment places a premium on sexual behavior. The need to perform sexually and to be sexually responsive are deeply ingrained aspects of popular folklore. Fantasies about sexual performance are written about regularly in a wide variety of magazines aimed at men and women; these subjects are also discussed on television talk shows and through other media that reach and influence popular culture. It is difficult for men and women to escape an awareness of sexual functioning as a strong concern of contemporary persons. And yet it is a subject about which people still hesitate. This does not mean that they are totally puritanical or benighted. It may reflect the conflicts they experience between this new openness and their own values, social beliefs or religious convictions. Counselors dealing with persons who have questions about their own sex drive are wise to remember that they are dealing with total personalities rather than with just the sexual dimension. To be truly helpful we must be able to catch the fullness of their lives, placing sexual concerns in a cross section of other varied experiences.

This is important because it is so easy for people to distort their own messages about their sexual experiences. Machismo still has its effect on men, for example, so that a great deal of the masculine boasting that goes on never loses its flavor of adolescent exaggeration. Sometimes human beings are anxious, feeling that they have something wrong with them because they do not react sexually quite the way culture and media make it sound that everyone should react.

In any case, counselors must listen carefully to the whole story in order to be able to respond to the sexual person rather than just to the sexuality of the person. There is an enormous difference between sexiness and sexuality. This is also important because complaints of excessive sexual drive or inadequate sexual drive may be surface symptoms beneath which more serious conditions, such as depression, may lurk. Counselors need not ask embarrassing questions in order to be alert to these potential difficulties.

The experience of sexual drive or, as it is sometimes called, *libido,* varies widely and is dependent on a complex of factors that may be quite different for different individuals at different points in their lives. There is no general way of describing for clients an ideal or an average amount of sex drive; neither is counseling a time for reassurances or encouragement.

For example, when people complain about the sudden increase in their sexual drive, counselors should take this perception seriously and attempt, through careful listening, to discover its full meaning for them. At times a person's perception of his or her sex drive and the actual reality of the sex drive are two quite different things. It is possible that a reported increase in sex drive may be more apparent than real. This makes no difference to the psychological world of reality of the person perceiving it. Such persons feel it is true and react as though it were. Any report of a sudden increase in libido can indicate a serious underlying psychological or physical problem. Such complaints must be distinguished from the sexual boasting referred to previously. The tone and described circumstances will be far different in the rather imaginative accounts given by persons who want to impress us with their sexual potency.

Dr. Thomas P. Detre of the Yale School of Medicine (*Medical Aspects of Human Sexuality,* Sept., 1973) describes several conditions in which the experience of excessive libido is associated with serious problems. He notes, for example, that an increase in libido may be reported in pathologically elevated mood states such as *mania* and *hypomania.* Increased libido may be one facet of a generalized increase in the characteristically frenzied activity of such a situation and points to the underlying mood disorder far more than it defines a sexual problem in itself.

So too, excessive libido is frequently associated with the *anti-social personality.* The latter is the personality disorder that has at various times been described as *psychopathic* or *sociopathic.* Such extra libido has, curiously enough, been glorified in certain fictional or historical figures who are admired in popular culture for their incredible sexual exploits. *Don Juan* and *James Bond* are merely two examples of characters who may well have anti-social characteristics in their personality makeup. They move from one sexual conquest to another without signs of either concern or fatigue. This kind of activity excites the imagination of ordinary people but very few relatively normal people could possibly live this way. The consequences of this style of behavior would generate other conflicts with which people could not comfortably live. Although the idealization of this behavior is unfortunate there is little that can be done to control the readiness of a mass market to absorb such stories. The reality is something far different.

How can one tell if the complaint about excessive libido is related to anti-social personality? Counselors must discern the quality of the relationships in which this excessive sexual drive is expressed. Anti-social personalities may present a charming facade. This is one of the reasons that they can seduce people, both physically and psychologically, with great success. Beneath this veneer of charm, however, one can detect a lack of anxiety about behavior that would cause anxiety or the experience of genuine guilt in most persons. This lack of conscience is one of the chief clues to this type of personality. Anti-social persons also have a need for immediate gratification. They cannot postpone getting what they want even for a few moments. They react very much to their impulses and move immediately into action. Put this picture together and the pathological conditions of the sexuality of the anti-social personality can be understood much better.

Counselors must ask themselves what the total person is like instead of closing in too sharply on individual sexual experiences. What is actually going on in their lives during the time of complaint about sexual excess? When something important is taking place in the person's life he or she may change their self-presentation to some extent. For example, at certain early stages in a psychological illness persons may seem to display more sexual behavior than was characteristic of earlier periods in their lives. They may seem more sexually interested, not because there is a true increase in their sexual drive, but because something else is happening to them that makes them lower previously well established defenses. As their anxiety increases, such persons may seem to be more sexually intimate when they are really only interested in more emotional support. Their reserve diminishes but it is in search of protection rather than increased sexual activity.

Persons experiencing the first effects of a brain syndrome may well exhibit sexual curiosity and behavior that was never present before. This is frequently a sign of an impairment in their social judgment related to brain damage rather than to any real increase in their sex drive. So too, in schizophrenic states, an increase in sexual interest or behavior is often an effect of the emotional illness rather than of any absolute increase in libido. Such behavior constitutes only one aspect of a range of inappropriate behavior which is noted in severely disturbed personalities.

A new and uncharacteristic report of apparent or real increase in sex drive may be the first signal of an underlying physiological or psychological disorder. This increase in libido is to be distinguished from minor, somewhat rhythmic increases in sexual interest which characterize most people. This latter normal variation in sexual interest is of a different nature altogether. Most people understand that there is a periodic quality of their sexual interest and, while at times they may wish to discuss this with a counselor, they are not describing a sharp and unprecedented experience of sexual interest or activity. It is clear, however, that if a person expresses an excessive anxiety about what amounts to a normal rhythm of sexual interest, this situation needs to be explored. It may be related to factors that will be discussed in later chapters.

A diminution in sex interest or drive can be associated with many physical and psychological conditions. It frequently becomes a source of anxiety, especially in men who feel that such changes threaten their sense of themselves. Again this may be one aspect of a more generalized attitude toward themselves and, in all these cases, the person's overall self-estimation needs examination. It is very difficult to assist somebody with problems of self-esteem by focusing only on the sexual aspect of personality functioning.

One must distinguish between an absolute lack of sexual drive and an inhibited condition which may be explained psychologically or physiologically. An absolute lack of sex drive is, according to Dr. Martin Goldberg of the University of Pennsylvania Medical School, an example of *primary impotence.* This is a condition in which an individual has never experienced sexual drive nor any successful physical sexual reactivity. This is distinguished from *secondary impotence* which occurs in a person who has previously been sexually potent (*Medical Aspects of Human Sexuality,* Aug., 1973).

Primary impotence may be explained by certain physiological factors, such as endocrine disturbances. The determination of an absolute lack of sexual desire as primary impotence should be made only after a thorough physical and psychological examination.

Far more common are disturbances in potency in which decreased sexual interest is the presenting complaint. This may also be caused by basic physiological problems, including an imbalance of endocrine. Other contributing factors include the experience of some terminal or wasting disease or severe malnutrition. A lack of sexual desire has been reported, for example, among people barely surviving in concentration camps. In many of these cases, of course, the physiological condition aggravates the psychological adjustment and it is difficult to separate out the amount of causation due to one or the other factor.

Other physiological factors that may affect the experience of sexual drive include congenital abnormalities which affect sexual development. However, the presence of even severe congenital problems does not mean that a person will not experience sexual desires. Very strong sexual desire can be present in persons who are physically incapable of sexual relations.

Perhaps more common—and certainly more the concern of counselors

—are examples of psychologically-induced diminution of sexual drive. The most frequent cause of a reported lack of sexual drive in persons is the experience of *depression.* When depression is deep and pervasive the loss of interest in sexual activity is very common. Depression affects the individual's overall zest for life and has its effect on other appetites, such as for food and recreation, quite as much as it does on sex.

The counselor must be ready to sense the causes of the underlying depression and to respond to these rather than merely to the symptomatic decrease in the strength of libido. Counselors should ask: *What has this individual lost in order to make this complaint?* The possibilities are many. Impotence may occur after the death of a loved one, the termination of a job, upon retirement, or at the end or close of any event that casts a shadow on a person's self-image. Whenever individuals have an experience that threatens the integrity of their personalities it is not surprising to find them complaining, not only about a decrease in sexual potency, but also about other esteem-sensitive aspects of life.

Other psychological causes for a lessening of sex drive include some temporary preoccupation caused by *situational stress.* These may include divorce, a change of jobs, problems at work or with child raising, or any of a number of the other stresses that are common in contemporary society. The multiplying effect of more than one stress being experienced at a time is also significant in this regard.

Such problems are by their nature ordinarily self-limiting; usually counselors need not involve themselves in trying to make basic changes in the life of the counselee. Rather, they serve the function of helping the stressed persons put their overall experience of psychological pressure into clearer perspective and of offering support to them through critical phases of their lives.

It has been the contention of various research reports that the regular use of some drugs taken as aphrodisiacs often results in temporary experiences of impotence. Claims have been made in this regard with respect to the regular use of marijuana. All the research evidence is not in, but it is clear that counselors should be alert to the possibility that clients may be using a certain drug, or combination of drugs, which inhibit sexual performance.

This issue can become complicated because there are almost always psychological factors involved in a person's decision to take drugs. An exploration of the basic psychological need may be as important as establishing the physiological basis for the need for drugs. Here again a person's perception of reality and the reality itself may differ considerably because of the effects of auto-suggestion, expectation, and other psychological aspects of the overall experience.

The use of alcohol has long been known to inhibit sexual performance. Shakespeare spoke of drink that "provokes and unprovokes, it provokes the desires but takes away the performance. Therefore much drink may be said to be an equivocator with lechery." People experience an increase in sexual desire because of the loosening of their inhibitions under the influence of alcohol. They find, however, that sexual performance may be markedly affected. Individuals with severe drinking problems—those who might be classified as chronic alcoholics—often have difficulties in sexual functioning.

Impotence fits in frequently with their more generalized difficulties with *self-esteem* and *dependence*. Counselors must always be alert to the range of dynamics in any situation in which self-esteem is at the core of the problem. Self-esteem is far more important to most people than anything else. To many a capacity for sexual experience is an important element in maintaining their self-image. Obviously, extensive counseling is needed for those whose self-esteem has been under attack and who need to find new sources of self-worth. It is more important for counselors to treat self-esteem than symptomatic impotence.

References

Adams, W. J. "How Hidden Feelings Spoil the Sex Act." *Sexology.* 35 (Nov., 1968), pp. 220–22.

Arafat, Ibtihaj and Yorburg, B. "Drug Use and the Sexual Behavior of College Women." *Journal of Sex Research* (Feb., 1973).

Detre, Thomas, M.D. *Medical Aspects of Human Sexuality* (Sept., 1973).

Gray, G. R. and Sheppard, C.W. "Sex-Crazed Dope Fiends: Myth or Reality?" *Drug Forum.* 2 (Winter, 1973), pp. 125–40.

Goldberg, Martin, M.D. *Medical Aspects of Human Sexuality* (Aug., 1973).

Golden, Joshua. "Sexual Frustration." *Medical Aspects of Human Sexuality* (Dec., 1973).

Gould, J. A. and Iorio, J. *Love, Sex and Identity.* San Francisco: Boyd & Fraser, 1972.

Hastings, D. *Impotence and Frigidity.* Boston: Little, Brown & Co., 1966.

Henslin, J. (Ed.). *Studies in the Sociology of Sex.* New York: Appleton-Century, Croft, 1971.

Kelly, G. L. "Impotency." *The Encyclopedia of Sexual Behavior,* Vol. 1. New York: Hawthorn Books, 1961.

Kirkendall, L. A. "Sex Drive." *The Encyclopedia of Sexual Behavior,* Vol. II. New York: Hawthorn Books, 1961.

MacKinnon, R. A. and Michels, R. *The Psychiatric Interview in Clinical Practice.* Philadelphia: W. B. Saunders, 1971. See esp., "The Depressed Patient" and "The Sociopathic Patient."

Maslow, A. H. *Motivation and Personality.* New York: Harper, 1954.

Money, J. and Yankowitz, R. "The Sympathetic-Inhibiting Effects of the Drug

Ismelin on Human Male Eroticism, with a Note on Mellaril." *Journal of Sex Research.* 3 (July, 1974), pp. 331–47.

Murstein, B. I. "Sex Drive, Person Perception and Marital Choice." *Arch. Sex. Behavior.* 3 (July, 1974) pp. 331–47.

Whalen, R. E. "Sexual Motivation." *Psycho-social Review.* 2 (1966), pp. 151–63.

Willis, Stanley, "Sexual Promiscuity as a Symptom of Personal and Cultural Anxiety." *Medical Aspects of Human Sexuality* (Oct., 1967).

—— — —— —

SEVEN

Sex and the American Neurosis

OBSESSIVE-COMPULSIVE problems have been described by many observers as the most common of all psychological difficulties experienced by Americans. It is also a difficulty which, because of its convoluted intellectual defenses, is hard to treat effectively. There is a wide range of behavior that can be termed obsessive-compulsive. We speak here, however, about fairly firm patterns of adjustment marked by rigid thinking, perfectionism, a need for control, and the particular joylessness that this seeds in people who suffer from it.

These external characteristics are not the core of the problem. They are what we see on the outside, the scaffolding for the psyche on which a conflict that cannot be faced directly is translated symbolically into rituals and preoccupations that, difficult though they are to bear, people find easier to suffer than to face the truth of their central conflict. Like all neurotics, obsessive-compulsives translate their inner problems into symptoms which puzzle everybody including themselves. Even when they are capable of intellectual insight into their difficulties, that is usually not enough for them. They stay away from emotions and they go to great and complicated lengths to protect themselves from the anxiety they would suffer if they had to face their basic psychological dilemma.

It is not surprising to find obsessive-compulsives translating their inner conflicts into sexual difficulties. Sexuality is a special and highly sensitive language; because it is an area of behavior that demands intimacy, it is highly threatening to obsessives. They approach it with their defenses up and with a great need to protect themselves in an activity which, in order to be successful, demands that they reveal something of their inner selves. The obsessive-compulsive is caught in his own defenses.

Counselors frequently hear symptoms from obsessive-compulsives or from their spouses which may seem very bewildering. The symptoms describe outer problems, but it is only as we sense the psychological style of obsessives that we can see beneath the presenting symptoms of sexual difficulty and observe the strife within. We cannot treat only the symptoms of the sexual difficulties of obsessives. This would lead us into a complicated and self-defeating search for the kind of perfect and controlling solution to life which obsessives themselves desperately seek, in one way or another, all their lives.

Counselors must gives obsessives the understanding they need to translate their sexual problems so that they can respond to them more accurately. Obsessive-compulsives have to get beyond their own rituals. They are constantly giving out symbolic messages both to themselves and to those around them. They hide behind these messages. The counselor's fundamental task is to be able to sift through these in order to discover and to convey the true meaning back to the client.

Obsessive-compulsives are caught in a conflict between being obedient and being defiant. Such a problem has its origins in their early home life, especially in situations in which great demands for specified kinds of behavior were made on them; they reacted accordingly in order to feel that they were accepted or loved. Unfortunately, in order to get these rewards they had to be something other than themselves. They spend a lifetime continuing to be this way.

The conflict between wanting to please and wanting to rebel is intense and they cannot face it directly without experiencing overwhelming anxiety. Their whole lifestyle becomes their effort to manage this conflict. They try to master existence so that nothing can go wrong. As Dr. Leon Salzman has noted, an obsessive seems to have a need to "gain control over oneself and one's environment in order to avoid or overcome distressful feelings of helplessness. The concern about the possibility of losing control by being incompetent, insufficiently informed, or unable to reduce the risks of living causes the greatest amounts of anxiety. The realization of one's humaness —with its inherent limitations—is often the basis for considerable anxiety and obsessive attempts at greater control over one's living."

Obsessive-compulsives are marked with the following traits: They experience cognitive rigidity, approaching life in a stiff and restricted manner. There is little elasticity to their thinking because they have to interpret everything in accord with a very limited style of reflection. They are preoccupied with stressful, driven activity that is paired with a restless inability to take time off or to enjoy leisure hours. They are indecisive and put off decisions to prevent them from being wrong. They worry constantly and they cannot seem to do without this. They are out of touch with life and devote excessive concern to things that may have the most remote chance of happening to them, such as accidents or illnesses (E. B. McNeil, *Neurosis and Personality Disorders.* Englewood Cliffs, N.J.: Prentice-Hall, Inc., 1970, p. 39ff.).

Obsessive-compulsives bring this whole way of dealing with life into sexual relationships. Since they are rigid and concerned with details and because they have a great need to defend their inner selves, they are particularly vulnerable to the demands of sexual activity. Their sexual activity is inseparable from their personality difficulties and from their problems in relating to people in general.

Sexually, obsessives are just the way they are in any other situation. Their difficulties cause distress to their spouses and puzzlement to themselves. They cannot master this sexual area and this increases its threat for them. Their defenses keep getting in the way with the result that they experience a mechanization of sex as well as a number of other individual problems that are directly connected with their personality style. As Dr. Joseph Barnett notes: "These include problems with impotence, premature ejaculation, retarded orgasm, and compulsive genital activities, such as masturbation" (Joseph Barnett, M.D., "Sex and the Compulsive Person," *Medical Aspects of Human Sexuality.* Feb., 1971). While these problems can occur in other persons for different reasons, counselors who can relate these presenting difficulties to an obsessive-compulsive character structure are on the right track in trying to be genuinely helpful.

Obsessive-compulsive persons are afraid of being shamed or having the truth about themselves exposed to others. This is precisely what they try to avoid and why they develop such complicated behaviors to protect themselves. This is also why the intimacy that is associated with sexual experience is so psychologically demanding on them. The more they enter into intimacy the more they are threatened. Closeness upsets them and they must attempt to re-establish distance in order to defend themselves.

Sex, then, is especially dangerous unless it is totally impersonal. If sex and true personal intimacy are tied together, as presumably they would be in any healthy relationship, the obsessive finds this a very difficult task with which to deal. Sexuality, Barnett observes, "is highly revealing of needs, impulses, and attitudes about self and others. Sexual performance is largely dependent on the ability to assert one's wants directly. Ideally, sex evokes spontaneous thoughts and feelings which are expressive and abandoned. The very self-expressiveness and self-exposure implicit in such behavior is threatening to the obsessive" (p.36).

The solution employed by obsessives is similar to those they use in other life situations. They must protect themselves against feeling their own emotions and so they use a psychological protective system to separate their sexual from their emotional needs to cover up their feelings while they are involved in sexual activity. The result is that their sexual behavior is awkward, rigid, and ritualized. It is the only kind of sexual style with which they can be comfortable.

This is not to say that obsessives are failures at sex. They may perform well enough but their sexuality will be lifeless and without spontaneity. They are really not in relationship to their spouses in their sexual relations. They are tied up in their own troubled emotional lives, protecting themselves against revelations that are too anxiety laden for them, and they are quite unaware of the effect they have on others. Obsessive-compulsives may be puzzled because they have worked so hard at performing adequately and cannot understand why their spouses get an impersonal message from them.

Such ritualized, impersonal behavior leads to marital difficulties or at least to complaints about sexual life. These are the kinds of things that may be brought to a counselor by the obsessive's spouse or, more mechanically, by the obsessive. Counseling, like sex, is an area that demands spontaneity and a willingness to let oneself be known. Obsessives bring their typical defenses against self-revelation into therapy. They are preoccupied, they intellectualize, and they frequently attack the therapist in subtle ways in order to protect themselves from letting anything out that would embarrass or shame them. They are not easy to work with and their number is large.

Barnett suggests that the obsessive-compulsive may lead a secret life of sexual fantasy in which he or she is able to isolate "those aspects of the emotional life which are connected with shame, like aggressive impulses or the need for nutrients." This is a highly organized world and it is kept at quite a distance from one's ordinary life with other persons. Obsessives are not fully aware of this fantasy life themselves, especially if they are deeply defensive. This may take the form of obsessive daydreams or it may appear in the form of unconscious fantasies, the content of which the patient cannot report clearly.

Moreover, Barnett notes that "sexual and aggressive impulses often emerge in the secret life of the obsessional." The fantasy life serves to deal with these impulses which are so threatening in their regular life and sexual contact. They are afraid of the hostility that they might reveal in an intimate situation and so it finds expression in this very private world of imagination. The roots of a somewhat bizarre fantasy life can well be found in the conflict at the base of the obsessive's adjustment to life. It is clear that counselors can never focus too closely on those things that are only the end products of long and complicated psychological chains.

Because obsessives experience an inner conflict between obedience and rebellion, anything related to this in a sexual experience will also cause trouble. One of the dynamics that touches this off is dependency. The obsessive depends on others to convince him of his worth and this, as Barnett notes, places "him in a bind in which he feels insignificant if no sexual demands are made of him, but anxious, inadequate, and resentful if they are made." He therefore tries to establish emotional distance in sexual relationships in order to hide his dependency needs.

This is sometimes revealed in the passive way in which obsessives enter into sexual relationships as well as in the manner in which they can put such a strong premium on the performance rather than on the intrinsic meaning of sexuality. They can perform but this takes the place of expressing themselves to another person in a free and unguarded way. If they perform sexually according to what they consider to be an adequate standard, they feel safe and protected from the dependent side of their nature. The real messages cannot be hidden, however, from the spouse who, despite the seeming competence of the sexual performance, will also feel the distance and the defensiveness. This is a very real and difficult area in the sexual relationships of the obsessive-compulsive.

Obsessive-compulsives do not relate to other persons freely and warmly. They act out a role and this imposes a certain false character on their sexual relationships that they cannot disguise or cover up. They cannot explain, even to themselves, and so asking direct questions of people whose behavior can only be explained by unconscious dynamic mechanism is a useless occupation.

Sometimes obsessive-compulsives show a decrease of interest in sexual activity. This, as in other situations, is frequently related to the kind of depression which they experience as part of their whole style of obsessive living. They pull back into a world of their own and, just as interest in many things around them wanes, so too does their interest in sexual activity. Here, of course, it is the depression that needs response before a counselor tries to do anything to assist the obsessive-compulsive person with his lowered interest in sexual activity.

Counselors themselves will feel one of the other dynamics that affects the sexual life of obsessives. Obsessives need to control the relationships into which they enter in order to protect themselves from being lost in them. They bring this style to sexual relationships and they bring it to the counselor's office. That is why they may attack, questioning the counselor's competence to be helpful, or asking other questions that tend to interfere with the counselor's concentration. This is just one aspect of their psychological need to master every situation so that nothing surprising or disconcerting can happen to them. It is very difficult for them, then, to play anything but a controlling role in sexual activity.

Within this context it is not surprising to discover complaints such as premature ejaculation. As Barnett notes, these people are very upset by such difficulties but they have no idea of their true cause. "Deeply distrustful of women, the man in these cases labors under a constant apprehension of rejection, and is unable to depend on the continuity and stability of the woman's presence for the duration of the sexual act. The occasions of precipitate orgasm cause shame and humiliation about his failure, adding to the existing anxiety and intensifying the problem." The task for the counselor is not to focus on the individual sexual failure but to reach the anxious person beneath the elaborate intellectual defenses and the rigid lifestyle. It is not enough to teach the obsessive some relaxing exercises; he will attack them with an effort to master them just as he does everything else.

Although this obsessional difficulty is more often seen in men, female obsessive patients do have similar difficulties with orgasm. Detached and restrained in their experience of sexuality, these women often experience difficulties in achieving orgasm. This does not mean that they are impotent. It is merely another reflection of their whole personality style. Complaints of retarded orgasm in obsessive women cannot be treated separately from their whole personality.

Impotence, a failure to be able to complete the sexual act, is common in this obsessive approach to sexuality. It is a symbolic activity representing a pulling back from intimacy and a restraint of emotion in any atmosphere of closeness with another. Such impotence also reflects the underlying "sense of inadequacy and incompetence in interpersonal relations characterizing the obsessive's early family experience" (Barnett, p. 43). It also mirrors the obsessive's fear of dependency needs. A couple may be caught in a conflicting sexual situation and never suspect the underlying obsessive dynamics that cause it.

Obsessives may well attempt to rationalize or intellectually interpret their sexual problems. This, however, is only another way of putting distance between themselves and their own feelings. It does not improve the situation. They may read scientific books and discuss obsessiveness with intellectual cleverness, but it only makes them seem more remote in relationship to their spouses and more inaccessible to any kind of deeper treatment. Obsessives' defenses can be very strong and only a counselor who recognizes the overall pattern can see beyond the presenting sexual problems and respond to the troubled person within.

Other behaviors that are sometimes evident in the sexual lives of obsessives are compulsive genital activities which include masturbation and promiscuity. There is very little enjoyment or even sexual interest involved in such activity; for obsessives, these are repetitive acts that flow from underlying dynamics basically unrelated to sex. Acting out sexually in a compulsive manner can also rise from these psychological dynamics. The style of promiscuity, for example, reveals this; there is no real closeness and the activity seems more an effort to save the self from isolation. The intimacy is not, therefore, successful and delivers very little satisfaction. A long list of sexual symptoms can flow from obsessive inner dynamics. Most patients have no idea of the relationship of their difficulties to their obsessiveness. If these sexual problems are not to be treated directly, what can counselors do to respond to persons with whom the establishment of close relationships is so intrinsically difficult?

Counselors need a great deal of patience in dealing with obsessives because they have so much masked anger. Counselors may well feel this anger but be unable to pinpoint or understand it. They do not know what is happening to them until they catch some glimpse of the obsessive-compulsive dynamics behind the defenses they experience in the counseling situation. Until they do, such counselors may try to be logical only to find that they are caught up in the intellectual presentation which is so characteristic of the obsessive. Counselors who get caught in these defenses have a very difficult time getting out. Counselors feel the hidden anger even though it is expressed subtly, as in the obsessive-compulsive effort to control the counseling or to keep the counselor at a distance so that he or she does not ask too many intimate questions. This is what angers counselors. It is not a good idea to try to push obsessives too hard, or coax them into revealing themselves, or to get defensive ourselves in dealing with them. It is certainly not a good idea to get angry at them.

Counseling these persons can be very trying precisely because they are so skilled at avoiding the emotional contact the counselor wishes to establish. In other words, they do to the counselor what they do to everybody else, including their spouse. As counselors are able to appreciate the way in which obsessives avoid emotional material, they begin to understand better their whole style and this enables them to avoid being caught up in it. Hearing the right messages—and being particularly alert at the beginning and end of the session—may help the counselor slowly and sensitively to form a therapeutic alliance with the distressed person. To accomplish this counselors must observe and control their own reactions since these can so easily become negative in dealing with these persons. Obsessives work at keeping us at a distance and they work especially hard to convert their sexual problems into intellectual riddles. When counselors can anticipate this challenge they are far less likely to complicate the therapy with their own confused counter-transference feelings. They may have to settle for limited gains and few cures but this is far better than being trapped in the infinitely complex web of defenses that obsessives so easily spin.

References

Balswick, Jack and Peek, Charles. "The Inexpressive Male: A Tragedy of American Society." *The Family Coordinator* (Oct., 1971).

Brenton, Myron. *The American Male.* New York: Coward-McCann, 1966.

DeMartino, M. F. (Ed.). *Sexual Behavior and Personality Characteristics.* New York: Grove Press, 1966.

Ellis, Albert. *The American Sexual Tragedy.* New York: Grove Press, 1962.

Grunwald, Henry A. (Ed.). *Sex in America.* New York: Bantam Books, 1964.

MacKinnon, R. A. and Michels, R. *The Psychiatric Interview in Clinical Practice.* Philadelphia: W. B. Saunders, 1971. See esp., "The Obsessive Patient."

Richardson, Herbert W. *Nun, Witch, Playmate: The Americanization of Sex.* New York: Harper & Row, 1971.

Winik, Charles. *The New People: Desexualization in American Life.* New York: Pegasus, 1968.

Zax, M. and Stricker, G. (Eds.). *The Study of Abnormal Behavior.* New York: The Macmillan Co., 1964.

EIGHT

Sex and Depression

DEPRESSION is anxiety's chief rival in the list of reported psychological symptoms. Every human being sooner or later feels, to some degree, the anguish and suffering that go along with just being alive. While depression and anguish are not the same, the feelings do have a certain similarity. Depression is not that normal, easily recognizable reaction that follows a loss, such as that of a loved one, or prolonged stress. Such reactions are usually time-limited to the precipitating incident or a reasonable period of recovery and re-integration afterwards. Depression is something else and since it can afflict almost everybody it is important for all counselors, even those who function only part-time, to read its identifying signs accurately.

This has added importance because of the relationship between sexual difficulties and depression. Sexual conflicts and complaints at all ages on the developmental scale may have depressive results or features; sexual problems, whether they are physical or psychological in origin, may give rise to depressive reactions and depressions, whatever their source, may reveal themselves in the disguise of sexual complaints. There is no easy rule of thumb for the non-professional counselor to follow in dealing with the complications that arise in these situations. The capacity for a sensitive reading and understanding of the complaint combined with good judgment about treatment possibilities constitute the best response for the para-professional helper. The latter is frequently the first outsider that family members contact when they are concerned about changes in the attitudes or behavior of one of its members. Some diagnostic sense is invaluable in being able to interpret the evidence correctly and with real understanding and appreciation for the feelings of all involved. Very few of these problems fail to have repercussions in the lives of those closest to the suffering person. People who are themselves emotionally involved in the conflict frequently misread it, distorting a true understanding of it with their own anxieties. The doctor, the member of the clergy, the teacher: these may be the ones who, instead of offering mere reassurance, may be able to make out at least the outlines of the problem and lead the concerned person to the correct next step.

Depression and its various manifestations are frequently misunderstood. Hence the need for counselors to understand its nature and the faces it can assume in human problems. In general, depression, the symptoms of which range along an extensive continuum, is manifested in feelings of sadness, a detachment from friends and relatives, and a break in the capacity to enter into and enjoy work or other activities. Self-esteem is involved and failure to care for the self may be one of the first clear signs of depression. Classic to the experience of depression is the report of insomnia, with the affected individual sleeping for short periods and awakening very early in the morning. There may also be a loss of appetite and a loss of weight as well. Mild depressions are marked by a certain dullness, as though the edge had been taken off life with a consequent loss of spontaneity and a need to make a constant effort to keep up with obligations. In a serious depression the symptoms are more marked: the person may be quite despondent and complain of serious physical ailments. Depressive symptoms often mask anger that has not been expressed and that, according to the classic psychodynamic theory, has been turned inwardly against the self.

The depression is sometimes evidenced only in "equivalents," that is, symbolic complaints that give voice to the depression—although these would not ordinarily be considered as symptoms of this problem. These include unusual complaints about pain or other somewhat vague if intensely felt hypochondriachal difficulties. At times the depression comes out in drinking or, as noted before, in sexual difficulties. Individuals suffering from depression may, for example, begin to act out sexually in a way that does not fit in with their previous modes of activity.

It is important for even para-professionals to be acquainted with the distinction between exogenous and endogenous depression. Exogenous depression refers to reactions associated with neurotic complaints, grief reactions, and the depressions that can follow certain illnesses or the taking of certain drugs. Persons suffering from this form of depression ordinarily have a life history which is marked with neurotic conflicts and complaints.

The endogenous classification is divided into unipolar and bipolar depressions. Unipolar depression, as noted by psychiatrist M. J. Martin of the Mayo Clinic, "may occur later in life than psychoneurotic depression, and is characterized by recurring episodes of depression which are usually of psychotic proportions" ("Impulsive Sexual Behavior Masking Insidious

Depression," *Medical Aspects of Human Sexuality,* March, 1976, p.50). Bipolar depression, also known more popularly as manic-depressive reaction, is classified as an affective disorder which, as Martin puts it, "produces alterations in mood with depressive bouts alternating with pathological euphoria and hypomanic activity." Research has shown that hereditary factors are associated with this disorder. It is this form of depression that has been treated successfully with lithium carbonate. Because there is much discussion about this treatment, it is vital for counselors to understand something about it and those situations in which it is effective.

Para-professional counselors often work with persons who have only heard something about a new treatment on the radio or television or from a newspaper article, and they must fill the role of educators and translators, assisting these individuals to understand that there is no magic cure waiting for most of them and that other treatment procedures may be indicated. The misunderstanding about the use of lithium to treat all depressions is an example of a situation that para-professionals can easily clarify.

Depression can occur at any time in the life cycle and sexual behavior is often the focus of its expression. Thus, for example, one can observe depressive reactions even in young infants, especially when they are deprived of the mothering figure. Depression does not look the same in infants as it does in adults but the depressive equivalents have a familiar ring to them. Observable changes occur, as for example, in the absence of the kind of behavior that is expected and is appropriate for the age of the infant. Feeding problems are also common.

Sexual problems as signs of depression must be understood in this perspective throughout the developmental period of infancy and childhood. As psychiatrist Dommena Renshaw of Loyola Medical School in Chicago has observed, there is an absence or an excess of the normal kinds of sexual expression that are expected at any particular phase of growth ("Sexuality and Depression in Infancy, Childhood, and Adolescence," *Medical Aspects of Human Sexuality,* June 1975, p 24, ff.).

The appearance of depressive symptoms in infants is significant in itself and for what it portends about later sexual development and conflicts. Infants, for example, who are deprived of the mothering figure for an extended period of time and for whom no adequate substitute is provided, become apathetic, eat poorly, respond socially in a remote and indifferent way, do not smile, and are even subject to more infections. Significant for the present discussion is the fact that poorly mothered infants suffer a generalized psychomotor retardation and, as Renshaw observes, "the depressed baby fails to engage in overall self-exploration as well as in genital exploration. This loss of normal pleasurable auto-eroticism is amplified by the loss of total body sensorimotor experience which results from being handled fondly by the mother" (p.29). In other words, the experiences essential to a full sense of the self and a normal capacity to experience and express sexuality are affected by this deprivation. This shows up in the children's subsequent difficulties with forming their "body image, self-esteem, the capacity to relate to others, and for later sexual adjustment."

Para-professional counselors need an understanding of these symptoms and of the fact that these difficulties do not take care of themselves. All too often well-meaning advisors—even physicians at times—offer reassurance that the child will "grow out" of the difficulty. This may be true in certain problem areas but it does not work out successfully when there is evidence of this type of depression. Many of the adult difficulties with sexuality can be traced to early life problems. If even a fraction of these can be avoided it is a distinct advantage for a great many persons, including all those who will be affected, in one way or the other, by the adult sexual adjustment of the infant. And treatment is possible, especially if the symptoms are recognized in time. The role of the para-professional counselor may be that of urging responsible persons to look more deeply into the situation when these symptoms seem to be present. The nonprofessional may not be the agent of treatment, but may well serve as the effective agent of referral.

As Renshaw observes, treatment "of depression in infancy is really treatment of the mother. It is therefore important to establish the reason for any long separation between mother and baby." While death, institutional placement and desertion may explain it, other conditions in a present mother may also be important. Thus, psychiatric problems such as "rejection of the infant, drug addiction . . . severe depression, inadequacy, sociopathy, or psychosis may be other causative factors that effectively separate her emotionally from her infant . . ."(p.32). Working toward treatment for the mother, which may include educating her in the tasks of motherhood and the provision of a mother substitute, are two possibilities of which non-professional counselors should be aware.

During this period, ranging roughly from the third to the thirteenth year, the clinical evidence may vary greatly. The implications of the presence of depression with its effect on and expression through sexual behavior remains quite important. Counselors need not indulge an unhealthy curiosity in any of these situations; they are not out to offer advice that is unsought or unwelcome. The fact is, however, that the nonprofessional counselor is the person to whom concerned family members may first turn when they notice something troubling in their child's behavior. This is particularly true when there is a sexual dimension to the disturbance.

Children can exhibit depressive problems through behavior as varied as temper tantrums, headaches, vomiting or through fighting or poor school performance. Sometimes the child engages in aberrant behavior, stealing or running away from home, in order to attract some attention or recognition. The depression is connected with sexuality because it can, if it is of long duration, further inhibit the normal types of developmental activity which are important for adequate adult sexual adjustment. If the child is depressed, for example, he or she may be less spontaneous than their companions and may, as a result, have poor relationships with them. They may remain somewhat isolated and fail to participate in the normal kinds of discussions or exploratory behavior related to sexual awareness and growth.

A child may attempt to ward off depressive feelings through self-stimulation. Masturbation may be viewed by the parents as evidence of some moral disorder rather than as a symptom of intrapersonal conflict. Reactions that generate shame and guilt only complicate the problem for the child and may deepen the underlying depression. Counselors who are sensitive may be able to interpret the child's behavior in a different light, assisting the parents to understand and to modify their pattern of reactions accordingly. If the counselor is a member of the clergy the positive effect of an informed understanding of masturbation as a symptom rather than a sign can be enormous.

Much that has been noted about masturbation holds true during the adolescent years as well. Instead of being a problem in itself it can at times be a sexual reflection of another condition that needs attention in an understanding manner. However, not all masturbation signifies a struggle against depression. In fact, at the time of adolescence the lack of masturbation—or a lack of any sex play or interest in the opposite sex—*may* be an indication of a depressive difficulty.

Depression in the adolescent years is a serious problem. Suicide, as Renshaw notes, rises dramatically in the fifteen to eighteen year age group. Catching the signals early and interpreting them correctly takes on added importance.

What does depression look like during this period? It may resemble, in its symptomatic translation, the evidence already noted in the period of childhood, including difficulties in school, physical complaints, and running away. Sexually, there may be a lack of interest on the part of a person who had previously seemed normal in sexual awareness and development. There may be excessive masturbation, activity that goes beyond the masturbation that may be expected during this period of personal growth and identity consolidation. In adolescent girls there may be promiscuous sexual behavior which represents an effort to ward off depressed feelings. This problem may be related to the girl's poor self-image, her seeking of popularity, or her fear of loneliness.

As a boy gets into the later stages of adolescence he may suffer greatly from the effects of the depression on his self-esteem and his sexual interest. Depression, as it can in later life situations, may lessen sexual feelings or sexual reactivity. The boy becomes more bewildered and may try the kinds of remedies that, despite the supposed sexual revolution, are still commonly offered in his peer group. He may, for example, try the use of amphetamines or alcohol or the use of some spurious aphrodisiac suggested or sold to him by a companion. Failing again, the depression worsens and the sexual difficulty assumes an even greater role in sharpening his sense of failure. The possibilities of the manifestation and exaggeration of the depressive problem are numerous and counselors should attempt to understand any prolonged bizarre behavior or evidence of social withdrawal.

While weight loss traditionally goes along with depression, adolescents may gain weight, using the gratification of food as a means of trying to handle the difficulty. This can be the problem of obese girls, for example, who have negative attitudes toward their body-image and who may try to use sex as a bartering agent for social acceptance.

What advice can the nonprofessional counselor offer if there is some suspicion about problems of this nature? The best recommendation is for a thorough examination, both physical and psychological, with a careful history recorded in order to get as complete a picture as possible of the possible conflict beneath the symptoms. Understanding support to the individual and to the family members, who may well benefit from some group form of therapy, are also significant roles which non-professionals can fill in these circumstances.

Depression is often the result of sexual problems in the later years of life. In a culture in which sexual performance is prized so highly, the first hint of some faltering in sexual functioning can have enormous psychological impact on both men and women. Human beings remain highly vulnerable to depressive reactions to sexual conflicts throughout their lives. Helpers do well to understand something about the process of aging and its effect on sexuality as well as the psychological complications associated with the multiple crises of passing into and through the middle years of life. Perhaps the most basic learning centers on the changes in sexual performance that can be related to the aging process as distinguished from those attributable to emotional causes. Quite often middle-aged people are helped a great deal when they are enabled to identify and to accept the inevitabilities of growing older without feeling their sexual identity is thereby threatened.

While males may retain their capacity for sexual relationships well into old age, there are some changes that can be expected after the age of fifty. There is a slowing down in almost all phases of the sexual act, from the capacity for stimulation and erection, through climax and the refractory phase before sexual activity can be undertaken again. These are facts and they are not attributable to depression, although the latter may have similar effects. Slowing down can be depressing in itself. The difficulty arises when men are unprepared for such changes and are made anxious by them. They can make the problem far worse for themselves through efforts to "will" their way out of it, or to "prove" that they are as virile as they were when they were young men. If counselors are well-informed and understanding they can offer helpful education to these troubled men and assist them to work through their anxieties and adjust to a somewhat modified but by no means totally impaired sexual functioning.

Genuine depression causes sexual dysfunction of a different kind. A lowered interest in sexuality is more frequently attributable to depression and therefore to more remote psychological causes. Other indications that the problem is psychogenic are found in secondary impotence; that is, an inability to perform sexually that has no physical origin but is related to diminished self-esteem or other psychological causes. So too, depressed women may experience orgasmic dysfunction although they have never experienced this difficulty before. When persons use compulsive masturbation to try to get to overcome a problem with insomnia, depression should be suspected. Promiscuity as a means of handling depression is also a signal, as are the alternating periods of intense sexual activity and no sexual activity at all which go with bipolar depression (Renshaw, *Medical Aspects of Human Sexuality,* September, 1975, p. 53).

Here again, a careful history is essential if a humane and helpful diagnosis is to be made. This is the business of medical and psychological experts; but the role of the para-professional in hearing out the difficulties and making a sensible referral is highly important. It is still difficult for many persons to speak about their sexual conflicts or doubts, and it is harder still when people are trapped in depressive reactions which rob them of much of their previous interest in life.

Depression, with its effects on sexual and other activities, can arise from many causes, even at times from succeeding too early in life. The depressive reaction to early success—the no-more-worlds-to-conquer syndrome—is not uncommon. It is quite as crippling psychologically as real or perceived failure. Middle age is itself the setting for a number of adjustments and depression is not at all unusual during this time. The sexual life of human beings is particularly sensitive to overall personal problems and helpers who can sense the depression beneath the sexual complaints—and who can distinguish these from the ordinary changes that go with aging—can be enormously helpful. They fill an equally important role when the depression is the result rather than the cause of the depressive reaction. Being attuned to the many combinations of experiences that can affect middle-aged persons helps counselors to avoid giving old-fashioned and ill-informed advice and enables them to assist persons back to a healthier and happier life adjustment.

References

Bowlby, J. "Grief and Mourning in Infancy and Early Childhood." *Psychoanalytic Study of the Child* (1960), 15:9.

———. "Separation Anxiety: A Critical Review of the Literature." *Journal of Child Psychology and Psychiatry* (1960), 1:251.

Dement, W., et al. *Sleep and Altered States of Consciousness* (1st Ed.). Baltimore: Williams & Wilkins, 1967.

Jacobson, E. *Depression.* New York: International Universities Press, 1971.

Kiev, A. "Depression and Libido." *Medical Aspects of Human Sexuality* (Nov., 1969), 4:235.

Kinsey, A., et al. *Sexual Behavior in the Human Female* (1st Ed.). Philadelphia: W. B. Saunders Co., 1953.

———. *Sexual Behavior in the Human Male* (1st Ed.). Philadelphia: W. B. Saunders Co., 1948.

Linn, L. "Clinical Manifestations of Psychiatric Disorders." *Comprehensive Textbook of Psychiatry* (2nd Ed.). Baltimore: Williams & Wilkins, 1975, p. 811.

Masters, William H. and Johnson, Virginia E. *Human Sexual Inadequacy* (1st Ed.). Boston: Little, Brown & Co., 1970.

———. *Human Sexual Response* (1st Ed.). Boston: Little, Brown & Co., 1966.

Paykel, E. S. and Weissman, M. M. "Marital and Sexual Dysfunction in Depressed Women." *Medical Aspects of Human Sexuality* (June, 1972), 1:73.

Renshaw, D. C. "Depression in the 1970s." *Journal of Nervous Mental Disorders* (July, 1973).

———. "Depression in the Young." *Journal of the American Medical Women's Association* (Oct. 1973).

Spitz, F. R. "Hospitalism." *Psychoanalytic Study of the Child.* 1:1945.

Winokur, G. "Diagnostic and Genetic Aspects of Affective Illness." *Psychiatric Annals* (Feb., 1973), 3:6.

NINE

Transference in Sex Therapy

A SITUATION that can be overlooked by those wanting to help persons with sexual difficulties centers on the psychological implications of any relationship which is close, intense and highly personal. Some commentators overlook or discount what we can describe as the invisible but very real factors in the interplay of those who help and those who are helped. Transference and counter-transference feelings, as psychology has termed them, are powerful factors in any therapeutic relationship, however, and they cannot be ignored, especially when counseling persons with sexual conflicts. The reciprocal feelings, many of them unconscious, are important in this area which is necessarily sensitive and intimate and therefore the perfect atmosphere for the development of such feelings.

Transference, as most helpers understand it, refers to the feelings which clients experience toward counselors in the course of therapy. These feelings are actually reactions appropriate to previous, significant persons in the client's life, such as, for example, parents or surrogate parents. Such feelings out of the past—they may be positive or negative—are transferred to the counselor. Technically speaking, then, these are feelings from a previous period in the individual's life which are now applied unrealistically to the therapist. It is important for counselors to understand that they themselves are not the real object of these feelings and that some understanding of these patterns of reaction on the part of their clients is essential if they are going to make progress.

In a classic definition of transference Fenichel says this: "The patient misunderstands the present in terms of the past; and then instead of remembering the past, he strives, without recognizing the nature of his action, to relive the past and to live it more satisfactorily than he did in his childhood. He 'transfers' the past attitudes to the present" (*Psychoanalytic Theory of the Neurosis,* New York: W. W. Norton & Co., 1945). Psychiatrist Richard D. Chessick has observed: "Transference is a form of resistance in which the patient defends himself against remembering and discussing his infantile conflicts by reliving them, but it also offers a unique opportunity to observe the past directly, and thereby to understand the development of the conflict."

Transference is a complicated subject and there is extensive literature on it in the textbooks on therapy, especially those of a psychoanalytic nature. While most counselors will not be engaged in long term therapy with individuals who have sexual conflicts, and therefore will not need to be experts on the subject, they must know enough about it to recognize its presence and its implications in their therapeutic work. Transference is a core feature of most of our relationships in life. We bring up things out of the past toward present figures all the time. We use the style of relating we developed in our earliest years. We do not want to get too self-conscious about the fact, but we cannot ignore it nor try to impose an excessively rational grid on life so that we miss the unconscious psychological determinants of many of our relationships. Transference and counter-transference constitute the aura of a therapeutic relationship much like a field of electricity which cannot be seen but whose effects cannot be denied.

The development of transference feelings in the client provides counselors with a window through which they can see more clearly the psychological style of the individual. In psychonalytic therapy it is the transference that is analyzed so that the person can surrender unrealistic patterns of relating and adopt new and more mature ways of relating to other persons. People are not cured of transference feelings but they are helped to lay down the burdens of their past lives.

Counter-transference feelings are also significant. These are the emotional reactions—again, positive or negative—of counselors to their clients, feelings ranging from strong attraction to rejection. Such feelings are also informative because they tell us about ourselves as counselors and provide us with a measure of our own style and the depth of our involvement in the current relationship. Once again, counselors must not try to purge themselves of all counter-transference feelings. They must be able to understand the feelings and achieve some insight into their origin if they do not want to be controlled by them.

As psychiatrist Jon Meyer of Johns Hopkins University observes: "The expression of reaction patterns, affects, and fantasies in a current time frame, with immediacy, and in a personalized context is the living experience of the transference. A transference brings vividly alive, in a controlled and observable setting, both the unsatisfied claims for love and sexual release and the prohibited aggressive feelings. This phenomenon offers opportunity for real work. One cannot dismantle a neurotic construction purely in retrospect or, as Freud put it, 'in absentia'" (*Comprehensive Textbook of Psychiatry*, Vol. II, 2nd Ed., Baltimore: Williams and Wilkins Co., 1975, p. 1552).

Counselors use accepted techniques to deal with the transference phenomenon, attempting to match their interpretations of its deeper significance to the capacity of their clients to understand and accept and therefore modify their own expectations of the relationship and of life in general. Special challenges arise when working with people with sexual difficulties. Perhaps the most common manifestation of transference feelings is the patient's falling in love with the counselor. This is not unusual in therapy in general but, unless counselors have some grasp of what is really taking place, they may mistakenly identify themselves as the true object of these feelings and fail to see this as a transference phenomenon.

There are those who popularly suggest that it is therapeutic for therapists to respond to these erotic feelings with physical manifestations of love. This unfortunate but widespread notion is ethically, morally and psychologically disastrous. Psychiatrist William Masters has publicly suggested that any counselor who indulges in sexual relationships with a client should be considered a rapist, and recent well-publicized legal cases suggest that the courts may also regard such relationships in the same light. It is not simply a question of taking advantage of a vulnerable person in therapy. That is reprehensible enough. However, the fundamental failure lies in the lack of appreciation of the erotic component of the transference/counter-transference relationship. It is a profound professional failure. A patient may have sexual feelings toward a therapist and a therapist may well have them in response to a patient. Sorting these out, however, and seeing them in perspective is an essential demand of good counseling. Acting out these impulses is both bad morals and bad therapy. No rationalization, however glib it may be, can justify this behavior.

Erotic satisfaction only seems to be what the client wants in the transference feelings toward the helper. In fact, the outcome is frequently to defeat the therapist when he supplies what he thinks the other person wants. This destroys the relationship and compounds the difficulties of the person coming for help. The exploration and interpretation of the transference, as well as the identification of the infantile strivings that are its constitutive elements, require a disciplined counselor who is both sensitive and knowledgeable.

Dr. Meyer feels that special problems exist in helping persons with sexual difficulties because "sexuality is plastic and multifaceted, involves other people through their representation in fantasies, and is non-obligatory for an individual's life." He suggests that at times "the most effective progress is made by direct pursuit of history and fantasies related to the sexual disability; in others, consideration of more peripheral material is highly therapeutic." He cites some of the areas in which counselors may find themselves and mentions the central themes that require identification in order to work through the transference feelings successfully.

He suggests, for example, that if a person has not resolved an experience of grief related to early separations of losses, or because of being brought up by parents who maintained emotional distance, the individual may have problems in learning to trust enough to experience mature intimacy. This grief, he suggests, must be dealt with because the client experiences a "constant fear of repeated loss, human relationships being approached with detachment, isolation and a facade of independence." Counselors must be prepared during the treatment phase to confront this sense of deprivation and the anger that flows from it. "In this situation," Meyer suggests, "the reliability and punctuality of the therapist are essential."

He also observes that the frankly sexual material that comes out in counseling frequently has "Oedipal shadings." Meyer suggests that "desires for physical and emotional possession of the therapist are pursued not simply for personal satisfaction alone but also in the context of a presumed competition with other patients or other figures in the therapist's life." Counselors who are unaware of how complex these transference feelings can be will hardly understand the kinds of emotional transactions that may be carried out in the course of therapy. This may be a special difficulty for counselors who have gained some recognition for working with people with sexual problems. They may be especially vulnerable to these kinds of fantasies and they may feel pressure from their patients who would like to be perceived more as associates and helpers to the counselor than as persons with problems of their own.

It is not at all unusual for contemporary counselors to work with individuals who are or have been part of a "swinging scene." These individuals describe their lives as filled with relationships. These developments are related, of course, to earlier conflicts in their lives.

As Meyer suggests: "The swinging provides the element of risk-taking so addicting in neurotic and perverse sexual lives, it offers far easier gratification and discharge than is possible through a therapeutic process, it operates in the service of denial, it provides narcissistic rewards."

Counselors, in other words, must be aware of the factors operating below the surface in "swingers" who present sexual problems; they must be attuned as well to the particular transference feelings that may arise and which may have the flavor of some of the conflicted material that has just been described. Unwary counselors can be caught up or incorporated into this—which would be equivalent to being caught up in their clients' superficial fantasy and self-gratifying lives; and this is clearly not therapeutic.

A subtle issue that counselors working with people with sexual problems face is the possibility of complications after short-term re-educative counseling has been employed with sexual problems. In other words, if counselors try to confine their treatment in the behavior therapy approach to sex problems, they may ignore or factor out the possibilities of transference phenomena. This does not mean that these are not present. To ignore them does not cause them to vanish or to lose their power. Indeed, the clients may not experience emotional realities occurring within them until some time after the briefer, behaviorally oriented therapy has been completed with apparent success. Meyer indicates that either one or both partners "may realize for the first time the presence of internal resistance to working through a problem initially seen as educational and mechanical." He feels that such issues will become more common as shorter term, educationally oriented sexual therapy is employed.

When persons come to the realization of the need to work through these recently discovered internal resistances, they frequently return to therapy. Three elements, Meyer notes, must be recognized if this takes place. First, a return to therapy may be based on an accurate understanding of a genuine personal difficulty. Second, it may involve the operation of transference. Third, it may be related to the psychological problem of separation.

Meyer suggests that if the person returns to the original counselor, referral to another therapist would be in order. If the original counselor agrees to see the client again, he should be aware of the presence of these factors, especially of those related to a transference begun in the original counseling and never worked through. He says that "the patient will have an unresolved transference and expectation based on a previous and different therapeutic encounter with the therapist; second . . . considerations about his abilities as a lover and teacher will pertain; and, third . . . the patient's spouse will have more than the usual questions about events in the treatment situation."

Counselors are naive to assume that any relationship can be kept on a strictly objective, unfeeling plane. Something always happens when persons interact on an intimate level and this, of course, is necessarily the case when therapy centers on the sensitive area of sexual difficulties. Counselor and client are not two machines digging impersonally at the turf of the psyche. As human beings they live and move in the clouds of emotional impulses that we communicate all around us all the time. Counselors, even when they wish to minimize the effects of transference, must be aware of its possibilities and must learn to read the unconscious language of the transference/counter-transference reality.

Counselors who are not working full-time as therapists or who see persons for extremely limited courses of counseling, must sensitize themselves to the reality of transference so that they will be able to identify the first signals of its development and will have some sense about how to respond to it. They must also, in fairness to themselves and to their clients, judge how deeply they can commit themselves to persons with whom they are going to work only on a short-term basis. It is all very well to say that we must build rapport, seem personalistically concerned, and make ourselves totally available to others; that is a romantic counseling ideal that does not work well in the close quarters of intense therapy with persons with sexual conflicts. The possibilities of transference are many and the complications are obviously numerous and frequently beyond the competence of the counselor to understand or manage.

It is the height of personal concern and respect to make understanding judgments about the therapy in which we engage and to conduct ourselves so that the human and ethical values we believe in are upheld with both grace and dignity. It does not help others to get over-involved when there is no possibility of follow-through. It is a distinct disadvantage to stir up the phenomena of transference and counter-transference without having sufficient time or skill to work them through. There is no dishonor in tempering our counseling style to fit the realistic possibilities of our work situation.

The more sensitive a counselor becomes to the way transference/counter-transference feelings develop, the sooner in the course of the relationship will he pick up the subtle signals that foretell something of the potential direction and depth of these feelings. A wise counselor reads the unconscious messages early in order to make a more informed—and therefore more understanding—judgment about the way in which the counseling should be conducted. Just a sensitivity to transference in its most undefined form is extremely helpful to the concerned helper. Freud was supposed to have suggested once that a therapist should not trouble the transference until the transference troubles him, but counselors definitely need some awareness—a feel for it, one could say—of its nature before proceeding far into therapy.

Transference will trouble the counselor who chooses to act as if such a phenomenon did not exist or did not enter into even brief, intensive therapy. The problem will be there but the naive counselor will not know what it is or where it came from. He may misinterpret the client's apparent interest in him, may get embroiled in the defenses rather than the substance of therapy, and may even do things to encourage these puzzling but enjoyable feelings. In limited therapy it is easy to see how the client may begin to generate transference feelings and not get a chance to identify them or even begin to work them through. Such clients, their unconscious stirrings suddenly cut off, are the kind who may have to take up therapy again at a later date in order to complete what was begun but not attended to in the earlier counseling.

Common sense, as much as anything else, suggests that those who counsel as part of other responsibilities need at least a practical working knowledge of the world of transference. They need not be masters of psychodynamics to appreciate that such feelings can arise, that the feelings are out of the past and not directed toward them, and that they need to calibrate their self-presentation to the circumstances and possibilities of their work.

As mentioned earlier, one of the most common forms of transference/counter-transference emotions is the stirring of sexual feelings in client and therapist. This phenomenon may seem natural enough; indeed, some therapists seem pleased that they can react sexually and can cause others to react sexually to them. They are curious, somewhat titillated by what seems to be a combination of risk and novelty in an otherwise burdened day. Therapy, of course, does not exist primarily for the entertainment of the counselor.

Other counselors, especially part-time ones, have very different reactions. Some are terrified by their own sexual reactions, feel guilty about them, and may struggle to suppress them. Some people, despite the supposedly enlightened age, find it difficult to talk about their own sexual reactions; they try to carry on despite them, disowning them as temptations or alien aspects of the self. It is clear, however, that any person who works closely with another person will be subject to the possibility of some sexual reactivity. This does not make either party evil, adulterously inclined, or a psychosexual pervert; neither is it fuel for the fires of machismo.

Whenever there is an intense relationship people react totally to each other, whether they intend to or not, and sexuality is necessarily a part of this. The presence of sexual feelings cannot be ignored; in fact, counselors must attend to them in order to see their relationship to the transference situation. They need to be read and understood for their significance in the overall relationship. In order to be able to do this, counselors need some understanding of the erotic aspect of transference. They also need to understand the dynamic reasons for not acting out their own sexual feelings in relationship to the patient.

As psychiatrist Leon Saul has observed, it is a mistake to give any encouragement to a client to use the therapist as a source of gratification for his or her sexual and dependent love needs. This is a blind alley, the kind the client may have been pursuing in other ways all through life. The counselor does not help by providing these gratifications; he only helps, as Saul notes, by assisting the client "to find the satisfaction in real life that is craved . . . by helping her in removing the inner blocks" (*Psychodynamically Based Psychotherapy,* New York: Science House, 1968, p. 334).

It is also vital for counselors to appreciate the substance of the erotic transference feelings which only seem to ask for a sexual response. These are actually feelings out of the past directed on an unconscious level to other persons. Part of extensive therapy is allowing the patient to feel these historic feelings in the present toward the counselor so that they can be understood. The therapist, in other words, is substituting for the original parent figure and, no matter how the sexual urges are rationalized on the surface, there is an unconscious incestuous reality that must be acknowledged. Even though the patient consciously claims to have affection for the person of the therapist, something else is taking place at the unconscious level. As Saul observes, the apparent love for the counselor is ". . . the child's wish for the good parent. . . . Hence to the patient's unconscious any unsublimated sexual gesture is like a similar gesture by a parent toward a very small child. . . . Any sexual element, however appealing to the patient's mature ego, can only be a threat to the small child within" (p. 336).

Yet a third reason for seeing the erotic aspects of transference in better perspective is suggested by the way such feelings can intensify the client's involvement in the transference. In other words, persons try to get out of the transference what they should be getting out of life itself; they cannot live in the transference and make progress in the area of general living. This causes additional confusion and makes the task of seeing the transference phenomenon in proper perspective extraordinarily difficult.

Add to this what Saul describes as "the often deeply repressed hostility and guilt which are probably always hidden behind, but intrinsic to, the sexual desires toward the analyst" (p. 337). All counselors can learn from Saul's injunction to be wary of what may seem the self-enhancing sexual interest of the client. "In the face of sexual love needs, he should remember that what the patient puts forward may mask the opposite, and in fact regularly does so . . . no matter how obvious eros may be, hostility is the inevitable middle link. Hostility arises from dependence and weakness and libidinal frustration . . ." (p. 338).

The counselor's objectivity is also destroyed by a faulty interpretation of erotic transference and any ill-judged responses, even very mild ones, to it. This makes the counselor's value as a helper highly dubious. Add to these psychological reasons the host of ethical and moral considerations important to both parties, and the case for proceeding with caution and insight into transference realities becomes even more clear.

It may be that not many counselors will find themselves this involved in the complications, erotic and otherwise, of transference. Nevertheless, the situation of dealing with persons with sexual conflicts minimizes the possibility of these feelings developing at least in inchoate form. Helpers cannot be blind to this and they must keep clearly in mind their goal of establishing a relationship with the healthy part of the client's ego. The helping link goes from what is healthy and strong in them to the strengths, rather than the confusions or weaknesses, of the other. Only when transference phenomena can be accurately sensed and understood can this mature bridge be built.

References

Arapz, Daniel. "Marital Transference." *Journal of Family Counseling.* 2(2):-55–63.

Aronson, Gerald. "Some Types of Transference and Countertransference." *Bulletin of the Menninger Clinic* (1974), 38(4):355–59.

Blum, Harold. "The Concepts of Eroticized Transference." *Journal of the American Psychoanalytic Association* (1973), 21(1):61–76.

Daniels, R. S. "Some Early Manifestations of Transference: Their Implications for the First Phase of Psychoanalysis." *Journal of the American Psychoanalytic Association* (Oct., 1969), 17(4):995–1014.

Farwell, G. F., N. R. Gamsky and Mathieu-Coughlan (Eds.). "Commonalities and Distinctions Between Counselling and Psychotherapy." *The Counselor's Handbook.* New York: Intext, 1974.

Frank, Jerome D. *Persuasion and Healing: A Comparative Study of Psychotherapy.* New York: Schocken, 1973.

————. "Therapeutic Components of Psychotherapy: A 25-Year Progress Report of Research." *Journal of Nervous and Mental Disease* (Nov., 1974), 159(5):325–42.

Garfield, Sol. "What Are the Therapeutic Variables in Psychotherapy?" *Psychotherapy and Psychosomatics* (1974), 24(4–6):372–78.

Hurn, Hal. "Adolescent Transference: A Problem of the Terminal Phase of Analysis." *Journal of the American Psychoanalytic Association* (1970), 18(2):342–57.

Klopfer, Walter and Max Reed. *Problems in Psychotherapy: An Eclectic Approach.* Washington, D.C.: Hemisphere Publishing Corp., 1974.

Robinson, K. E. "The Dimension of Reality Satisfaction or Frustration in Transference and Countertransference." *Comprehensive Psychiatry* (1969), 9(4):349–57.

Sahakian, William (Ed.). *Psychotherapy and Counselling: Studies in Technique.* Chicago: Rand McNally, 1969.

Sandler, J., C. Dare and A. Holder. "Basic Psychoanalytic Concepts"; "Working Through"; "Interpretations and Other Interventions." *British Journal of Psychiatry* (Jan, 1971), 118(542):53–39 and (Dec., 1970), 118(541):617–21.

Scher, Maryonda. "The Process of Changing Therapists." *American Journal of Psychotherapy* (Apr., 1970), 25(2):278–86.

Shave, David. *The Language of Transference.* Boston: Little, Brown & Co., 1968.

Sorell, William. "Basic Concepts of Transference." *Diseases of the Nervous System* (1973), 34(4):;58–159.

Strupp, Hans. "Basic Ingredients of Psychotherapy." *Psychotherapy and Psychosomatics* (1974), 24(406):249–60.

————. " 'Spontaneous Remission' and the Nature of the Therapeutic Influence." *Psychotherapy and Psychosomatics* (1974), 24(406):389–93.

Weinshel, E. M. "The Transference Neurosis: A Survey of the Literature." *Journal of the American Psychoanalytic Association* (1971), 19(1):67–88.

TEN

Sex Problems in Marriage

ALMOST anyone who counsels, even only part-time, spends many hours with married couples. Frequently the presenting problem is sexual in nature. There are as many depersonalized "cures" for sexual problems as there are examples of depersonalized sexuality. To avoid excessive concentration on the sexual "problem" counselors must carefully determine the nature of the complaint and its relationship to the personalities of the married couple. Few experienced counselors are naive enough to think that marriages can be set straight merely by a few sexual readjustments, although this is the popular impression left by many best-selling books on sexual compatibility. Such books sell well precisely because so many men and women seek answers to their more fundamental interpersonal difficulties by solving the sexual difficulties that are only symbolic of deeper problems. These books not only help people to get more pleasure out of their sexual activity, but also to hold the promise of strengthening or healing the marriage relationship itself.

Counselors keep the relationship in proper perspective by understanding that the sexual complaints are more likely to be symptomatic of deeper difficulties than they are to be the total problem in themselves. Although the details of sexual difficulties can be fascinating, sensitive helpers always listen for what lies beneath these complaints. The task of the counselor is to sense the psychological drift or pattern in the couple's married relationship and to respond to that more than to individual complaints about sex.

Clients are often puzzled by their sexual problems; they are distressed by the difficulties and cannot see them as part of a symbolic language through which they unconsciously express conflicts. The counselor is a translator of these problems, helping those suffering from them to better understand all of themselves. This is readily done by counselors who are prepared, in what can become quite complex therapy, to hear both sides of the question. It is always tempting to ally oneself with the aggrieved or more complaining partner in a marriage. The first one who gets to the counselor frequently paints a very convincing picture in order to enlist the helper on his or her side. This is especially dangerous in situations in which sexual difficulties are described. Counselors may easily choose sides before hearing from both parties because the stories can be interesting and deeply touching. It can seem clear, especially to the inexperienced, where the blame lies.

It is commonplace for accusations to break like waves across the counselor's desk, with both wife and husband accusing each other of being responsible for their sexual incompatibility. Who started it and for what reasons requires a patient kind of unraveling that cannot take place in a few moments or even a few sessions. Listening to the way a couple relates, even as they charge each other with responsibility for their problems, gives the counselor the flavor of their emotional interlocking. Hearing this gives us important clues to the symbolic meaning of their specific sexual conflict and helps us to decide far more wisely on the goals of therapy and related questions, such as the desirability of referral.

Those who have had experience with marriage counseling understand that human beings have remarkably keen communication systems which enable total strangers with the same difficulties to find each other even in the vast crowds of modern civilization. People send out signals to each other which are picked up at a nonrational level. Immature persons can find other immature persons without trying very hard. They marry each other, or think that they do, not to enter into a stable relationship, but to preserve their own immaturity or to gratify their childlike needs. Persons with neurotic difficulties somehow unfailingly locate other neurotics who seem to match their needs.

Although counselors need not suspect that every marriage is a mismatch, they must be prepared, especially when sexual complaints are in the foreground, to listen carefully for the dynamics that identify personalities in conflict. Charles Llewellyn, Jr., a psychiatrist at Duke University, suggests that helpers who want to discern the true picture of the personalities involved must ask themselves questions: "What is each partner getting out of this relationship even though they have persistent sexual difficulties?" "Why has this relationship continued despite the intense difficulties?" "Why are these people coming to me now?" (*Medical Aspects of Human Sexuality,* Aug. 1973.) The answers to these questions provide the counselor with a feeling for the relationship that is both informative and helpful.

Dr. Llewellyn has described a number of types of persons who enter into mismatched marriages largely because of their psychological difficulties. Among the personality types suggested by Llewellyn are the following:

THE NARCISSISTIC PERSON

The narcissistic personality, a subject of recent intense study in psychiatric circles, may not seem maladjusted at all to the casual observer. Narcissistic persons can, in fact, seem fairly normal even though they seem self-preoccupied. What we cannot appreciate is their utter failure to learn that there is a difference between them and the outside world. Everything exists for them and they cannot differentiate psychologically with the result that they are concerned almost exclusively with the satisfaction of their own needs. Even when they do something which seems generous it is usually a calculated political move which brings them some kind of reward.

It is only logical, then, that when narcissistic persons marry they expect their spouses to meet their needs completely. There is no question that their needs come first and it seems entirely appropriate that the partner should gratify them. Such narcissistic self-investment is clearly revealed in sexual relationships where the narcissistic person's partner feels frustrated and left out. The narcissistic person seeks to get but not to give pleasure. The sad part is that narcissistic persons frequently seem to find immature spouses who, in the beginning of marriage, seem to derive emotional support from them. It is not long, however, before their mutual inadequacies become apparent.

The sexual area cannot help but reflect clearly the total selfishness of the narcissistic person. The sexual area is not, however, the problem in itself. Although the affected spouse may complain of a relationship that is "one-sided," and although we may feel very sympathetic to this person, the situation is not quite so simple. It is not merely a question of encouraging the man and woman to work out a balance between their emotional needs. Narcissistic persons cannot understand this kind of talk because they have no real perception or appreciation of any needs but their own.

No one can rush to a quick diagnosis of a narcissistic personality merely on the basis of a few complaints about a relationship that is emotionally distorted. Counselors should, however, look for manifestations of narcissistic self-preoccupation in other areas of the individual's life. It is vital to understand the need that united these people in the first place and keeps them, howsoever tenuously, together.

Because such narcissism is a personality disorder its accessibility to treatment is unlikely. A decision about continued therapy for one or both partners is, however, far more preferable than trying to work out some kind of sexual bargaining or settlement that cannot and will not work. There is no simple answer to the sexual or deeper emotional problems of such a couple. Shifting the focus to their larger problems and supporting them through more intensive therapy is indicated.

THE WITHDRAWN PERSON

Withdrawn persons frequently enter a marriage in order to get away from some other situation. They may have been dominated at home and see marriage as fresh air after a long period of strangulation. These persons are afraid of assertiveness and of their own aggressive or self-expressive behavior. That is why they cannot establish more independence at home. They have difficulty understanding or expressing their own feelings and are very wary of any relationship which would make the demands on them that are implicit in marriage. To be dependent on another and to allow another to be dependent on them is frightening because if this happens they lose emotional control of the situation. They become anxious because they feel that their own identity may be submerged or that they may be manipulated or used by the other. These unconscious dynamics take over when they get married.

Their presenting difficulty may be frigidity or impotency, a reluctance or an inability to have sexual relationships. Obviously this difficulty, so closely linked to their personality problem, would be oversimplified if it were reduced merely to the individual's uneasiness about having sexual relationships. Counselors must try to see the many other aspects of the person's life and not tighten the focus on the sexual problem to such an extent that the broader issues are distorted. No effort should be made to respond directly to this sexual problem before the fundamental emotional problems are sensed more accurately.

Here again the psychological factors which brought these people together in the first place are extremely important. Therapy on an extended basis will lead them more deeply into themselves and will necessarily cause them to explore far more than their presenting difficulty of sexual incompatibility. Deeper therapy to strengthen the overall personality of the withdrawn person gets first priority over any effort to solve individual sexual problems.

THE COMPETITIVE PERSON

Sometimes the upbringing of an individual offers conditioning to competitive behavior that becomes a permanent part of all their activities, including their sexual life in marriage. This is not an unusual problem although its true nature is frequently unrecognized by those couples whose conflict is precipitated by it. They may sense that they are always out to get each other or to put each other down or to seize the emotional advantage in one way or another. A lot of it can sound good-natured on the surface. Competitive persons are generally aware of their deeper need to come out first all the time. They cannot live unless they do this, generally to compensate for some underlying personal inadequacy. This is what drives them on and drives them into sexual problems in marriage. The competitive dynamic almost certainly sentences a couple to intense sexual difficulties. A markedly competitive person sometimes chooses a marriage partner who can easily be overcome; the partner so chosen may need to be put down or may be quite dismayed to find marriage such a one-way relationship. There is no remedy for the consequent sexual difficulties that do not take the personality mix into account. Helping the person or persons to come to a better understanding of their competitive needs is a prerequisite for resolving any of the couple's sexual difficulties.

THE SADISTIC INDIVIDUAL

Sadistic individuals adjust to life by expressing their hostilities to those around them. This difficulty, which ordinarily afflicts men rather than women, clearly indicates a need for deep psychiatric help. These persons cannot experience sexual satisfaction unless they relate it in some way to the pain they cause their partner. This may occur through treating the partner rudely or, in an extreme, by hurting a partner both physically and psychologically. The tension that is generated by this activity seems necessary for these persons to experience sexual satisfaction.

When a couple comes in with stories about sexual difficulties that involve violence, counselors should be alerted to the possibility of pathological sadism. The sexual dimension of the sadistic personality becomes an outlet for the expression of a basic personality disorder. To try to treat the difficulty in marriage without recognizing its long and intertwined roots would only make the difficulty far more serious. Such persons cannot be urged to be more gentle nor can couples be encouraged simply to be more understanding. Any hints of sadism in the sexual life of married couples should alert counselors to the need for continued psychological help, including the probability of referral.

THE MASOCHISTIC INDIVIDUAL

Masochists seem to try to wipe away guilt or to achieve acceptance or forgiveness from the marriage partner through actions that amount to debasement on a regular basis. They always blame themselves or cast themselves in the role of the villain in life. They need to atone for their guilt. They may need the partner to sexually abuse them, to strike them or speak vile words to them in order to experience sexual excitement. When this is part

of the presenting problem, counselors are again alerted to the fact that they
are not dealing with a problem that can be separated from the personalities
of the individuals in the relationship. Something more than advice about a
specific sexual difficulty is called for. The counselor's role will be to define
the problem in sufficient depth to help the person take advantage of continu-
ous therapeutic treatment. In other words, work toward a referral if you are
not ready to work at length.

THE OBSESSIVE COMPULSIVE

Obsessive persons, full of rituals and repetitive behavior, bring these
along like excess baggage, into marriage, often incorporating these patterns
into sexual behavior. They need to carry out their rituals in an exact way
or they cannot have sexual relationships at all. This is merely one aspect
of an overall pattern of obsessive behavior, evidences of which are observable in other aspects of their lives. The obsessive person, as noted in chapter
seven, is characterized by repetitive worries or thoughts that leave little
room for anything else. Such persons are bound to have difficulty in the
sexual area of marriage. Just the preparations they go through before sex
relations can cause discomfort to their partners to such an extent that the
enjoyment of sexuality is notably diminished. It is clear counselors will not
help obsessive persons merely by giving them new rules to follow in their
sexual lives. They have to see more deeply into them than that. So too, it
is with obsessive persons who may be haunted by some thought (for example, that they will give veneral disease to their partner) that interferes in a
noticeable way with any free and spontaneous sexual activity. Extended
therapeutic help is appropriate. The obsessive person is discussed in greater
detail in chapter seven of this book.

THE EXHIBITIONISTIC PERSON

Exhibitionism, ordinarily a difficulty associated with males, is evidence
of a major psychological problem that is not cured by marriage. It is
generally found in insecure persons who need reinforcement for their masculinity; their inner conflict is expressed through displaying their genitals
to other persons. The underlying complexities that give rise to exhibitionistic behavior cannot be treated lightly nor merely with reassurance. A person
with this difficulty needs ongoing psychiatric treatment.

A form of exhibitionism is frequently seen in hysterical women who
appear to be very seductive; they dress in a sexually exciting way and may
be very flirtatious. They attract and excite men but they are incapable of

genuine sexual experience and, despite their provocative behavior, they want fatherly comfort from a mature husband rather than sex. They are unresponsive sexually despite all their teasing and superficially erotic behavior. Their exhibitionistic way of presenting themselves is sometimes pleasing to men who feel that their own self-esteem is increased by being with them and who settle for this secondary gain even when they cannot have a satisfactory sexual life with them. Here again, counselors need a sensitivity that allows them to see in the seemingly sexy woman the little child who needs intensive help.

THE PHOBIC PERSON

Phobic persons suffer from a neurosis through which they distract themselves from the true sources of their anxiety, turning it onto something in their environment. It is easier, for example, to be afraid of climbing stairs than it is to look directly at one's inner conflict. Phobic difficulties are functional but crippling. When phobic persons enter into marriage they project much of their fear out onto the environment in which they are living. This results in enormous difficulties with intimacy, because closeness causes them anxiety by threatening their underlying conflict. It may well be, for example, that a woman who is afraid of having children because of the traumatic impressions she had of this in her own impaired background, may be terrified of even the prospect of sexual relationships. She projects onto the arena of sexuality the unresolved conflict that is within her. The sexual problem cannot be treated successfully unless the internal conflict is first understood and healed. That conflict becomes a chief concern of counselors working with persons who express an inordinate fear of sexual relationships.

SERIOUSLY DISTURBED PERSONS

It is not unusual for psychotic persons to enter into marriage. It happens, in fact, all the time. Their profound personality disorder manifests itself clearly in sexual difficulties. Sexuality for them is merely another aspect of the disturbed kind of communication which they reveal in other areas of their lives. Sensitive counselors recognize and deal with such gross disturbances rather than just with the symptomatic sexual difficulties that may be found in their marriage. There is no easy cure for the kind of sexual difficulty that is rooted in a psychotic personality and counselors should be very wary of attempting one.

Counselors must be ready to read the symbolic signs of the sexual difficulties that are presented to them by married couples. Not all of them will necessarily signify personalities such as those just discussed. Helpers will, however, be led in the right direction by looking beyond these symptoms to their deeper roots. They will avoid mistakes in counseling by recognizing these serious cases and not responding to them in an oversimplified way. Not everything expressed sexually is a sexual difficulty. It is a personal difficulty spoken in a special language that counselors must train themselves to hear and translate accurately.

References

Ard, Ben and Constance C. (Eds.). *Handbook of Marriage Counseling.* Palo Alto: Science Behavior Books, 1969.

Baruch, D. and Miller, H. *Sex in Marriage: New Understandings.* New York: Hoeber, 1965.

Boyd, H. "Love vs. Omnipotence: The Narcissistic Dilemma." *Psychotherapy.* 4 (Dec. 1968), pp. 272–77.

Boxer, L. "Mate Selection and Emotional Disorder." *Family Coordinator.* 19 (April, 1970), pp. 173–79.

Christensen, Harold T. *Handbook of Marriage and the Family.* Chicago: Rand McNally & Co., 1964.

Dedek, John F. *Contemporary Sexual Morality.* New York: Sheed & Ward, 1971.

Eysenck, H. J. "Personality and Attitudes to Sex." *Personality.* 4 (1970), pp. 355–76.

———. "Introverts, Extroverts and Sex." *Psychology Today* (Jan., 1971), pp. 49–52.

———. "Hysterical Personality and Sexual Adjustment, Attitudes and Behavior." *Journal of Sexual Research.* 7 (Nov., 1971), pp. 274–82.

Gould, James A. and Iorio, John J. *Love, Sex and Identity.* San Francisco: Boyd & Fraser, 1972.

Green, Bernard L. (Ed.). *The Psychotherapies of Marital Disharmony.* Glencoe: The Free Press, 1965.

Llewellyn, Charles, Jr. *Medical Aspects of Human Sexuality* (Aug., 1973).

Mair, Lucy. *Marriage.* New York: Penguin Books, 1971.

Olson, David H. "Marriage of the Future: Revolutionary or Evolutionary?" *Family Coordinator* (Oct., 1972).

Robertiello, R. C. "Masochism and the Female Role." *Journal of Sexual Research.* 6 (Feb., 1970), pp. 56–58.

Spanier, Graham. "Romanticism and Marital Adjustment." *Journal of Marriage and the Family* (Aug., 1972).

Taizman, L. *The Obsessive Personality.* New York: Science House, 1968.

Tharp, R. G. "Psychological Patterning in Marriage." *Psychological Bulletin.* LX (Mar., 1963), pp. 97–117.

ELEVEN

Marital Infidelity

MARITAL infidelity, and the complaints associated with it, constitute one of the areas in which it is most important for counselors to be sure of their positions, official and personal, as well as of the complex of feelings that bubble up from various levels of awareness when this experience is discussed.

The question of marital infidelity is now set in a web of cultural shifts which has accented and explored the possibilities of infidelity as a new way of life. "Open marriages," nonexclusive commune-style marriages, and extra-marital relationships are all involved in this issue. But there is also a current trend to re-examine the arguments for commitment and fidelity. At the same time there is the lingering discussion on the "benefits" of infidelity in preserving marriage. Opinions and feelings obviously abound in this area. Counselors must not only be aware of and ready to deal with these assorted problems, but they must also have integrated their own notions on this matter.

Frequently lawyers, teachers, and clergy represent, because of their authoritative positions, traditional ethical and moral stands on the question of fidelity. Whatever their personal convictions, such professionals are perceived by many clients as essentially *conservative* in function and therefore supporters of fidelity in marriage. Are clients coming to hear counselors reinforce traditional viewpoints? Is it possible that the aggrieved partner perceives the counselor as an agent for reforming an unfaithful spouse?

A couple may also come, whether they intend to or not, to advertise the problems of relationship which may have influenced the infidelity in the first place. They may come to deal with guilt or they may be prepared to deal with the deeper causes of their estrangement. It is not unusual for erring partners to court the counselor to secure some official influence in seeking forgiveness from the spouse and reconciliation or preservation of the marriage. On the question of preserving marriage, motives can be as tangled as electronic circuitry. Some people genuinely want to take a deeper look at and solidify their relationship while others may have an interest in preserving the marriage for extrinsic reasons.

Do the men and women seeking help have some sense that the infidelity may signal deeper problems to which they must attend? Are they more concerned about getting at these or do they focus more on refashioning the surface of a damaged relationship? In these situations counselors may ask whether they should themselves take the initiative in probing more deeply into underlying causes. They may want to leave this up to the couple and merely provide the atmosphere in which such a choice can be made with the assurance that as counselors they are fully prepared to follow through therapeutically.

It is also possible that only one partner may come to the counselor. What is the significance of this? This raises the issue of whether the other spouse should be brought into the counseling or whether, indeed, the other spouse should be told of the infidelity at all.

Counselors must be prepared for an unpredictable array of circumstances. They cannot presume too much in advance and they should not quickly offer solutions to couples—for example, encouragement about deepening their sexual relationship or having a child—until they have a real feeling for the relationship and the factors that affect it.

Counselors should try to be unambiguous, then, about the goals they feel that they can achieve in this counseling. They may not be able to depart from their official role as putative representative of a conservative tradition but they still may be able to convey therapeutic understanding while upholding a familiar teaching. Others experience conflict in trying to maintain these two positions at the same time. Counselors must be clear about the advantages or limitations of their roles and, in a brief way, structure the relationship so that the couple coming for assistance will understand what kind of help the counselor is ready to offer.

Fidelity and infidelity are seldom found in the table of contents of psychology textbooks or even in tracts on marriage. The nature of fidelity in any human relationship can be quite complex. It is possible, in the view of some, for people to be unfaithful to each other without being sexually unfaithful. There are subtleties in the range of commitment and the possibilities of violating it through inner attitudes as much as external behavior. The inner attitudes are always important, of course, but for the sake of discussion here, we limit our considerations to those violations of fidelity which include concrete elements of adultery. As psychiatrist Leon Salzman has noted, infidelity may be defined as "sexual behavior with other partners, either overt or covert, of married or unmarried people exclusively committed to each other" (*Medical Aspects of Human Sexuality,* Feb., 1972). This includes most of the situations in which counselors will presently find themselves involved in our culture.

There may be no other field of human behavior in which rationalizations are used more freely than in the question of infidelity. And the important thing to remember is that the defense of rationalization is quite functional in many situations. Rationalizations are offered not only by individuals but by the entire surrounding contemporary culture. Such defenses deny guilt, keep persons from experiencing anxiety, and tend to enhance their image of themselves. This is particularly true at the initial stages of infidelity which may have thrilling or exciting aspects precisely because, as an experience, it breaks the chain of repetitiveness and dullness that people report after they have been married for some time. That is why some persons do not feel much anxiety about their infidelity. They worry about being caught but they do not let themselves think about the deeper implications of what has happened.

Contemporary culture has emphasized sexual adventure, sex as recreation, and other sexual behavior that could be described as old fashioned lust in a way that has minimized anxiety. Such comforting notions have been portrayed in various magazines and movies not only as acceptable but as sophisticated and attractive as well. Many immature people succumb to what amounts to a cultural invitation to uninhibited sexuality. Counselors who recognize rationalization beneath these notions may be strongly tempted to confront persons and point out the fallacy in their reasoning. This may not always be the most desirable thing to do even though the facts of the situation seem to justify it. Premature confrontation contains a particular danger for the self-righteous in an area in which people have strong personal convictions. There should be great personal convictions. There should be great hesitation about breaking through people's defenses before they are ready to put them aside themselves.

Counselors must also be sensitive to the kind of anxiety reported by persons involved in infidelity. Sometimes this anxiety centers on the fact that they have been caught and is more akin to fear than to guilt. At other times the anxiety is the reflection of superego pressures rather than more deeply internalized moral or ethical principles. In either of these situations it is clear that the counselor's sensitivity to the source of the anxiety is extremely important if the person is to resolve the difficulty and gain some insight into the situation. It is also possible, of course, that the person may be reporting guilt as a genuine personal reaction to moral failure that is perceived as such in a fairly accurate and mature fashion. Counselors must obviously be clear about whether they are acting as agents of absolution, reconciliation, or counseling in a strictly psychological sense in their work with these people.

Salzman says that no matter what explanation or rationalizations are offered, "in most persons the experience of multiple sexual partners does represent a degree of alienation and a crisis of commitment." Something is going on, in other words, in the personalities of the couple and in their relationship with each other. A man and woman may look the same but it is not likely that they will be the same after an experience of infidelity. It may well be the occasion for the strengthening and deepening of their relationship, but it is also possible that infidelity will leave lingering scars, changed attitudes, or force new styles of relationship that may significantly alter their marriage.

Psychiatrist Bernard Greene of the University of Illinois, discusses the issues underlying infidelity in his book *A Clinical Approach to Marital Problems* (C. C. Thomas, 1970). He found in 750 couples that infidelity was the seventh most common verbalized complaint by 230 spouses; an additional one-third of the men and women of 500 cases seen in therapy reported that they were or had been unfaithful but that their spouse did not know of the situation. Noting his own surprise at the willingness with which spouses seem to forgive infidelity, Greene also observes that the majority of the couples underwent a real marital crisis. He divides the dynamics of marital infidelity into those which are conscious and those which are unconscious.

Dr. Greene lists the conscious causes of infidelity in the following order:

1) *Sexual frustration.* This, reported by seventy percent of the spouses and in a ratio of two males to one female, was the most common complaint.

2) *Curiosity.* With the ratio of two males to three females, just over 50 percent of the spouses reported this as a cause for infidelity.

3) *Revenge.* The sexes were equally divided with forty percent of the individuals reporting this as a motive.

4) *Ennui.* This, according to Greene, was also equally distributed between the sexes and was defined as "monotonous, bored, tedious, and square."

5) *Recognition seeking.* With equal frequency among the sexes this was a conscious reason for infidelity in twenty percent of the relationships.

In terms of their frequency, Dr. Greene lists the following as unconscious determinants of adultery:

1) *Seeking "stroking" of the "inner child."* This is clearly a strong motive but one not readily accessible to consciousness. It is the kind of motive that drives people toward infidelity and other behaviors that diverge from their normal pattern of life. Because it is unconscious it needs to be rationalized. That is one of the reasons, along with the following motives, that the defense mechanisms are employed so widely in situations of marital infidelity.

2) *Rage at partner or parent.* Once again, anger that may have nothing to do with the partner but actually be the acting out of previously unresolved conflicts toward the parents, is a powerful motive on the unconscious level. The rage may be directed at the spouse but because it is so unacceptable to consciousness it is denied. The infidelity then becomes a symbol as well as an instrument of hurt.

3) *Proof of masculinity.*

4) *Expression of an immature personality.*

5) *A partner acting out an "unconscious homosexual defense"* against the spouse or a denial of unconscious homosexuality.

It is clear that counselors who do not understand the possibilities represented by these motives would be naive indeed to try to settle the sexual problems and relationship problems associated with infidelity in simple logical or moralistic terms. Any genuine progress is very difficult until people begin to get some appreciation of what drives them into these situations. One of the complaints that is often heard by counselors is that the wandering spouse doesn't really understand how the infidelity got started. Rationalizations may explain it for them on the surface but they are genuinely lost at penetrating their own unconscious life. Counselors may be the first persons who possess enough psychological skill to assist them in exploring this level of motivation.

Salzman, examining the situation from a slightly different viewpoint, speaks of three main causes of infidelity. He feels that the causes are interrelated and that they "represent increasing degrees of alienation and lack of involvement which may represent a character fault in one of the partners, or an inability to make the relationship function properly because both are uncommitted and therefore unwilling or unable to make necessary compromises required in any stable and fidelitous relationship." Salzman lists the following causes, using the word "failure" quite consciously in describing them.

Dr. Salzman believes that many marriages are undertaken even though the partners are not at all clear about the issues of love and commitment. People get into marriages for reasons extrinsic to what they mean to each other. As an example, he cites the obsessional marriage as one in which a person fears committing the self and taking the risks of making a mistake in life. Such a person feels that any mistake can be undone by a divorce; this attitude builds a condition into commitment right from the start. This obviously undercuts the notion of continuing marital fidelity. It is clear that should infidelity occur in such a situation the underlying problem must be addressed by the counselor. It is not the act of infidelity but the attitudes which may have predisposed one or the other of the marriage partners to engage in it that must be examined.

Salzman concedes that such marriages frequently look very good at the start. The elements of devotion and genuine commitment seem to be present and it is only as the personality differences of the partners become more apparent and more abrasive that infidelity becomes an option. Infidelity arises when people are disappointed in each other or when they make demands on each other that they cannot really meet. In such circumstances the sexual life of the couple becomes routine and one partner looks around for novelty or new excitement. Frequently neither partner wishes the marriage to be dissolved. In these relationships some of the more common rationalizations are employed: that adultery supports the marriage rather than harms it, etc.

Salzman lists here a number of psychological difficulties which make fidelity almost impossible between man and woman. Here he mentions the antisocial personality, for example, or the manic individual as well as the paranoid or the "pathologically vindictive or jealous" spouse. Here too are included immature persons who have never learned to delay gratification nor to limit their own needs or desires. The narcissistic personality, for example, also fits well here. Salzman feels that the motives of some persons in this category are not too hidden from them. He feels that although "infidelity may be part of neurotic or psychotic development . . . more often it represents a rational or comprehensible piece of behavior in a so-called normal person."

Bernard Greene further lists a number of psychological disturbances that are accompanied by infidelity. He includes the hypomanic phase of the manic depressive psychosis or the paranoid state of psychosis in which the complaint is delusional. Greene also mentions the depressive reactions in which the person becomes unfaithful in order to ward off depression. Chronic alcoholism can also cause unfaithful behavior. Salzman adds that there are a "number of physical disorders ranging from cerebral arteriosclerosis to endocrine malfunctioning in which infidelity is a symptom. This should be suspected when the behavior is alien or widely incongruent from the more circumspect behavior in the past."

Given this wide range of possibilities it is wise for counselors to make their way slowly as they attempt to grasp the circumstances and personality factors that have led to the infidelity in question. Many of these conditions cause sexual incompatibility or clashes at other intimate points in a marital relationship. The counselor's focus must be wide enough to get the marital interaction in perspective before reasonable goals for counseling can be established.

References

Denfield, D. "Dropouts from Swinging." *The Family Coordinator.* 23 (January, 1974), pp. 45–49.

Ellis, A. and Abarbanel, A. (Eds.). *The Encyclopedia of Sexual Behavior.* New York: Hawthorn Books, 1961. See esp., Harper, R. A., "Extramarital Sex Relations."

Goldberg, Martin, M.D. (Moderator). "A Roundtable on Marital Infidelity." *Medical Aspects of Human Sexuality* (Oct., 1973).

Greene, B. *A Clinical Approach to Marital Problems.* Springfield, Ill.; C. C. Thomas, 1970.

Hunt, Morton M. *The Affair: A Portrait of Extramarital Love in Contemporary America.* Cleveland: World Publishing Co., 1969.

Masters, W. and Johnson, V. (with Robert Levin). *The Pleasure Bond.* Boston: Little, Brown & Co., 1975.

Neubeck, Gerhard. *Extra Marital Relations.* Englewood Cliffs, N.J.: Prentice-Hall, Inc., 1969.

Otto, H. A. (Ed.). *The Family in Search of a Future.* New York: Appleton-Century-Crofts, 1970.

Pineo, P. L. "Developmental Patterns in Marriage." *The Family Coordinator.* 18 (April, 1969), pp. 135–40.

————. "Disenchantment in the Later Years of Marriage." *Marriage and Family Living.* 23 (Feb., 1961), pp. 3–11.

Salzman, Leon. "Female Infidelity." *Medical Aspects of Human Sexuality* (Feb., 1972).

Spanier, G. "Romanticism and Marital Adjustment." *Journal of Marriage and the Family,* (Feb., 1970).

Stinnet, N., Collins, J., and Montgomery, J. "Marital Need Satisfaction in Older Husbands and Wives." *Journal of Marriage and the Family.* 32 (August, 1970), pp. 428–34.

TWELVE

More on Marital Infidelity

IN the preceding chapter the subject of marital infidelity and its possible causes was discussed. It may well be that the fragile nature of many contemporary relationships—the quality that makes them vulnerable to the assault of infidelity—is explained by the generally immature outlook of the man and woman toward each other and toward the nature of marriage itself. Whenever getting married is perceived as a solution for loneliness, lack of intimacy, or lack of full identity, it is almost certain to be a disappointment.

People often enter marriage expecting it to be some kind of magical state that will answer all their questions and respond to all their needs. Not perceiving that the actual work of building a deep relationship commences in many ways on the day of marriage itself, they are upset by the developing annoyances, misunderstandings and, finally, open conflicts that occur in even the closest of human relationships. They find the experience estranging as well as upsetting; it may be the first occasion for examining their own personalities and their relationship in greater depth. This is a moment in which one partner may find justification for experimentation outside the relationship on the grounds that a mistake has been made and that, with a little extended searching, he or she will discover the person with whom true happiness can be found.

This flirtation or actual experience with infidelity may be the immature reaction of a person who simply fails to understand that marriage is not magic and that relationships are built on the misunderstandings and conflicts of life; these occurrences are not ruins but the possible elements of foundation for a deepened relationship. When men and women are too impatient to take on the real work of growing together they may turn to other persons for the gratification they can no longer find with each other. This is a form of extended immaturity, however, which will involve them in a vicious circle rather than a deeper relationship.

It is clear that counselors who recognize this style of immaturity cannot deal only with the symptoms; their concern must be with the basic problems of a lack of development on the part of the husband and wife. As psychiatrist Larry Feldman of the Family Institute of Chicago has observed: "What most couples need is a set of skills which will enable them to deal with their conflicts in such a way that the relationship grows through the process of conflict-resolution. As this occurs, the amount of pleasure which each spouse derives from the relationship also grows, and the desire for extramarital affairs diminishes" (*Medical Aspects of Human Sexuality,* Jan., 1974, p.95).

When counselors sense that the infidelity is set against a broad background of undeveloped or failed communication, the focus must be more generalized than the clients sometimes make it. The dynamics of their mutual attraction, their goals and their relationship styles as sources of information about the motivation for infidelity—all are areas that deserve exploration. It may be that a counselor would profit from using the techniques of family therapy or would wisely refer such a couple to a therapist with those therapeutic skills.

Should the partner be told? This is a question that is brought up whenever the issue of marital infidelity is discussed. It is frequently mentioned by the partner who has committed the infidelity, especially when he or she feels that confession would be good for the soul and would eliminate some of the guilt. There are opinions on both sides of the issue but a majority of experts seem to feel that there is no need to insist on divulging information about the infidelity to the other partner. Each situation should be seen individually, however, and counselors should try to evaluate the meaning of the person's desire to acknowledge or unwillingness to admit this to the marriage partner.

Counselors cannot insist that their clients adopt their viewpoint about this issue. There is no way to settle this confidently beforehand. In the long run, it must be the decision of the person involved; a counselor's best service in such circumstances is to assist this person to understand fully the motives that may sway him or her in one direction or the other. There are almost as many motives for wanting to tell the spouse as there are for the act of infidelity itself.

As with any major decision in life, then, the individual should be allowed to face and take responsibility for any revelation of this material. The counselor's continuing role in helping the partners to explore further the significance of such a happening is clearly crucial. The matter will not be settled merely by getting it out in the open. This may, however, be the beginning of helping a man and woman to work through the important aspects of their relationship. But it could be quite the opposite if the signals are not read clearly.

The dilemma of to tell or not to tell is a confusing one, a fork in the path where either road has its particular snares. Just as the motivations for the infidelity are scrambled and complex, so too are the impulses to confess or seek confrontation on the issue. Many of these strands of dynamic reality are drawn together in framing the question of whether the failure of fidelity should be admitted or confessed. What are some of the many possibilities to which counselors should remain sensitive?

The impulse to confess frequently proceeds from a deep experience of admitted guilt on the part of the erring partner. Guilt is a multi-faceted phenomenon, however, and soothing though confession may be to the person racked by guilt, some exploration of the nature of this emotion may be in order. It may be that the confession will relieve the tension generated by guilt in the offending partner but what about this guilt? As psychiatrist Harold Winn has noted: "The person wishing to confess must examine why, if there is so much guilt, it did not prevent the infidelity" (*Medical Aspects of Human Sexuality,* May, 1970, p.8). It is possible that the guilt and the relief of it through confession may be part of a manipulative style that is part of the person's own self-contained "narcissistic game of doing bad, feeling remorse, confessing and then getting forgiveness in order to repeat this manipulation over and over. . . ." Such a person may have no recognition of the feelings of the spouse and may, in fact, merely be acting out in a different way the role that has imperiled the marriage relationship from the start. Such persons resemble the gambler or the alcoholic or the collectors of pornography who periodically destroy their collection only to return to assembling it again. Confession of this sort obviously does not touch the basic situation and may be destructive because it serves the needs of the offending partner but fails to address more basic causes for the behavior.

Confession may also be diluted or tainted by the need to express unconscious hostility. While confession can be good for the soul, the individual must be aware of the way in which he or she is using it. If, for example, the confessing individual can be helped to understand the hostility that motivates the impulse to confess, it may be possible to get a better look at the nature of the whole relationship. This type of insight may prove the basis for working out deeper difficulties.

Other elements of motivation may be entwined with the need to confess and to involve the other party in the infidelity in a psychologically complicated manner. Describing vivid details of the infidelity may, for example, serve sadistic or masochistic needs that have determined the previous nature of the relationship. The infidelity and its confession may, in other words, just be outcroppings from a more fundamental set of dynamics. Encouraging or discouraging open confession will not touch these dynamics and they are, in fact, the material with which the partners must ultimately deal.

It may also be helpful to examine the kind of "honesty" related to the need to confess or to promote some kind of "openness" between the partners in a marriage affected by infidelity. Honesty, many contemporary therapists claim, is the best policy no matter what the consequences may be. This is not as simple as it appears. Honesty needs examination, especially when it is insisted upon as the overriding motive for confession.

Honesty based on the conviction that total openness is a romantic therapeutic ideal may, in fact, serve the needs of the offender more than the good of the total relationship. Such a commitment to honesty may not be a commitment to the whole truth about the marital relationship. Truth is a deeper and wider reality that includes the perspective of the offended party as well as the root causes of their marital conflicts. Honesty can be used as a weapon because it can inflict injury while it confers absolution on the offender. This is so when the person is immature and when the guilt that is confessed is of a shallow, resourceful variety rather than that based on a true analysis of one's behavior and a determination to search for underlying causes.

The excessive honesty, like the ill-motivated "confrontations" advocated by amateur therapists, may derive, as Leon Salzman has observed, "from the individual's obsessive concerns about his or her behavior. He or she needs to preserve the illusion of total honesty, and the consequence of confession on the partner is not considered at all" (*Medical Aspects of Human Sexuality,* May, 1970, p. 14). This kind of confession tends to turn the tables, making the offender the one demanding absolution on the grounds of "total honesty," even though he or she has not looked deeply at the basic motivation. As Salzman writes, the confessor may "feel hurt and betrayed if the partner gets angry, or offended, leading them to say, 'Well, if you react this way, then the next time I will not tell you the truth. Would it be better if I lied?' " Victim is turned into offender and vice versa. This is a way, Salzman concludes, of telling the truth and perpetuating a lie.

Most psychodynamically-oriented therapists believe that there is no such thing as a truly accidental disclosure of infidelity. The partner who leaves telltale clues around, even subtle ones, is delivering a message from the unconscious. Such partners want the spouse to know about their infidelity. Why is the message delivered indirectly and what does this tell about the person who delivers it or about the general state of communication in the marriage? Is this an extension of an expression of anger or hostility, a test of devotion, or does it have some meaning that is impossible to understand except in the exact context of this relationship? Counselors should listen for the answers before deciding.

This is a difficult question which has been raised only recently in the light of more open discussions of homosexual behavior in our culture. A widely circulated woman's magazine asked a well-known homosexual writer to deal with this subject in an article. The article proved to be sympathetic to the homosexual partner and left the impression that such behavior need not necessarily totally damage or destroy a marriage. This is a superficial and somewhat politically motivated view and it is clear that such behavior cannot be dismissed or rationalized away as if it did not have deep meaning and wide ranging consequences.

For a woman to be married to a man who is homosexual and who is unfaithful to her with homosexual partners involves a counselor in a complex of therapeutic encounters which cannot be settled with popular slogans. It is clear that no resolution of such a situation can be accomplished without some exploration of the dynamics which brought this man and woman together in the first place and which sustained their relationship through the years. What role did the erring partner's sexuality play in the marriage and what significance does a lack of fidelity have in this kind of relationship? Those who believe that homosexuality is just an alternative lifestyle might easily ignore the deeper and possibly quite involved dynamics. These would have to be sorted out in order for one to come to a satisfactory solution of such a conflict. There is no way of reassuring people or giving simple answers; this needs response in depth.

Do marriages improve because of infidelity? In most cases, the infidelity itself does not cause the marriage to improve. But it is important for counselors to ascertain the whole setting for the infidelity and the willingness of partners to explore the factors in their own relationship which may have occasioned the initial infidelity. Frequently persons mature a great deal through making a mistake and a marriage that was previously shaky may be stabilized because people have to face the hard truth together. The continuing role of the counselor in the lives of people who come with a presenting problem of infidelity is very significant. This may be particularly true at a time when so many cultural pressures already drain men and women of their emotional resources. They need supportive understanding to be able to reach each other and to work through what can quite conceivably be a decisive event in deepening their relationship.

It is also true that the possibility of infidelity among women is much greater than it has been in past times. Formerly, the man was thought to be freer to commit adultery than the woman. Reliant and convenient contraceptives, the women's liberation movement, and other similar factors (which I shall discuss more fully in the next chapter) have brought about a re-evaluation of this. These factors must be kept in mind by counselors who are concerned with the aftermath of the experience of infidelity in a marriage.

Because there has been some shift in this, it may be important to review some of the effects which a wife's infidelity can have on a husband. There is not an extensive literature on this subject but psychologist James L. Framo of Temple University in Philadelphia recently explored the reactions of husbands to infidelity by their wives in a small sample of marriages (*Medical Aspects of Human Sexuality,* May, 1975).

According to Framo, husbands react in very different ways to the news that their wives have been involved in an affair. Some of them seem to be delighted while others can be driven to psychosis or suicide by the news. Framo notes that sexual infidelity is still an event of the most serious proportions for most people. It can be emotionally devastating to men and may release in them very strong feelings of jealousy, revenge, and depression. He notes that "one can often detect in these people who react so extremely a kind of mourning and grieving, tied in with the theme of lost love. These extreme reactions are usually a function of earlier, unconscious reactions being stirred up."

Other husbands who take the news without becoming too upset initially find that the impact strikes them more forcibly later on. They then become preoccupied with the event and with all the details concerning it. They are plagued with the question *why.*

Dr. Framo observed in his sample certain stages that the couple goes through after the revelation of an adulterous affair. At the beginning the husband feels that "he is in competition with the lover and has to prove he is better." There is a great deal of anxiety about his sexual performance and he is very anxious to know whether he seems as sexually competent as his wife's lover. This is a very difficult time for both husband and wife, a time in which the husband is tortured by fantasies about his wife's lover which are often wildly out of line with the truth.

Occasionally, Framo notes, husbands develop a close identification with the lover, imagining that they themselves are the lover in fantasies which can cause them great anguish. He feels that in most cases "the men are far more furious at the lover than at the wife, probably because it's safer that way; the feelings toward the wife are very mixed, because she is still needed, whereas the feeling toward the lover can be experienced as pure hatred."

Others are more directly angry at their spouse, sometimes because the revelation has forced them to share in the guilt of the situation. They begin to realize that they had some part to play in the infidelity of their spouse. This is very hard for them to absorb and integrate into themselves. They also become very concerned about who else has knowledge of the affair; who knew about it while they, in the role of the betrayed spouse, were still ignorant of it.

It is sometimes true that the adultery is committed in an effort to terminate a marriage. This is a symbolic statement about the marriage and is designed to make a final, formal break inevitable. Although this is sometimes successful, it often happens that one spouse wants to hold on to the marriage just as strongly as the other wants to get out of it. Their motives for coming to therapy are then quite different. One wants the therapist to recommend divorce; the other wants the therapist to reinforce the marriage bond.

When the infidelity has been on the part of the wife and she clearly wants to get out of the marriage, the husband is in a disadvantageous position. He can see his marriage coming apart bit by bit; he feels humiliated and helpless but he does not seem to be able to do anything about it. His self-esteem has been attacked and he does not feel that he can respond. Framo makes an observation in this regard that is worth counselors' consideration. "Deeper exploration can reveal, moreover, that having a man in this humble position represents to the woman a neurotic payoff and triumph over, say, a father who once rejected her. The man, too, may be re-enacting some earlier situation in his life." He feels that the real reason most women involve themselves in an affair is to attract the husband's attention and interest. Once this is accomplished, the women frequently have no continued interest in infidelity. Others feel that this is a somewhat oversimplified masculine interpretation of the event.

Infidelity is frequently just one of many significant occurrences in a marriage relationship that is under stress. The infidelity cannot be treated separately from these causes and counselors must be ready to explore very complicated and at least partly unconscious motivations in order to help people understand what they are doing to each other. Framo's own treatment methods include "working with the couple as a unit, helping the partners to develop clear and more honest communication with each other, and coaching the couple in their efforts to deal with the real issues between them." He also describes techniques which involve bringing the family of origin in each of these adults into therapy as well as of group therapy in which several couples work together "to develop more realistic expectations of marriage."

Counselors must feel comfortable in exploring the many levels of psychological reality with men and women in whose marriage infidelity is a problem. If counselors feel that they do not have sufficient skill to go this deeply into therapy, they can work toward a good referral and may themselves serve as a bridge into a deeper kind of uncovering and reconstructive therapy.

Virginia Johnson comments on infidelity in her recent book, *The Pleasure Bond* (written with Dr. William Masters): "Infidelity is a very chancy and very unreliable means to use in searching for one's identity, in exploring one's true emotions, in struggling not only to find out what one's deepest feelings and beliefs and responses may be, but also communicating them to someone else. This is true for many reasons, including the fact that a man and a woman who are involved in an affair generally have different investments in their relationship, and these affairs are most often conducted under less than encouraging conditions.

"In addition, social attitudes—including those internalized by both the man and woman—make it certain that in a good number of cases the individuals will have to cope with feelings of guilt, one way or another. Either the guilt will intrude on their ability to accomplish their goals—to discover dimensions of their own personality—or it will require them to deny that the feelings exist, and in doing so to sweep other feelings under the rug along with the discomfort of guilt. . . .

"Making do in a marriage is not fulfillment through marriage. Even if infidelity represents the first step in a positive direction—toward making do instead of making war—it is still a long distance away from the goal of becoming committed: true to oneself and loyal and vulnerable to one's partner." (*The Pleasure Bond,* pp. 128, 139)

References

Edwards, J. N. "Extramarital Involvement: Fact and Theory." *Journal of Sexual Research* (Aug., 1973), 9:210–24.

Framo, L., Ph.D. "Husbands' Reactions to Wives' Infidelity." *Medical Aspects of Human Sexuality* (May, 1975).

Harper, R. A. "Communication Problems in Marriage and Marriage Counseling." *Marriage and Family Living* (1958), 20:107–12.

Johnson, R. E. "Some Correlates of Extramarital Coitus." *Journal of Marriage and Family* (Aug., 1970), 32:449–56.

Lederer, W. J., and Jackson, D. D. *The Mirages of Marriage.* New York: W. W. Norton & Co., 1968.

Libby, R. W. and Whitehurst, R. *Renovating Marriage.* Danville, Calif.: Consensus Publishers, 1973.

Masters, W. and Johnson, V. (with Robert J. Levin). *The Pleasure Bond.* Boston: Little, Brown and Co., 1975.

Neubeck, Gerhard (Ed.). *Extramarital Relations.* Englewood Cliffs, N.J.: Prentice-Hall, Inc., 1969.

Otto, H. A. *More Joy in Your Marriage.* New York: Hawthorn Books, 1969.
———(Ed.). *The Family in Search of a Future.* New York: Appleton-Century-Crofts, 1970.
Peterson, J. A. *Married Love in the Middle Years.* New York: Association Press, 1968.

THIRTEEN

Women's Liberation and Sexual Problems

WOMEN'S liberation is a potent cultural force that has had widespread repercussions on the sexual lives of many persons. Not all of these problems are understood by those who experience them nor do they fully understand the relationship between their difficulties and the movement itself. Certain effects of the feminist movement are far more obvious. These are generally the results of extreme positions taken by certain advocates of women's liberation, positions that have been counterpointed by a massive negative masculine reaction that can also be observed in subtle forms of hostility, as in the kind of jokes, etc., made about the movement and those who participate in it. Feminism is a presence in the lives of contemporary Americans, and counselors must understand the movement and also the psychological dynamics associated with it in order to be able to respond adequately to persons with sexual conflicts that may be related to or intensified by it.

The solution to conflicts caused by Women's Liberation is not found in new sexual techniques nor in sexual therapy clinics. The roots of the problem must be appreciated in the interplay of the man and woman whose relationship is affected by the philosophy or in and through the behavior of those who commit themselves to this movement in one way or another. Obviously, not all sexual dysfunction at the present time can be attributed to feminism, but there is a sufficient amount of uneasiness connected with it to turn the attention of counselors to the unconscious dynamics beneath the sometimes noisy surface arguments.

Extremists in any movement manage to alienate many of the very people they are trying to convince. The extremist platform in Women's Lib is intrinsically threatening both to men and to women who support some traditional concept of sexual roles in our society. Extremists who, for example, champion lesbianism as the ideal feminine lifestyle and who regard men

97

as useful only as sperm donors so that women can carry on the race unshackled by the so-called chains of traditional heterosexual matrimony, present ideas that both anger and frustrate other persons.

Feminists who present their arguments in such a hostile manner that any dialogue becomes impossible also alienate people. This generates hostility in the response and makes it easy for critics to caricature the whole movement as one that is dominated by poorly adjusted persons. This explains that bitter edge on much of the humor directed at Women's Lib. It also explains why counselors may see a certain amount of acting out of these extreme positions that, in fact, does not liberate the women involved nor make them feel more adequate or independent as human beings.

When women make excessive sexual demands or use sexual denial as a political weapon they tend to isolate themselves and to suffer the inevitable psychological effects of this maneuver. The amount of bile and black smoke generated make it difficult for people to discuss the movement without concentrating on the extremes; it also makes it difficult for them to examine their own feelings because their irritation with extreme positions frequently gets in the way. And when the discussion stops short at extremist positions it adds to rather than lessens other problems.

Counselors, like everyone else, need a careful examination of their own convictions in this area. They may be heavily committed to feminism and its aims in a balanced way or they may find that their own feelings are deeply involved and that they have, in effect, been politicized. Counselors may also have a wide variety of ill-defined feelings about the movement in general; these feelings are operative even when they are not acknowledged. They may range from hostility, through support, to apparent indifference, but they are nonetheless present and have their effect on the work of counseling. Difficult as it may be, counselors obviously must search out their own reactions and have them clearly understood before they can deal with relationships in which feminism has been a source of stress and has caused sexual difficulties. Women's Lib, caught in so much unresolved feeling, can easily generate counter-transference feelings of a very strong nature.

Counselors who wish to be effective in this static-filled area help themselves when they reflect on the underlying psychological issues more than when they focus only on the surface political slogans. To recognize the essential aims of the women's movement as furthering the opportunities for women to experience and explore their full possibilities as women in relationship to men in society, and to acknowledge their sub-goals of economic and social equality, counselors may need an appreciation of what psychiatrist Alexandra Symonds of the New York University School of Medicine describes as the *neurotic dependency* into which women have been forced and which, through the women's movement, they are trying to resolve.

Distinguishing between healthy and unhealthy dependency, she suggests that the stereotyped role of neurotic dependency has caused women widespread difficulties that have issued into severe sexual problems. Dr. Symonds sees the effects of this neurotic dependency in the way women have feared loneliness and hostility. The fear of loneliness has driven some women to accept marriage, quite often at an early age, as the institution that would save them from social isolation. All too often these women discovered that they had really purchased a closed world in which it was difficult for them to identify and express their own desires for fuller personal growth. Because they are afraid of the hostility that this situation generates, Dr. Symonds feels that this anger has been expressed indirectly through a variety of psychosomatic symptoms. Such problems, of course, complicate the domestic life and sexual relations of men and women even though they may not be identified as the basic causes.

If Dr. Symonds is correct, then it is clear that some of the underlying dynamics are both powerful and pervasive and that there is no easy way to handle these without some in-depth counseling. Many women do not understand or do not have a way of verbalizing these psychological conflicts. They feel that the movement is right but they are not quite sure what the issue is which they are attempting to resolve. If the counselor has some idea that in a relatively normal woman the commitment to feminism may, in fact, be evidence that she is working toward a healthier balance of independence and dependence in her life, the counselor will be far more able to assist her in exploring the relevant psychological issues. Such a counselor will be sensitive enough not to tangle the live wires of these unconscious issues.

Counselors may end up dealing with the loose ends of the complaints made by some women and the effects that such stirrings cause in the lives of their husbands. It is clear, for example, that when a woman begins to shift in her traditional role the effects radiate out to all those with whom she has previously been in relationship. She is disrupting and destabilizing something to which husband, children and friends may have become quite accustomed.

The effects of such unbalancing are frequently felt in the sexual life of the man and woman. It would be unusual if they were not. The man, unsure of what is happening, may find that he is not able to perform sexually as he did before. He is not relating to quite the same person and this may trip off uncertainties and insecurities in him. A temporary kind of impotence in the husbands of women who shift their lives around in the name of a healthy readjustment is not uncommon. Unless the couple is helped to understand the real psychological transaction that has taken place, it may only be complicated by bitterness and hostility on the part of the man. This is a problem that can occur, as has been mentioned, in the lives of non-extreme people. It is the kind of thing that happens, in one way or another, whenever there are shifts or changes in the personalities of people who live very closely to each other.

It is clear that such a difficulty cannot be solved merely by rational discussion. It is not something that stands to reason because it is a highly emotional and largely unconscious kind of activity. The counselor's task in dealing with what seems to be a straightforward sexual problem is to hear the overall context of the difficulty and to help the man and woman to hear it themselves. Husband and wife caught in such a conflict communicate to each other symbolically far more than they do in words. Counselors must be prepared to catch these symbolic communications, many of them non-verbal, and to see them in relationship to the other dynamics that are operational between husband and wife. Something important is happening, in other words, and it can, with successful counseling, be the occasion for greater growth for both husband and wife and for an ultimate deepening of their relationship. As Dr. Symonds has observed, repressed hostility on the part of the woman will subtly infect the sexual relationship anyway and, in the long run, will do far more harm than a more clearly expressed difficulty in sexual relationship that can then be associated with the appropriate dynamics.

Counselors should not focus so closely on the specific sexual problem that the true issues cannot emerge. Counselors who do not expect clearly reasoned arguments—and who keep the couple from engaging in political debate—have a far better chance of helping the real problems to surface. A wide angle is needed to create the counseling environment in which this can happen.

Most reasonably healthy men can, with some counseling help or with their own common sense, work their way through the challenges and difficulties posed by Women's Lib. If they are sensitive and capable of expressing tenderness, they will actively seek an understanding of what is taking place and will respond by trying to grow themselves. This does not occur without a struggle, however, and the role of the counselor in facilitating this is highly important.

It is possible, however, that the spouse's ego is not strong enough to sustain what seem to be the frontal attacks of the Women's Lib philosophy. The stress caused by this problem may reveal personality weaknesses that were not previously apparent. Such a man may need considerable support as he confronts conflicts or uncertainties only dislodged by the pressure of his wife's new self-assertiveness.

The sexual difficulties for a couple affected by Women's Lib are severely complicated if either of them is suffering with a problem of *gender identity.* The threat of the movement will set off anxiety and, therefore, cause them to become quite defensive. One of the problems that counselors find here is the defensive style that highly threatened spouses may adopt in order to hold their sense of themselves together. It is not uncommon, for example, for men to employ *social withdrawal.* This defense represents a symbolic search for a renewal of self-esteem. This may lead a husband to affairs with other women or into other acting-out attempts to retrieve his wounded masculinity. He may become so depressed that there is a diminution in his interest in sex. It is also possible that a man could become quite hostile in order to punish the woman symbolically by acting out his own infantile notions in their sexual relationship.

Each case must be examined and understood separately. Counselors must find their way inside the relationship and avoid trying to give general answers or sexual prescriptions to couples experiencing these sorts of sexual conflicts. The fundamental challenge is to assist the man and woman to stay in relationship to each other during the crisis of readjustment that follows the wife's advocacy of new feminist views. The more the man and woman can perceive and respect each other as individuals, the more surely will they be able to work through the symbolic sexual problems which they may experience. The therapeutic emphasis must be on getting to the deeper levels of their psychological relationship. The external sexual difficulties that arise in the context of Women's Liberation cannot easily be solved in and of themselves, even by the newer sexual therapies. That, of course, is because they are not essentially sexual in nature.

It is also unwise for counselors to propose contract-like solutions which amount to cease-fires in order to try to improve the couple's sexual relationship. These arrangements, allowing for certain rights or duties on certain days or times across the whole range of domestic activity, also ignore the interpersonal factors that are at work, and so they provide a solution that runs the risk of making the couple slaves to rules. This only puts more distance between them. Rules can be used very effectively by people who want to be hostile toward each other; such legal-like arrangements only *seem* to settle things. The couple may gain some peace but these approaches do not touch the fiery core of their suddenly unsettled way of interacting. Getting beneath the sexual complaint to the real source of strain cannot be accomplished by drafting a new set of ground rules.

As man and woman attempt to resolve their relationship they are going to look different than they did before both to themselves and to others. Counselors should be prepared for the fact that the path toward a new and deeper kind of relationship between husband and wife is not one that is

easily traversed. One would be surprised if the struggle for greater individuality and a better relationship did not occasion at least some mild complications in the couple's sexual relationship. Counselors should resist the temptation to cure the sexual symptom right away; they do better to exercise
restraint in hearing the couple out and accompanying them on their difficult
passage toward a better understanding of the real factors that set them at
odds with each other.

This is complicated by certain other attitudes that have developed in the
wake of the sexual revolution. Perhaps the most difficult is the general
impatience that human beings have grown to feel with the whole idea of
being patient. This is particularly true of a younger generation of people
who, by and large, have been able to have most of their material wishes
gratified without much delay. This is far different from the older generation
which had to learn patience through the experience of a World War and
a Depression and which came to feel that there were many things that one
had to wait for in life and that there were some things one never got at all.
One of the reasons that people need sensitive counselors is precisely because
of their unwillingness to work through complex problems which take a long
time to unravel. If there is conflict they want it solved immediately and,
because of this tendency, they may demand or at least expect easy and quick
solutions to the kinds of sexual difficulties that arise as the symbolic signs
of interpersonal conflict.

It is not easy to help people adopt a new philosophy of life but counselors
can at least be on guard against being caught up in the impatience of their
clients. It may not be possible for helpers to educate their clients to a more
patient acceptance in working through difficulties that have deep psychological roots. There must be some effort, however, in this direction even if
it is only reflected in the counselor's own capacity to wait and to try to
understand in depth what is taking place between people. This may be one
of the most important contributions that effective counselors can make in
resolving the sexual conflicts that are revealed under the stressful impact
of movements like that of Women's Liberation.

While we have discussed some of the crises for which Women's Lib has
served more as an occasion than a cause, it would be unduly negative to
judge the process to be nothing but trouble. In fact, wise counselors understand that the rise of Women's Lib has spurred a great deal of positive
thought and action as well as a more dynamic and helpful style of relationship between the sexes. The leaders of Women's Lib, for example, have
emphasized their interest in total human liberation, male as well as female.
The fact that some men and women have begun to work toward shedding

the ancient stereotypes in order to deepen their relationships is a small but significant step in the right direction.

As of now, the media and popular impressions ignore this development and emphasize the conflict generated by the movement. And this general face of conflict has been sexually disruptive for many couples. Counselors obviously need a balanced view of the issues in order to respond to troubled persons against the background of a heated public discussion.

Some undisputed results of Women's Lib include an increase in sexual activity which is now more widely perceived as humanly significant and not as totally ordered to childbearing as it once was. We are witnessing now a pendulum swing away from some of the extreme positions of the Women's Movement. There is a softening in the almost harsh competition that was championed by some radicals. One can note that in the search for the kind of deeper values to which so many persons have turned in our society. Even some of the old slogans, like that centering on a woman's rights "over her own body," including the child in that body, have been opened up again with an awareness of the fact that the father has a role in conception and in a continuing relationship to the developing child.

Many women are tired of the battle for separation and fulfillment, noting an emptiness that seems to invade their lives when they have forsaken the possibilities of a relationship with a man. Counselors should read widely in this field to educate themselves and to increase their sensitivity to the developing issues. Perhaps the most important thing for counselors is the expansion of their own worldview so that they will not easily be trapped into taking one position or the other on a question that is too complex for simplistic answers.

References

Bardwick, Judith. *Psychology of Women: A Study of Biocultural Conflicts.* New York: Harper & Row, 1971.

Bengis, Ingrid. *Combat in the Erogenous Zone.* New York: Alfred Knopf, 1972.

Brown, D. C. "Female Orgasm and Sexual Inadequacy." *Analysis of Human Sexual Response* (R. Brecher and E. Brecher, eds.). New York: New American Library, 1966.

Callahan, Sidney. *The Illusion of Eve.* New York: Sheed & Ward, 1965.

Chapman, J. D. *The Feminine Mind and Body.* New York: Philosophical Library, 1967.

_____."The Woman in America." *Daedalus* (Spring, 1964).

Friedan, Betty. *The Feminine Mystique.* New York: Dell Publishing Co., 1963.

Gray, Madeline. *The Normal Woman.* New York: Charles Scribner's Sons, 1967.

Greer, Germaine. *The Female Eunuch.* New York: McGraw-Hill, 1970.

Horney, Karen. *Feminine Psychology.* New York: W. W. Norton & Co., 1967.

Hunt, Morton. *Her Infinite Variety: The American Woman as Lover, Mate and Rival.* New York: Harper & Row, 1962.

Janeway, E. *Man's World, Woman's Place.* New York: William Morrow & Co., 1971.

Kinsey, Albert, et al. *Sexual Behavior in the Human Female.* Philadelphia: W. B. Saunders Co., 1953.

Komisar, L. *The New Feminism.* New York: Franklin Watts, 1971.

Mailer, Norman. *The Prisoner of Sex.* New York: Little, Brown & Co., 1971.

Maslow, A. H. "Self-Esteem (dominance-feeling) and Sexuality in Women." *Sexual Behavior and Personality Characteristics* (M. F. DeMartino, ed.). New York: Grove Press, 1966.

McCracken, R. D. *Fallacies of Women's Liberation.* Boulder, Colorado: Shields Publishing Co., 1972.

Millett, Kate. *Sexual Politics.* New York: Doubleday & Co., 1970.

O'Neill, W. L. *Everyone Was Brave: The Rise and Fall of Feminism in America.* Chicago: Quadrangle Books, 1969.

Seaman, B. *Free and Female.* New York: Fawcett Publications, 1973.

FOURTEEN

Adolescents and Sex

ALL counselors understand that they live in a world in which the experiences of sex and marriage have increasingly been separated both in contemporary discussion and in practice. Like many others, they feel the steady pressures of a sensate society in which there is an intensive and steady presentation of sexual images as well as widespread availability of erotically oriented materials; they also feel that they are being swept along on a tide of social change which they neither fully understand nor endorse. If it is not easy to live, it is even harder to grow up in a world in which sex can be so sharply separated from love, value from action, and morality from any foundational principles.

The psychological bewilderment that attends our present situation does not cry out for counselors to become moralistic preachers or reformers. Neither does it summon them to stand at the opposite end of the continuum as though the listening attitude of counselors signified a passive acceptance and somewhat undefined indifference to the meaning and consequences of sexual behavior. Perhaps counselors have never been more needed as the agents of understanding of our culture's current experience. Counselors need to attune themselves to all generations and, with their special sensitivity, attempt to take the soundings beneath the surface of so much of our noisy and preoccupying contemporary activity. Only as they understand the underlying dynamics can helpers respond with a constructive operational understanding to the difficulties and questions, the doubts and confusions, that mark the lives of many people.

It is very important for counselors to understand the sexual experience of adolescents and youth. While the techniques involved in counseling younger people may be no different than those employed with any other group, the need to understand the world in which adolescents have grown up as *they* perceive it remains the keystone in helping them understand and resolve sexual doubts and conflicts. Counselors must avoid the temptation to sit in judgment on those youth viewed as disappointing or irritating, as well as the temptation to romantically over-identify with youth in general as an ideal generation.

While helpers focus primarily on the individual persons with whom they work, they are also challenged to sense and chart the socio-cultural context in which young people find themselves at the present time. Those who would be helpful must understand the place of traditional religious values and the search, often quite evident in young people, for standards on which to base their own decisions. Counselors also need an appreciation for the underlying motivation for much of the sexual activity of persons in their developing years. Often it is not aimed toward pleasure or toward human relationships. Sexuality for many young people is a vehicle for generating and maintaining self-esteem, a phenomenon that is used instrumentally in the search of the young for a firm identity.

Erik Erikson, in his classic exposition of the stages of human development, describes the period of adolescence as that in which young people must consolidate their personal identity. They must bring together the various aspects of their life experience and genetic inheritance so that they have a fairly clear understanding of their own individuality, some way of saying "I" and knowing what they mean. This is a necessary preparation, Erikson suggests, for their entrance into intimacy which takes place in young adulthood. The achievement of identity is no easy task. It is, in many ways, a compromise imperfectly achieved even when successful. It requires young people to throw themselves out of balance and, without rebelling totally, define themselves apart from their parents in order to fashion a new relationship with them. Unless they do this, their own capacity for self-reliance cannot be developed.

As many observers have noted, the peer group constitutes the critical surrounding environment during this phase of personal development. Adolescents feel that acceptance by the members of their peer group is crucial for an independent sense of self. As Erikson states: "To keep themselves together they temporarily over-identify to the point of apparent complete loss of identity, with heroes and cliques and crowds" *(Childhood and Society,* New York: W. W. Norton & Co., 1950).

Part of the identity involves the adolescent in an episode of reaching out to a member of the opposite sex or "falling in love," which Erikson says "is by no means entirely, or even primarily, a sexual matter, except when mores demand it. To a considerable extent, adolescent love is an attempt to arrive at a definition of one's identity by projecting one's diffuse ego image on another by seeing it thus reflected and gradually clarified."

If the passage to a solidified identity is not successful confusion can result. If this confusion persists the young person experiences great difficulty in establishing satisfactory relationships with other persons. Adolescents with diffuse identity find it difficult to cross the threshold into the stage of life in which they should be able to deal successfully with intimacy. They may, in fact, as Erikson observes, throw themselves "into acts of intimacy which are promiscuous without true fusion of real self-abandon." Adolescents do not pass easily through this stage and they pass at different rates. Some have greater difficulty than others in solidifying their sense of themselves. It is during the period of confusion, when their image of themselves is incomplete, that they may experience great pressure for sexual activity which promises, according to the judgment of their culture, the completed sense of identity which they have not as yet achieved.

Recently psychiatrists Michael W. Cohen and Stanford B. Friedman arrived at a list of nonsexual motivations for sexual behavior which may be observed during this adolescent period. These include the context of sociocultural influences in which young people find themselves today. An appreciation of these factors helps counselors to see the struggle of adolescents in better perspective and also to assist them in understanding the underlying causes of the sexual questions and uncertainties which adolescents may bring to them. Included in the list—which originally appeared in *Medical Aspects of Human Sexuality,* September, 1975, pp. 9ff.—are the following:

PEER APPROVAL

Peer pressure is an enormous influence in the adolescent culture because of adolescents' difficulty in defining themselves as separate from their families. The culture has underscored and exaggerated the tension between the generations and a sharp focus has been put on the experiences of young people both by those who sincerely want to understand them and by those who want to exploit them for commercial purposes.

Today's adolescents have developed, perhaps as no generation before them, a culture of their own. Inside its boundaries peer approval has enormous leverage on their lives. They feel isolated and alone when they cannot gain the approval of their companions. It is in this situation that adolescents may turn to sexual behavior in an effort to win the peer approval which they so desperately seek.

This is a complicated area and those who work with young people understand how large this issue looms in the adolescent perception of the world. To enter into and to be successful at sexual encounters seems to deliver to them a stamp of approval or some species of social status. Seeking out sexual activity for this motivation is clearly using sex in a self-contained way and in a manner which generates anxiety and causes ambivalent feelings about the whole experience.

Failure or discomfort in sexual activity at this time—when so much expectation surrounds it—takes an enormous toll on an individual's self-esteem. Efforts at sexual activity may be rebuffed and individuals find that, instead of securing identity more firmly, they have merely diminished their sense of themselves and their sexual abilities. This difficulty with self-esteem becomes crucial because it is at the heart of the main struggle of adolescence. Consequently, a vicious cycle may be set up which leads to a deepened rather than a lessened personal problem. The use of sex to solve personal problems is not limited to adolescents, of course, but it is important to understand how much weight this activity bears in the adolescent world.

REBELLION

Cohen and Friedman further observe that "sexual activity as a manifestation of adolescent rebellion is frequently noted in clinical histories" (p. 18). Parents feel that they must explain and support certain social limitations on their children's sexual behavior. They do this out of an ethical and religious tradition and because, despite the so-called sexual revolution, a great many people of the older generation are convinced of the value of sexual limits. The insistence on these values may have a reverse effect, however, because adolescents, whether they consciously intend to or not, feel that they must reject these values in order to act out their own rebellion and thus achieve a greater sense of independence. Perhaps they would not have felt it necessary to reject their parents' values if their parents had not insisted upon them so much. The crucial point, in other words, is not sex as much as it is the collision with parental rules. Sexual relations may not be entirely satisfactory when they are carried out for this reason and are sometimes coupled with other rebellious or deviant signs such as drug-taking or acts of delinquency.

EXPRESSIONS OF HOSTILITY

To have some feelings of hostility toward the older generation is not uncommon but, as the authors point out, "Some harbor these feelings to an extreme degree. The sources of this hostility may stem from issues based in reality to those fantasized by the youngster. Angry teenagers may be quite limited in their outlets of expression of these feelings. . . . These adolescents are extraordinarily sensitive to their parents' areas of vulnerability." Because they have this sense of where they can hurt their parents most if they wish to, their hostility may be expressed through their sexual behavior. This is a way of getting revenge more than it is any kind of true sexual experience. It is meant to be an insult to the parents.

ESCAPE

Sexuality is frequently used as an escape from other situations troubling individuals. Adolescents want to break out of the home in which they feel, for whatever reason, they are suffocated by restrictions or by unreasonable obligations. Adolescent girls, for example, may, according to the authors, "desire to get pregnant to force a marriage which would take them away from home. However, it appears as though marriages consummated for these reasons have an increased incident of marital discord" (p. 21).

Semmens and Lamers (*Teenage Pregnancy,* Springfield: Charles C. Thomas, 1968) describe three groups of teenage girls who become pregnant. First they mention the "intentional" group who were clear about their motivation in becoming pregnant in order to precipitate a decision about marriage or in order to harm their rejecting parents. Pregnancy is a way out of the house in which they may be very uncomfortable because they have responsibilities, for example, to raise the younger children. Secondly, Semmens and Lamers found the "accidental" group in which the motivation is not nearly so clear. The underlying dynamics, in other words, are not simply an escape. They may be related to the family pattern itself or to the culture in which these people find themselves. The motivation may be related to some of the needs already discussed, such as the achievement of identity or independence. A third group is composed of the "unknowing," and consists of the mentally retarded and those who are badly informed or hardly informed about the nature of human sexuality.

. It is easy to see that many factors combine to make pregnancy and marriage at an early age a seemingly desirable event. These are sought, however, not in and of themselves but because they offer the chance to escape from punishing or difficult circumstances.

A CRY FOR HELP

Cohen and Friedman suggest that sexual activity in adolescents, especially when there is no effort to hide it, may be their attempt to get their parents' attention so that they can receive psychological help. Many parents either choose to ignore or psychologically block out signals which may be very clear. They want to believe, for example, that this is just a phase through which their children are passing and they offer reassurance or hope that the matter will be taken care of by their teachers or by the counselors at school. The less the parents are willing to pick up the message of the young, the more the young may feel the need to act out their problems dramatically. They may leave evidence of sexual behavior around where it cannot be missed. Counselors should help parents understand that this sexual behavior may have as its principal motivation the teenager's own sense of needing something more than reassurance in order to deal with emotional confusion and problems.

Cohen and Friedman also suggest that some depressed teenagers may use sexual behavior in "an attempt at self-destruction" (p. 25). Sexual behavior may accompany other signs of depressive difficulties including the use of drugs, careless driving, or other acting-out suicidal behavior. Merely stopping the sexual behavior will not, in itself, clear up the underlying difficulty.

The use of sexuality may also represent a search for love. Young girls may desire a pregnancy in order to have a child who will become a source of love for them. As Cohen and Friedman contend: "They hope that the child will be an object to smother with love, and that in turn the infant will support their need for affection. This situation is fantasized and glamorized by the girl. Disappointment results after the birth when she is faced with the reality of the infant's normal demanding and dependent role. Because the mother's needs are not being met, she develops ambivalent and negative feelings about the infant. . . . This whole cycle is self-defeating."

Other motivations can also exist for sexual behavior during adolescent years. It is obviously naive to interpret all sexual behavior as evidence of a simple direct search for sexual experience on the part of young persons who have successfully achieved their identity. Counselors play an important role in sensing the true dynamics and in helping all those connected with sexually involved situations to understand what is actually taking place. It is also helpful to consult the studies which illustrate some of the concerns that exist strongly even in what many people consider the sophisticated college population of today.

A recent investigation by Lyon Hyams, M.D., revealed a number of the areas which cause anxiety in college women. Hyams, reporting on a three year study of college women (*Medical Aspects of Human Sexuality*, March, 1976, pp. 96ff.), suggests that the changes in sexual attitudes and behavior which many automatically accept as progressive also generate a number of problems. "Sex," he writes, "like love, loneliness, and death—with which it is inextricably linked—is more often characterized by anxiety." He maintains we need an appreciation of individuals and that we should not read or over-interpret reports on group trends as directly applicable to the persons with whom we work. Hyams proposes three underlying anxiety-producing themes which must be appreciated by those who work with college-age women: (A) fear of injury and death; (B) male-female differences; (C) search for normalcy.

Despite the supposed widespread contemporary dissemination of sexual information, Hyams found a great deal of anxiety about the potential dangers connected with sexual behavior. There was apprehension about the safety of birth control pills and about the possibilities of physical harm coming to women through the use of birth control devices. Even though a number of these fears are unrealistic the underlying apprehension was quite clear. Dr. Hyams also found a number of concerns about dangers to the unborn child, the difficulties of labor, and the problems of a Caesarean section and other issues connected with pregnancy and delivery. The young women also exhibited great concern about being harmed themselves during physical sexuality. Such subjects seemed to need both information and reassurance as well as an opportunity to explore their anxiety. Counselors may well find themselves dealing with such questions; they need to have both the information and the sensitivity to do so effectively and simply.

Despite the rage of "unisex" that has supposedly prevailed in recent years, many young women are concerned about the differences rather than the similarities between men and women, especially in sexual areas. They recognize, for example, that men seem to be aroused more easily than women but they have extensive concerns about the subjective experience of sexuality in men and how this may differ from their own experience of it.

Here again, there is a surprising lack of information about the sexual experience of the male. Some of the questions raised also suggest, according to Hyams, that there are still areas of sexuality that seem repugnant to college girls. They are concerned, for example, about the fact that men do not seem to require emotional involvement for sexual desire or performance although they, at this stage of their lives, may need these very deeply. There is, in addition, some anxiety about discovering that there are factors, physical and psychological, that do differentiate women from men in sexual responsiveness during the college years.

There is no easy way in which to answer all these questions or conflicts lurking beneath their expression. This does indicate that there are unresolved areas of great importance that many counselors would neither expect nor predict in sophisticated college groups. The capacity to listen and understand and to provide these women with both helpful information as well as the opportunity to search out their own feelings or conflicts constitute an important part of the counselor's work.

According to Dr. Hyams, the students he studied gave evidence of "a desperate search for standards upon which to base their behavior and judge their feelings. The search for 'normalcy' has two components. Girls want to know what they 'should' do and also, and perhaps more important, whether the way they feel and respond is acceptable or adequate" (p. 107). In other words, young women do not have all the answers although they are quite well acquainted with the current questions. They are not trying to answer the questions by themselves; they are searching for some foundation on which to build their own personal intimate lives.

Young people do not accept the promises of the sexual revolution any more than they accept the dictums of Victorian morality. It is clear that counselors who wish to help these young people must recognize this need for outside assistance and not use it as a road for moralistic evangelization as much as an opportunity to help them take more responsibility for their total lives. Girls at this age may become quite dependent on those who provide the answers to these questions; the wise counselor will especially help college-age women, through searching his or her own moral traditions and beliefs, to work through lasting answers of their own. Here again issues connected with self-esteem and identity are paramount.

Adolescents may well be in the grip of what Hyams calls our "cultural pathology" which he describes as "the need of external and absolute criteria to measure feelings and performance." They are still subject, in other words, to the tyranny of a perfectionism that contemporary attitudes about sexuality define as somehow outside of themselves. They feel this pressure and the need to meet expectations on their sophistication and performances. This is a complex area that reveals the uncertainty, the tentative quality of searching that characterizes adolescent young women and their need for counselors who will move slowly and sensitively with them as they try to resolve these issues.

References

Berger, A. S., Simon, W., and Gagnon, J. H. "Youth and Pornography in Social Context." *Archives of Sexual Behavior* (1973), 2:279–308.

Blos, P. *On Adolescence.* New York: Free Press, 1962.

Broderick, C. B. and Rowe, G. P. "A Scale of Pre-Adolescent Heterosexual Development." *Journal of Marriage and the Family* (Feb., 1968), 30:97–101.

Broderick, C. B. "Sexual Behavior Among Pre-Adolescents." *Journal of Social Issues* (April, 1966), 22:6–21.

Cutright, P. "The Teen-age Sexual Revolution and the Myth of the Abstinent Past." *Family Planning Perspectives* (Jan., 1972), 4:24–31.

Ehrmann, W. *Premarital Dating Behavior.* New York: Holt, Rinehart & Winston, 1959.

Glassberg, B. "The Quandary of a Virginal Male." *Family Coordinator* (Jan., 1970), 19:82–85.

Goldsmith, S. and Gabrielson, M. "Teen-agers, Sex and Contraception." *Family Planning Perspectives* (Jan., 1972), 4:32–38.

Hamilton, E. *Sex Before Marriage: Guidance for Young Adults.* New York: Hawthorn Books, 1969.

Hettlinger, R. E. *Living with Sex: The Student's Dilemma.* New York: The Seabury Press, 1966.

Josselyn, I. *The Adolescent and His World.* New York: Family Service Association of America, 1952.

Katz, J., et al. *No Time for Youth.* San Francisco: Jossey-Bass, 1968.

Kelly, H. "Adolescents: A Suppressed Minority Group." *Personnel and Guidance Journal* (1969), 47:634–40.

Offer, D. "Attitudes Toward Sexuality in a Group of 1500 Middle-Class Teenagers." *Journal of Youth and Adolescence* (1972), 1:81–90.

Rubin, I. and Kirkendall, L. *Sex in the Adolescent Years.* New York: Association Press, 1968.

Taylor, D. *Human Sexual Development.* Philadelphia: F. A. Davis, 1970.

FIFTEEN

More on Adolescents and Sex

IT may be helpful to observe that not all young people are searching for an undisciplined stamp of approval on their sexual behavior. Their search for standards, which in some ways may reflect their dependency needs, also indicates their desire to do what is right and to understand this and make it a basis for other decisions in their lives.

Adolescents sometimes sense but cannot quite clearly express the fact that they are not ready for adult sexuality. They feel intense pressure for participating in it from their peer groups and yet they hold back, heeding some inner messages about their own lack of maturity, their lack of readiness for sexual experience. It may be helpful for counselors to understand and reflect on some of the positive reasons for chastity in a world that hardly ever speaks about it. This is not to say that counselors should become the active proponents of a specific sexual morality.

Those who frequently counsel young people are official or semi-official representatives of a standard of morality which expects self-control and chastity as a part of a religious commitment. This is true for ministers and teachers in religious schools and institutions. Such people may need to distinguish any discussion of moral teaching from the process of counseling but counselors need not forsake their identity as trustworthy adults, as though they had nothing to say about their own convictions.

Counselors may, for example, turn to the ideas of psychiatrist Beverley Mead who reviewed a number of the arguments for premarital sex and raised, on purely psychological grounds, some counter-questions (*Medical Aspects of Human Sexuality,* January, 1970). Mead inspects, for example, the statement: "Sex is fun. Why should anyone avoid an easy source of so much pleasure?" He notes that "the boy may find pleasure without complications but, because a double standard imposes social penalties on girls who participate in premarital relations, the adolescent female would do well to be more cautious." He does not endorse the double standard but he feels we must recognize it as a continuing part of the reality of current life. Men can still get away with things sexually more easily than women.

Mead also argues with the notion that sexuality before marriage always delivers a kind of "Summer of '42." Young people say "at least I learned something." Mead, however, suggests that what the person learns may be far from the real facts of life or love. The information that develops from adolescent premarital sexual activity may be the wrong kind of information and may lead to disappointment and frustration about the subject of sex. "Sexual activity involves love, a sense of belonging, and a lasting relationship that," Dr. Mead points out, "are elements missing from much premarital sex."

Young people often say, "We can find out if we are sexually suited for each other" if we have premarital sex. But there may be many motives for seeking out sexuality at an early age, as noted previously. And premarital sex may not, in fact, provide the answer to the question of whether a young man and woman are suited for each other. In fact, when sex is experienced in pressured circumstances there may be more frustration than anything else and confusion, rather than a clear answer to whether a couple is personally and sexually compatible.

In analyzing the motivations involved in premarital sexuality, Mead cites the drive for emancipation discussed in chapter 14. "By having sexual activity they are proving a point; they are establishing independence; they are frustrating the establishment. It is obviously a way of using sex for nonsexual needs, which may indeed give satisfaction, but may turn out to be damaging to one's developing sexuality."

It is more difficult, Mead feels, to deal with the statement that begins like this: "We know each other, we love each other, we understand each other; and the sexual relationship is an obvious expression of our love for each other. There may be circumstances which delay or prevent marriage but we do not wish to deny ourselves the sexual part of a loving relationship."

What does one say in response to any of the many variations of this statement? Such judgments, Mead notes, "are often made by young people prematurely and impulsively, but, in all fairness one may have to admit that such social situations do occur." He advocates the case for chastity, however, on grounds that he feels are more substantial than some of the traditional arguments offered to support it. Many of the older arguments are based on superstition, threats of venereal disease, and other notions which are not as persuasive as they once were. Many young people get a good laugh out of the old warnings.

In proposing a positive look at chastity and its values for the individual and society, Dr. Mead offers an argument based on a sexual reason. He notes the wide variation in the degree of sexual responsiveness of different human beings and he says that this does not seem to be "simply physical or physiological. Our capacity for sexual pleasure or sexual response must be largely a learned or conditioned phenomenon. When certain activity is considered a very pleasurable one, it is usually because all the experiences of that type, particularly the earliest ones, have been very pleasant and satisfying experiences. It may be that such conditioning applies very significantly to sexual response.

"If certain first sexual experiences of an individual have been very pleasant, satisfying, or reassuring loving experiences which have not been followed by disappointment or disillusionment, then later similar experiences would tend to be just as pleasant and just as satisfying. It does seem reasonable that this might apply significantly to our attitudes toward our enjoyment of sexual activity. If true, this will offer an important reason for defending chastity. When young adolescents are experimenting with heterosexual activities, it is often under circumstances that do not allow for the happiest of associations. Excitement and desire may be present. But often there is much anxiety, worry about possible consequences, possible guilt and often a great deal of disappointment about the whole situation."

Mead suggests that it is quite often true that the boy may not feel disappointment with premarital sex unless it puts him in conflict with his moral values. The girl, however, "is much more likely to be disappointed. She has learned to think of sex as associated with love and may not understand that adolescent boys do not make this association. Consequently, her romantic ideas about the experience as being a wonderful, loving tender and exciting one, will not be fulfilled. She may feel disappointed, and in some cases may feel cheated or used, particularly if a boy does not become more romantically inclined toward her following the experience, and so often he does not."

Mead concludes that "there may be something to the argument, especially as applied to girls, that an easy surrender of chastity may condition a negative response to sexual activities later in life. This may be too strong a point of view, although it may be valid to say at least that in later life sexual response and attitudes might be more positive or even more meaningful if the early sexual experiences were more satisfying."

Gordon Jensen, M. D. and Myna Robbins, M.S. have offered some common-sense suggestions about attitudes that may be important in dealing with adolescents who have questions about sexuality ("Ten Reasons Why Sex Talks With Adolescents Go Wrong," *Medical Aspects of Human Sexu-*

ality, July, 1975. p 7ff). It may be helpful for counselors to reflect on these, especially if they have other occupations such as teaching or religious ministry in the context of which they frequently deal with adolescents curious or troubled about their own sexual vibrations.

Jensen and Robbins suggest what every counselor already understands: the first rule is to listen carefully and question completely. Counselors understand very well the part about listening carefully but they sometimes hesitate to ask clarifying questions. This can lead to grave misunderstandings that can interfere with the counseling in a notable way. A hesitation to propose questions may leave certain things undefined or ambiguous. The counselor may presume an understanding of a term which is meant in quite a different way. A story may be misinterpreted. It is far better to ask explicit questions about meanings that are not clear than to carry on with an uncertain sense of their significance.

Secondly, it is suggested that those working with adolescents should avoid a moralizing attitude. Most counselors already understand this but just as they should not hesitate to ask questions neither should they hesitate to present their own convictions and their own code of sexual morality. Adolescents expect that adults have thought these things through. They want to hear how adults have worked out their own answers to questions that vex them. When we can be honest and open and not just repeat the statements of others we can reach adolescents more genuinely and they may well want to incorporate our answers into their own moral decisions.

Counselors should be careful not to encourage sexual acting-out or sexual rebellion. In other words, as noted before, a rebellious reaction is often not directed at sexual restriction as much as to the fact that the adult rules something out or issues an order in regard to some adolescent behavior. As counselors we become accessories to the rebellion if we take too imperious a tone in our statements. This almost always complicates rather than helps to resolve things, especially where transference is concerned.

In addition, counselors should make sure that the sexual information they transmit is accurate. And they should not presume that the young are well or even accurately informed. Adolescents can still operate on some mythology current in their own peer group or on some new variation of an old wives' tale from another generation. These quaint notions have amazing staying power even in a sexually sophisticated culture. One cannot underestimate the lack of information and understanding that is still widespread among young people too embarrassed to admit that they don't know everything about sex.

Besides avoiding a shocked attitude it is important for counselors to understand and be self-possessed about their own sexual attitudes. Helpers always communicate their comfort or discomfort, their maturity or immaturity in this area whether they want to or not. The young are particularly good at picking up these clues. Unless they think these things through in advance, counselors may find themselves anxious and uncertain, a source of contamination rather than assistance at key moments in the counseling.

Confidentiality is also a very important element in dealing with adolescents. They are very sensitive to any violations of this, indeed to any way in which counselors might use the information to make a joke about them or to report on them to their parents or to others. Carelessness regarding confidentiality is never excusable. While it does not seem necessary to repeat this, the very sensitivity of adolescents who are still trying to bolster their self-esteem reminds us of its singular importance here. We have to accept them the way they are—sensitive, unsure and worried about our reactions. Just taking them seriously, without any hint of condescension, is a big help in itself. Another point centers on counselors not being curious about the details of the adolescent's sex life, probing for information that gratifies the helper somehow but does not do much to clarify the adolescent's difficulties. In short, the maturity of the counselor is the crucial variable in the highly important work of responding to the sexual questions, doubts, and difficulties of younger persons.

Adolescence is not an easy period; it is marked by self-consciousness and a great sensitivity to the factors which affect, in one way or another, self-esteem. Contemporary adolescents are also under pressure to seem knowledgeable about sexuality even when they are not; this merely intensifies their discomfort and increases their reluctance to put their doubts or conflicts into question form. It may be that counselors, whether they are teachers or religious figures, need to overhear adolescent concerns, that is to catch the clues, so often indirect and symbolic, about the issues that cause most adolescents concern. Of course, a fine line exists between sensing what young people are trying to say and imposing a faulty personal interpretation. An awareness of the more common—and frequently unspoken—difficulties of adolescents may help to tune counselors in to the correct content and the genuine measure of feeling connected with these issues.

Adolescents have no monopoly on a concern for their sexual normalcy; that is a doubt strung out across the generations into the sunset years. And yet adolescents do wonder, sometimes magnifying small doubts or fragmentary pieces of evidence, about whether they are like other young men and women in the range of their sexual awareness and experience. Counselors need to be well-informed about the boundaries of sexual normality as well as about basic medical and psychological data on human sexuality.

Perhaps the best preparation for dealing with the uncertainties of adolescence is a settled and accepting view of the human condition itself. Counselors who are not pushing their own cause and who have come to sensible terms with their own sexuality communicate an aura that is quite helpful to young persons. Adolescents deal much better with their problems when they know that they have not been rejected nor made to feel ashamed; they experience a vital confirmation of themselves through the generalized understanding of an attentive counselor.

What are the specific areas in which the compassionate and well-informed counselor should be ready to respond? Allowing young persons to express their anxiety about themselves without some mindless and over-hurried reassurance is a first step in assisting them to identify and to explore the sources of their uneasiness. Only they can tell us their particular view of things and they need time and room in which to do this. Gradually more concrete areas of conflict will be defined. Helpers must be keyed to the emotional context of these concerns as well as to their possible need for specific information.

Concern over masturbation continues to be a source of anxiety for adolescents even though the matter has received enormous public discussion over the past decade. It may be that old superstitions die only slowly or it may be that the individual adolescent views himself or herself as somehow different from their age-mates. The feeling tone of the counselor's concern is quite as important as the nature of the substantive inquiry. Most counselors realize that masturbation does not cause the long list of physical ailments that have been attributed to it over the centuries. What they need then is a heightened attentiveness to the concern of a particular adolescent seeking help from them at this specific moment.

Although the subject will be treated in greater detail in the next chapter, it may be important to note here that the fantasies accompanying the act of masturbation may provide clues about the deeper concern of the adolescent. Mere reassurance is not enough in such a situation. What is required is an ability to judge the potential of the fantasy as evidence of a more generalized sexual disturbance. Persistent homosexual fantasies, for example, would lead the counselor to evaluate the adolescent's concerns more carefully and to consider when further help may offer an opportunity for changing his or her life in a positive way.

Adolescents, already keenly aware of their body image and its approximation or non-approximation of some vague cultural ideal, are still specifically concerned about their sexual organs. This concern, like others discussed here, is not the exclusive worry of adolescents; this may merely suggest, however, that a concern which began around the time of puberty was never adequately dealt with for a number of adults. This further underscores the need for understanding and the sensitive communication of information about penis size or vagina adequacy.

As to the recurrent anxiety over penis size, there is abundant research that demonstrates that this is usually an unfounded worry. Masters and Johnson, for example, have found that a short male sex organ increases proportionately more in size in an erect state than a penis that is longer in a flaccid state. It is also important to realize that penile size is a minor factor in sexual stimulation of a female partner; it is not, in other words, the determiner of sexual adequacy. (See Masters and Johnson, *Human Sexual Response* and *Human Sexual Inadequacy*.)

Counselors must be sensitive to the larger concerns that may be behind these questions, especially when individuals are not reassured by accurate information. The concern about the sexual organs may be part of a deeper identity problem or a homosexual conflict. Counselors with even rudimentary sensitivity can catch these related anxieties and help people to begin some exploration of them. This readiness to move into a larger area of self-referent concern is important in all these issues.

Another common adolescent concern centers on the nature of sexual dreams. Sexual dreams are normal, as are experiences of seminal ejaculation for adolescent males during sleep. Being able to talk to an adult who does not become embarrassed at such discussions is extremely relieving for anxious young people. For normal persons this concern will disappear with open discussions with an adult. Here again, however, counselors should be ready to take persistent concerns more seriously, especially if the dream content seems to point to sexual dysfunction of a more generalized nature.

Adolescents are frequently troubled about whether they are homosexual or not. They may have homosexual feelings at times and they may feel that this indicates something about their overall sexual orientation. This concern is frequently a part of growing up, related to identity, body-image, and a number of other experiences—such as locker room contact—that increase during the adolescent years. Here again wise counselors can assist persons to express and to explore their concern; they may feel that it is right to offer them reassurance, for example, about the possibility of perfectly normal males experiencing homosexual feelings from time to time. This is an area, however, that requires a diagnostic sensitivity that neither pries where it should not nor overinterprets the material it does uncover. A sensible referral for a young person who is genuinely anxious about homosexual thoughts or behavior is obviously in order.

As mentioned earlier there is still widespread concern, complicated by mythology of a modern sort, about intercourse as a necessary experience if an adolescent is to be considered normal. The concern, for example, that young girls once had about being virgins has not reversed itself in some sectors of the population. Counselors need to see the larger issues attached to this worry and should assist young people in exploring them. These are frequently associated with peer expectation, self-esteem, a fear of losing popularity and being lonely, etc. Counselors help little if they contribute, by attitude or suggestion, to the idea that intercourse will solve the adolescent's problems.

All too often nonprofessional counselors—teachers, priests, and lawyers, as well as nurses and general physicians—find that the burden of sex education and counseling has somehow slipped largely onto their shoulders. This is particularly true, for example, in certain problem situations which the parents do not feel up to confronting by themselves. Parents may feel confused, responsible, or guilty about the problem that has arisen.

Frequently the sensitive tasks—even basic sex education—are left to the person fulfilling the role of counselor. In these circumstances it becomes important to work first with the parents to help them deal with their own attitudes and then to involve them in the discussions with the adolescent. Leaving the parents out of a situation of which they are very much a part does little to better things, especially when the intra-family dynamics are a possible key to understanding the adolescent's complaint or concern.

References

Berger, A. S., Simon, W., and Gagnon, J. H. "Youth and Pornography in Social Context." *Archives of Sexual Behavior* (1973), 2:279–308.

Blos, P. *On Adolescence.* New York: Free Press, 1962.

Broderick, C. B. and Rowe, G. P. "A Scale of Pre-Adolescent Heterosexual Development." *Journal of Marriage and the Family* (Feb., 1968), 30:97–101.

Broderick, C. B. "Sexual Behavior Among Pre-Adolescents." *Journal of Social Issues* (April, 1966), 22:6–21.

Cutright, P. "The Teen-age Sexual Revolution and the Myth of the Abstinent Past." *Family Planning Perspectives* (Jan., 1972), 4:24–31.

Ehrmann, W. *Premarital Dating Behavior.* New York: Holt, Rinehart & Winston, 1959.

Katz, J., et al. *No Time for Youth.* San Francisco: Jossey-Bass, 1968.

Kelly, H. "Adolescents: A Suppressed Minority Group." *Personnel and Guidance Journal.* (1969), 47:634–40.

Offer, D. "Attitudes Toward Sexuality in a Group of 1500 Middle-Class Teenagers." *Journal of Youth and Adolescence* (1972), 1:81–90.

Rubin, I and Kirkendall, L. *Sex in the Adolescent Years.* New York: Association Press, 1968.

Taylor, D. *Human Sexual Development.* Philadelphia: F. A. Davis, 1970.

—— —— —— ——

SIXTEEN

Masturbation

MASTURBATION is now recognized as a common occurrence and, in recent years, there has been a marked revision in medical, theological, and even common-sense thinking about it. Our purpose is not, however, to explore the moral issue as much as to note the fact that some lessening of the severity of judgment about the sinfulness of masturbation in theological dialogue. However, many traditional churches, like the Roman Catholic Church, have reiterated their convictions about the moral gravity of masturbation as a "disorder" that does not match the purpose of genital sexuality.

The question of masturbation does not, however, seem to be fully settled in the minds of many religious persons, including some Catholics. They experience some conflict and uncertainty in this area and it is with the psychological dimensions of these reactions that counselors are concerned. It is not the business of counselors, while they are functioning as counselors, to reform the moral traditions of the Western world. Their task is to respond sensitively and in a well-informed manner to persons whose doubts or emotional problems are set in the matrix of a culture caught in a century of moral re-evaluation.

Neither should counselors join themselves without reserve to the liberated views that have become fashionable lately. According to such views, not only is masturbation freed from the Victorian horror stories about its consequences, both physical and psychological, but the guilt and anxiety that have been associated with it in the past have been entirely exorcised. Many authorities, while less than evangelistic in the expression of their opinions, accept masturbation as normal and do not see it as a cause for excessive concern at any time during life.

Far to the left of these modern shapers of opinion stand those who, for the good of their own cause, have politicized sexual judgments. Here masturbation is presented as a social advantage, the best revenge that ultra-radical feminists can wreak on their natural enemy: chauvinistic men. Contemporary culture has also provided a context in which masturbatory scenes are displayed in mass circulation magazines and in movies as well as in a widespread literature about auto-erotic practices. There is, in fact, a certain romanticization of masturbation as an accepted component in a sensual age. There has been little speculation about the psychology of these attitudes or their possible significance as cultural signs.

And yet people still express concern about this subject even though they have received massive forms of reassurances about its unharmful aftereffects and its potential as a source of pleasure, a solvent for conflicts, and as an outlet to ward off depression and loneliness. A recent index of the present ongoing concern may be found in the report of TEL-MED, a public service program of the Chicago Medical Society through which persons may receive a recorded "health message" by dialing a local phone number and mentioning the subject of their interest. During its first three weeks of operation the subject of the message most frequently requested was masturbation with 1800 requests, over three times as many as the next subject (*Chicago Medicine,* March 20, 1976, p. 246). Despite the advent of new information and new opinions, masturbation is still a matter of serious concern for many persons.

It is possible to attribute the continued anxiety about this subject to the waning of a once rigid outlook on the matter that, although theoretically much diminished in influence, leaves an emotional residue related to early conditioning about the subject. In other words, guilt may remain a problem for many individuals even though society in general has learned to live more comfortably with the subject. In fact, the only counseling often recommended in connection with masturbation is designed to remove this aftermath guilt which is considered neurotic and unnecessary.

However, it is not clear that this is the explanation or the only possible explanation for this lingering uneasiness about masturbation. It is also possible that many persons wonder about its precise meaning in their own lives and whether it is an indication of other unattended problems. Others have found that masturbation has not been as liberating as they had expected and have grown concerned about its frequency or its implications regarding the loneliness of their own lives.

No one knows why the concern continues, so sensitive counselors must keep their minds open to their clients and their own stories about their subjective experience; counselors must allow others to take them into their own worlds of concern and neither anticipate nor pass judgment on the situation.

Sexuality is a subtle language and, as in all problem areas, helpers must pay attention to its varied moods and tones. Sexual activity can, after all, be initiated for a wide variety of motives, many of them nonsexual. We are still in the preliminary stages of understanding the meaning of sexuality and the human experiences of conflicts that radiate from it. For those who work closely with others a grasp of the significance, as understood so far, of all sexual activity is indispensable in assisting persons with sexual conflicts. Masturbation, for example, must be viewed in a developmental context.

Masturbation, in the form of self-stimulation of the genital area, begins early for both sexes. Such activity is evident in infancy and does not seem to indicate anything abnormal. Society chose not to examine the sexuality of childhood for many centuries and even now it has only begun to understand it. The pervasive nature of sexuality as a constitutive and sensitive element of our humanity is now, however, quite clear. Sexuality is not an alien force but one that is a rich part of human nature. It is not surprising to note sexuality as a self-referred phenomenon in the overall self-centered stages of human growth. Where else can human beings begin to explore their experience of existence except within their own world and with the focus on themselves? Narcissism is expected in the early stages of life. Adult growth dictates gradual capacity to move away from self-concern and self-pleasure toward others and toward sharing ourselves with them.

Adolescence is recognized as a highly significant stage in personal development. This is the time for the coalescence of individual integrity; included in this task is the consolidation of sexual identity. It is precisely in relationship to this that masturbation plays an important role. It can and should, first of all, be understood as a developmental phenomenon rather than as the work of evil spirits, a necessary kind of experience if a person is to achieve integrity of the self and pass on to the next phase of growth. Masturbation appears, in other words, as an element in the overall process of development, a factor in the search for a stabilized identity.

For a young adolescent boy, for example, masturbation is a suddenly and sometimes surprisingly discovered source of intense pleasure; this cannot be denied but likewise our understanding of masturbation cannot be limited to this perception. It means more than pleasure. Masturbation can be understood as a sign of a young man's dealing with the problem of his own growth; he is, in a very real sense, trying to work through that problem. Through masturbation he experiences himself in a new way, catching a glimpse of a portion of his future identity foreshadowed through this activity. He experiences himself, in other words, as a sexual being whose destiny is to grow toward sharing his complete identity through the genital expression of his sexuality. Masturbation may not be as disordered as those who view it outside a developmental schema would make it. It appears rather as a dynamic event, attesting to the individual's efforts to move beyond the regressive and primitive elements of sexuality that characterize it at an earlier stage in life. It is instrumental in breaking away from narcissism.

Masturbation may be understood, then, as a sign that the individual is getting himself together in order to be able to move forward in the life cycle. He is doing something about his identity in a profound way, accomplishing a task that is important for his further development. Viewed in this way, masturbation can be seen as an indication of growth under way, a sign of a person seeking himself in the only way that is available as far as the complicated process of human growth is concerned. This is an important aspect in this transitional growing together of the sexual elements of his personality. Thus, psychoanalyst Peter Blos observes: "Masturbation normally promotes new shifts, linkages and delineation of mental images and their cathexes; it consequently stabilizes object and self-representations, thus facilitating the approach to genitality" (*On Adolescence,* New York: Free Press, 1962, p. 161). Masturbation during adolescence plays a distinctive role in helping the individual progress from the pre-genital to the genital stages of development.

This is not to say that this passage to greater development is free of conflict, nor to claim that it always progresses without incident or without interferences by other factors. Life is complicated and many influences can have an effect on the consolidation of identity and the manner in which masturbation functions at this stage. There is nothing automatic about this transition as one can see from the widespread difficulties many persons experience with their identity and with the sexual dimension of their lives.

For this reason sensitive counseling is extremely significant during this period; and overgeneralized advice or ill-conceived stands for or against masturbation may not be helpful in the long run. Counselors need to focus on the growing individual rather than on the masturbation itself; this perspective enables them to sense the struggle for identity and the possible positive role of masturbation in it. Excessive concentration on masturbation itself, for whatever reason, distorts the picture and the psychological meaning of the occurrence in the person's life. The counselor's role is not that of the advocate nor of the moral judge or censor; it is that of the competent and mature adult who has an appreciation for the process of growth.

In summary, then, masturbation at the adolescent stage may contribute to an important transition, the big step from self toward others, the transformation from narcissism to relationships with others in an adult mode. As Dr. William T. Moore notes: "The important effect of this complex (sexual identity, ego ideals, and character traits) on the final ability to choose a heterosexual love object occurs through a series of object transitions in fantasy accompanied by genital masturbation. Without the masturbation-fantasy complex it is doubtful whether the essential transition from Oedipal to heterosexual love object could transpire as it does" ("Masturbation in Adolescence," *Masturbation From Infancy to Senescence,* Marcus and Francis, Eds., New York: International Universities Press, 1975, p. 261).

Masturbation is still part riddle as far as our complete psychological understanding is concerned. Perhaps we are wisest as counselors when we at least realize that we do not know the answer to the riddle before we even hear it proposed. Modesty of statement becomes the minister, educator, or other professional who may be presented with an individual's troubles or doubts about a masturbatory situation. What can the rule be for persons who want to help and who do not merely wish to repeat the conventional and generally clouded wisdom of the culture?

Some sensitivity to the role of masturbation in human developmental dynamics is obviously essential. That does not mean, however, that helpers will not pick up clues from individuals that indicate that masturbation is not just a part of their adolescent growth but that it has an entirely different significance in their lives. Factoring out the meaning of masturbation in an individual's life takes patience and sensitivity; it may, indeed, take more time than many nonprofessional counselors have at their disposal. If they can catch indications that the conflict is more complicated than they had anticipated, or that it is not simply related to psychosexual development, they may be in a position to refer the person for more extended and intensive counseling.

Counselors must recognize that the content of the fantasies connected with masturbation is highly informative about the inner dynamics of the person seeking their assistance. When these fantasies are consistently regressive or primitive, when they do not move toward a heterosexual love object, questions may be raised about the meaning of the masturbation in the individual's life. The fantasy tells a story that is not always easy to decipher, even for skilled therapists, but counselors can recognize the bizarre and the morbid aspect of fantasies even when they cannot trace them down to their roots in the individual's psyche.

When the fantasy is regularly a regressive and infantile one, this is ordinarily the sign of a growth problem that cannot be considered indifferent or of no significance. A person whose fantasies are of a very undeveloped type of sexual activity—and if these recur in compulsive fashion—may well be struggling dynamically against some inner block to continued movement toward maturity. Blos writes, for example, of a person whose fantasy was that of committing fellatio on himself, and suggests that this indicates a struggle against homosexuality. "Masturbation," he writes, "assumes pathological features whenever it would consolidate regressive infantile fixations." Such fantasies would signal to counselors the need for psychological help of a continuing nature to deal with the total developmental problems of the individual.

It is also true, of course, that persons may, for brief periods of varying stages of their lives, be hosts to fantasies that are apparently quite bizarre and frequently unwelcome. Counselors understand that these transitory experiences do not necessarily indicate deep psychopathology; these fantasies often disappear as growth conflicts are resolved. Helpers do not search for a sick person behind every fantasy that may have regressive elements in it. What they can be attuned to, however, is the persistence of such fantasies, especially in connection with masturbation, and whether they are of a compulsive nature or not. Extended preoccupation with regressive erotic fantasy indicates the presence of a conflict at a deeper level and sensible referral is usually in order.

The subject of fantasy content is by no means simple and this is not an area into which self-confident amateurs should boldly march. The interplay of unconscious defenses and the fantasies associated with these can deliver messages that may only be unraveled slowly. Counselors who wish to be constructively helpful neither panic at such material nor dismiss it.

Perhaps still more common for counselors will be conflicts over masturbation in persons who feel that they have failed themselves, as well as their moral standards; who feel guilty and ashamed of the experience of masturbation in their lives. These feelings must be accepted and understood like any other feelings in the context of the individual's complete personality. Counselors, even when they see people only briefly, are consistently more helpful when they respond to the whole individual rather than just to the problem. This more generalized response helps persons with masturbatory conflicts to look at a wider range of their own behavior and feelings and to at least begin to see how the masturbation is connected with other aspects of their lives.

For example, masturbation may be used by some persons to deal with a loss in their life; others employ it as a prop to their self-esteem. Some are strongly discouraged because they feel that it is not only wrong but is also an obstacle to their moving out of themselves and toward other people. Still others discover masturbation as a residual after some major stressful life experience and they may feel that something has gone wrong with them when they are actually experiencing the vestige of a serious personal trauma.

Nonprofessional counselors encounter individuals with these difficulties quite frequently. These are the kinds of experiences people have in their individual struggles with life and they can be understood in perspective only if we are willing to listen, judgment suspended, with care and compassion. Counselors need to avoid the danger of trying to talk people out of their conflicts; reason, even when based on the best current information, does not work in trying to help with emotionally linked problems. We cannot explain to people that they need not feel ashamed or that they should not feel guilty when they do. They need helpers willing to accompany them on their search of themselves for clues to their reactions. With a little understanding they will be able to lead the way into their conflicts, and they frequently find that the conflict with masturbation has its roots in nonsexual situations.

Perhaps the greatest current temptation is to quickly reassure persons with masturbation conflicts without hearing them out, without giving them the opportunity to express themselves or explore their feelings deeply. Neither is it wise to give symbolic absolution to adolescents on the subject of masturbation. They are not seeking permission so much as understanding; they deserve the help that will assist them to make the move toward more adult sexuality. Providing them with excuses for not working through the larger issues of their identity—letting them indulge their narcissism instead of breaking through it—is not helpful.

Science has come only recently to observe and publicly acknowledge the fact that sexuality is not confined to the spring and midsummer of life. The sexual activity of older persons has been recognized, although it is still dealt with somewhat defensively. There are jokes about the activities after dark in Sun City retirement villages—a sniggering and somewhat embarrassed manner of dealing with the reality of sex as an enduring dimension of human personality. If people continue to be sexual into their older years they must also deal with all the impulses and conflicts, sometimes sharpened by the frustrations of the limitations caused by illness or diminished energy. So too, masturbation may continue as a means of sexual expression and a potential source of personal uneasiness. While we have devoted much space to understanding masturbation in adolescence it is not a phenomenon confined solely to that age level or developmental stage.

Counselors must be prepared to respond to persons across the whole continuum of aging on the undifferentiated problems of the human situation, including that of masturbation. It is not necessary to raise the subject or probe unnecessarily; rather, counselors should be prepared to hear about the conflicts, misgivings, or uncertainties associated with masturbation at any age, with any group of persons and in any profession. It may be important for helpers to clarify their own feelings about the persistence or re-emergence of sexual conflicts, including masturbation, in other than only the adolescent population. Masturbation can be understood in youth, especially as part of a developmental process, or at least as an aspect of emerging energies. But denial is used with other groups—with the elderly, the ill, the crippled, the single, or the widowed. That sexual experiences should persist in those who do not seem vigorous or young seems somehow scandalous; no wonder humor on the edge of bad taste is used to defend against it.

Counselors who are not surprised by what is human will have little difficulty in responding with understanding and compassion to persons of any age group who may wish to discuss their concern about masturbation. People at any age may feel guilty or disturbed that they have not overcome or outgrown a phenomenon which they still associate with sin or immaturity. A calm ability to let persons investigate their conflicts and the territory of their shame and anxiety is extremely healing for persons of whatever age or situation.

Frequently, the human support that comes from someone prepared to listen without embarrassment or the need to judge is of enormous help to these persons. It helps them rebuild their self-esteem, accept the frequently mysterious reassertion of conflicts they thought settled long before and to carry on in greater comfort in life. The rules for nonprofessional counselors are no different with older people than with younger. One listens and attempts to understand the symbolic psychological meaning of whatever takes place, including sexual conflicts in persons in whom we feel they were or should have been resolved long before.

References

Berezin, M. A. "Sex and Old Age: A Review of the Literature." *Journal of Geriatric Psychiatry* (1969), 2:131–49.

Blos, P. *On Adolescence.* New York: Free Press, 1961.

Cowdry, E. V. (Ed.). *Problems of Aging.* Baltimore: Williams & Wilkins, 1939.

Feigenbaum, E. M. and Lowenthal, M. F. "Aged Are Confused and Hungry for Sex Information." *Geriatric Focus* (1967), 5(20):2

Frank, S. *The Sexually Active Man Past Forty.* New York: Macmillan, 1968.

Hammerman, S. "Masturbation and Character." *Journal of American Psychoanalytic Association* (1961), 9:287–311.

Harley, M. "Masturbation Conflicts." *Adolescents* (S. Lorand and H. I. Schneer, Eds.). New York: Harper & Row, 1961.

Kay, P. "Development in Childhood Pre-adolescence." *Handbook of Child Psychoanalysis* (B. Wolman, Ed.). New York: Van Nostrand Reinhold, Co., 1972.

Kleeman, J. A. "A Boy Discovers His Penis." *Psychoanalytic Study of the Child.* New York: International Universities Press, 1966, 20:239–66.

————. "Genital Self-Discovery During a Boy's Second Year." *Psychoanalytic Study of the Child.* New York: International Universities Press, 1966, 21:358–92.

Lauter, M. "The Body Image, the Function of Masturbation and Adolescence."

Psychoanalytic Study of the Child. New York: International Universities Press, 1968, 23:114–37.

Marcus, I., M.D. and Francis, J., M.D. *Masturbation from Infancy to Senescence.* New York: International Universities Press, 1975.

Nagera, H. "Autoeroticism, Autoerotic Activities and Ego Development." *Psychoanalytic Study of the Child.* 1964, 19:240–55.

Rubin, I. *Sexual Life After Sixty.* New York: Basic Books, 1965.

Spitz, R. A., "Autoeroticism Reconsidered." *Psychoanalytical Study of the Child.* 1962, 17:283–315.

SEVENTEEN

Sexual Fantasies

YOUNG people have a wide variety of feelings about their participation in sexual activity. Sometimes they feel they are not quite ready for sex despite the expectations of their culture. It is their own feeling of hesitation that they wish to explore with a counselor. Sometimes these are feelings which they should trust and follow. These young people are wiser than some of their elders in recognizing that they are not yet mature enough to enter a sexual relationship. Sometimes young persons are hard pressed to find counselors willing to listen to their misgivings. This is a very sensitive area, however, and counselors, without dragging extraneous subjects in unnecessarily, should make sure the person can survey all aspects of the question.

This is one of the reasons counselors should realize that many young people are eager to explore the whole area of peer pressure and cultural expectation. They want to understand the relationship of these forces to their own developing personal identity and to their long range sense of themselves. When people are hesitant it is the hesitation that needs to be sifted through rather than smoothed over.

Closely related to these are the many young people who feel intimidated and somewhat estranged by what they perceive to be the general attitudes toward sex in those around them at school or in their neighborhood. Many of these are people afraid to admit that they do not feel the same way that others expect them to. They cannot discuss it readily without fearing that they will be ostracized from their group. They may perceive themselves as different or feel that there is something wrong with them because they do not seem to go along readily with the prevailing fads.

Counselors are present at defining moments in young people's lives when they are exploring these important feelings about themselves and their own sexuality. They often wish, in this context, to explore their values. These can be as important as sexual information for them. Counselors cannot shrug off values as though they were only the private business of their clients. As long as there are conflicting feelings in the area of values, counselors can be extremely helpful in assisting persons to clarify them and to incorporate them more fully in their own personalities. The discussion of values should not embarrass counselors. Anything human is their business and this is especially so in the area of sexual conflicts. It is strange that some counselors are prepared to talk about the intimate aspects of sex but are uneasy talking about values.

You cannot be arrested, the old saying goes, for what you are thinking, but you may well feel bad about it. In fact, some people are terribly disturbed by their thoughts and fantasies. Counselors recall that human beings are capable of a wide range of stimulation and that many fantasies and images can spring to mind unbidden in the course of one day. It is reassuring to people to help them understand that they are not the only ones who may experience bizarre or unsettling dreams and daydreams. This is an important educative function of well-informed counselors.

Counselors should also be ready, however, to let people explore what these fantasies or other experiences may mean to them. Counselors should not be overwhelmed or seem surprised; neither should they stop short at mere reassurance. People may want to talk about their fantasies and it is good to let them do just that. What about the character of the fantasy? Perhaps it is something that seems to upset them or to cause them to ask disturbing questions about their own adjustment. Counselors who do not allow people to go more deeply into these unsettling images may fail them at an important moment. Don't brush off these people; go with them in their questions.

Homosexual fantasies, for example, are not uncommon among heterosexual men. As psychiatrist John Schimel notes, such fantasies are not "the great problem" of life. They do tell something, however, about the problems a person has in living. Counselors must be alerted to the possibilities of some unconscious conflict which the persons cannot face directly and traces of which they see only in their disturbing fantasies. Sometimes the fantasy of homosexual activity in an otherwise normal person's life is associated with an experience of stress. It may really stand as a symbol for another kind of worry about dependence, submission or humiliation. This may be related to an experience at work or some other real life incident in which the total self-esteem system of the person is involved. It is also possible that sadistic or masochistic material may be present in these fantasies. This is not unusual, especially in obsessives who are preoccupied with power and its exercise in relationship to other persons. Such fantasies may also occur in the lives of persons who are confused about closeness. They may need closeness but find it hard to achieve successful intimacy in their lives. This conflict then manifests itself symbolically and the only trace that the individual sees of it is in the fantasy.

Cultural pressures can also cause persons to experience these fantasies. American culture, despite the sexual revolution, still offers the stereotyped ideal that the man is always supposed to experience sexuality adequately. The man is supposed to be able to provide the stimulation for the orgasms which the woman is supposed to enjoy.

This new-found imperative, spread across popular magazines and heard even in casual conversations, makes people examine themselves if they cannot react automatically and consistently in one of these ways. A man who feels that he cannot perform adequately sexually worries about it and it is a short step for him to begin to wonder about whether he is a homosexual or not. Fantasies about homosexuality have a story to tell but we must be patient if we are going to understand just what that story is and be able to help other persons understand its real source in their lives. As Schimel notes: "The homosexual fantasy in the heterosexual male is rarely what it seems to be; it is a signal that something is going on within the person; it is worth investigation, but it is not an embodiment of the person's real problems in living" ("Homosexual Fantasies in the Heterosexual Male," *Medical Aspects of Human Sexuality,* Feb., 1972, p. 151).

Sexual feelings are almost infinitely varied. They can range from anger to sadness. They can be surprising or disturbing. One of the most common of sexual feelings is that of homosexuality. Here again cultural pressures are important. We have witnessed the politicization of Gay Liberation with its insistence that people with homosexual leanings should declare themselves publicly. This has in recent years put the question sharply into the minds of persons who might never have asked it of themselves previously. Does their experience of homosexual feelings really mean that they are homosexual? Should they, in fact, present themselves as such in society instead of holding back?

Whether or not this question presents itself, the agony of doubt experienced by many young people is intense enough to bring them to discuss such matters with counselors. Here again counselors need to understand the medical and physiological facts but, more importantly, the psychological roots and implications of such difficulties. Counselors should expect young people to be anxious when they come to them to talk about such feelings. Their whole image of themselves is, after all, deeply involved and they see their identity at stake. If these people are self-referred the counselor can safely leave it to them to begin the exploration of these feelings in their own way.

Dr. Robert Einstein, psychiatrist at Yale University, describes four different types who typically seek assistance in understanding their homosexual feelings ("Homosexual Concerns of College Students," *Sexual Behavior,* Dec , 1971). Noting that many students regard any feelings of homosexuality as evidence of abnormality, Einstein lists the following groups as those to whom counselors should be sensitive in this area.

First of all, there are people without conscious homosexual feelings who have had difficulties with heterosexual adjustment. Because they do not get along well with girls, they begin to question their masculinity. This becomes a source of intense anxiety for them. It is clear that the issues are much larger than those of sexual preference. Their whole picture of themselves is involved and it is to the entire person that the counselor must be sensitively attuned.

Secondly, there are people who are aware of some kind of sexual attraction to members of their own sex, but they are not overtly involved in homosexuality. These feelings may be fleeting, but they are quite disturbing. Here again people's sense of themselves is threatened; they need to explore not only the occurrence of the feelings, and perhaps be reassured that these are not unusual, but also the implications of their concern about their sexual identity.

Thirdly, there are people who have had one or two homosexual encounters, sometimes early in adolescence and sometimes in college, who are concerned about the implications of even this limited kind of behavior. Here the problem is far more conscious and the issues must be clarified in a more intense counseling relationship.

Fourthly, there are relatively active homosexuals who are not concerned so much about changing as they are about the way they are going to adjust in life. They are far more open now to choosing a homosexual lifestyle rather than trying to mask their homosexuality under the facade of a heterosexual adjustment. Here again, however, the person may be quite uncomfortable in this role and may want to go more deeply into his sense of self in psychotherapy.

It is clear that counselors cannot answer the kinds of questions that these young persons bring only with reassurance or popular notions. This is especially true when the pressure of Gay Liberation makes them seriously wonder whether there is some inner core of homosexuality within their psyches. Other young persons are intensely intimidated by the sexual boasting that continues to go on in their environment and with which they cannot comfortably identify. In a different kind of way girls may have similar problems in understanding and integrating their own developing sense of themselves.

Both groups can be caught up in faddish notions about a desirable sexual adjustment. In recent years there has been some pressure, for example, for people to choose a bisexual life style. This causes confusion and uncertainty in persons, especially in those who have felt both homosexual and hetero-sexual impulses in their lives. The politicization of sex has caused great pressures to accumulate on persons who are uncertain about themselves. It remains clear that the issue that is important for counselors is this basic uncertainty. What are the perceptions and concerns of these young people and how can counselors help them, despite the pressure they feel, to go more deeply into themselves in order to understand their own sexual identity and their self-esteem?

Such concern is almost always present here waiting to be responded to; people are not asking for much when they ask if we can hear and understand it.

Central in the experience of most of us—and vital for our human survival—is an adequate and competent sense of ourselves. Self-worth is frequently the issue beneath specific questions about troubling sexual feeling. Clients want to solidify their sense of themselves and reassure themselves that they are basically OK. Their anxiety about their fundamental soundness brings them to present questions about sexual identity to counselors. Sexuality is the focus because it reflects deeper concerns; it becomes the avenue through which they tentatively approach themselves.

But the core issue remains their overall identity rather than just some problem about an unusual sexual fantasy. "Who am I?" "What am I like?" These are the questions that these individuals must sooner or later ask if they are going to get to the heart of the matter. Brief counseling may not offer them time to find completely adequate answers but they can at least make a beginning and can move beneath their concern for sexual symptom-like phenomena. Counselors should not keep a tight focus on sexual questions if clients are ready to explore more profound aspects of themselves.

As the counselor helps clients to get more deeply into themselves clients will put the specific sexual complaints into much better perspective. They will be able to see, for example, that the sexually difficult is but one aspect of their overall style of meeting and dealing with people. They may be able to look through the sexual symptom and see the role their total personality plays in giving rise to it. They sense that there is more to them than just this specific sexual problem and this represents a big step for people at any age. Sexual problems out of perspective have a way of tyrannizing people, of overwhelming their consciousness and blocking people from seeing other aspects of themselves. This is typical during a period of maturing experience, as during adolescence, and can be greatly relieved by responses to the total person.

References

Abraham, Karl. *On Character and Libido Development: Six Essays.* New York: W. W. Norton & Co., Inc., 1966.

Bieber, I. *Homosexuality.* New York: Basic Books, 1962.

Blos, Peter. *On Adolescence: A Psychoanalytic Interpretation.* New York: Free Press, 1962.

————. *The Young Adolescent: Clinical Studies.* New York: Free Press, 1972.

Einstein, Robert, M.D. "Homosexual Concerns of College Students." *Sexual Behavior* (Dec., 1971).

Erikson, Erik H. *Identity, Youth and Crisis.* New York: W. W. Norton & Co., Inc., 1968.

Gagnen, John H. and Simon (Eds.). *Sexual Deviance.* New York: Harper and Row, 1967.

Group for the Advancement of Psychiatry. *Normal Adolescence.* New York: Charles Scribner's Sons, 1968.

Maccoby, Eleanor (Ed.). *The Development of Sex Differences.* Stanford, California: Stanford University Press, 1966.

Marmor, J. (Ed.) *Sexual Inversion.* New York: Basic Books, 1965.

Money, John. *Man and Woman, Boy and Girl: The Differentiation and Dimorphism of Gender Identity from Conception to Maturity.* Baltimore: Johns Hopkins University Press, 1972.

————. *Sex Errors of the Body: Dilemmas, Education, Counseling.* Baltimore: Johns Hopkins University Press, 1968.

Rubin, I. and Kirkendall, L. E. (Eds.). *Sex in the Adolescent Years: New Directions in Guiding and Teaching Youth.* New York: Association Press, 1968.

Ruitenbeck, H. M. (Ed.). *The Problem of Homosexuality in Modern Society.* New York: E. P. Dutton & Co., Inc., 1963.

Schimel, John. "Homosexual Fantasies in the Heterosexual Male." *Medical Aspects of Human Sexuality* (Feb., 1972).

Schaeffer, Dirk. *Sex Differences in Personality Readings.* Belmont, California: Brooks/Cole Publishing Co., 1971.

Singer, Jerome. *Daydreaming: An Introduction to the Experimental Study of Inner Experience.* New York: Random House, 1966.

Terman, L. M. and Miles, C. *Sex and Personality: Studies in Masculinity and Femininity.* New York: Russell and Russell, 1968.

Wagner, Nathaniel. *Perspectives on Human Sexuality: Psychological, Social and Cultural Research Findings.* New York: Behavioral Publications, 1974.

Willis, E. S., M. D. *Understanding and Counseling the Male Homosexual.* Boston: Little, Brown & Co., 1968.

EIGHTEEN

Counseling Homosexuals

A NEW openness about homosexuality is but one index of the recent liberalized transformation in our communication about human behavior. The question of homosexuality is hardly settled but something is indeed changing. The old, tightly drawn lines of distinction that placed homosexuality and heterosexuality as opposites in human experience, emotional tone, and moral value have been redrawn. It is not an easy thing to offer a satisfactory definition of homosexuality. The experts themselves disagree; but counselors must have some ideas as well as some resources to serve as secure bases for whatever work they may engage in with persons who describe themselves as homosexuals.

Psychiatrist James C. Coleman is only one of those who has challenged the notion of a sharp distinction between homosexuality and heterosexuality. He has written: "Contrary to popular opinion, it is not possible to divide people into two clear-cut groups—homosexuals and heterosexuals. Rather, these labels signify extreme poles on a continuum; in between, we find many individuals whose experiences and desires combine both heterosexual and homosexual components" (*Abnormal Psychology in Modern Life,* Glenview: Scott Foresman & Co., 1972, p.481).

Most are familiar with the data presented by Kinsey and others that tend to substantiate this view. If these data can be accepted as reliable, a majority of American men experience some homosexual arousal some time after the beginning of adolescence; but these men are not and would not generally be classified as homosexuals. They are considered normal heterosexuals. The presence of homosexual impulse or even an incident of homosexual behavior is not sufficient to define a person as homosexual. It is also generally recognized that there is a phenomenon that can be termed situational homosexuality. This occurs when heterosexual deprivation exists, as, for example, in prisons, distant military posts, and in other similar situations. People who engage in homosexual activities in these very difficult circumstances are not regarded as "true" homosexuals. They take on homosexuality because of the social conditions in which they are forced to live. It is a form of social adjustment; a complicated one that we do not fully understand.

Psychoanalyst Irving Bieber, in a now famous study of 106 homosexual patients, has offered a definition of a homosexual as someone who repeatedly, over time, engages in overt homosexual behavior and never engages in heterosexual behavior ("Clinical Aspects of Male Homosexuality," *Sexual Inversion: Multiple Roots of Homosexuality,* Judd Marmor, Ed., New York: Basic Books, 1965, p.248). Judd Marmor, who has written extensively on the subject and who took a leading role in modifying the way homosexuality is listed in the Statistical and Diagnostical Manual of the American Psychiatrist Association, offers a different and more expanded definition. He feels that a psychodynamic definition of homosexuality "cannot ignore the element of motivation and should combine the operational and motivational aspects of homosexual behavior. Homosexuality, as a psychosexual phenomenon, ought to imply the same kind of strong and spontaneous capacity to be aroused by members of one's own sex as heterosexuality implies in regards to the opposite sex. I prefer, therefore, to define the clinical homosexual as one who is motivated, in adult life, by a definite preferential erotic attraction to members of the same sex and who usually (but not necessarily) engages in overt sexual relations with them" (ibid, pp 304).

Psychiatrist John Cavanaugh considers homosexuality a way of being, something deeper than a life style. He writes that "it is important to accept the concept that homosexuality is a way of thinking and feeling; not merely a way of acting. . . . as a working definition, homosexuality may be defined as a persistent, post-adolescent state in which the sexual object is a person of the same sex and in which there is a concomitant aversion or abhorrence, in varying degrees, to sexual relations with members of the opposite sex" (*Counseling the Invert,* Milwaukee: Bruce Publishing Co., 1966, pp. 17, 18).

These definitions are broad enough to provide a frame of reference for most of the homosexual problems that are presented to nonprofessional counselors. Such counselors should also be acquainted with the change in the categorization, mentioned above, that was brought into effect by a vote of the American Psychiatric Association in 1974. Many persons, including psychiatrists themselves, have objected not only to this change but to the methodology through which it was achieved. A self-identified homosexual group raised the money for the necessary lobbying and the change was ultimately based on a minority vote of the members of the association. The political overtones of the discussion were very strong. Still it is worth noting what Marmor says about the subject.

This new category of *sexual orientation disturbance* is reserved, he writes, "for individuals whose sexual interests are directed primarily toward people of the same sex and who are either disturbed by, in conflict with, or wish to change their sexual orientation. This diagnostic category is distinguished from homosexuality, which by itself does not necessarily constitute a psychiatric disorder. Homosexuality per se is one form of sexual behavior and, like other forms of sexual behavior which are not by themselves psychiatric disorders, is not listed in this nomenclature of mental disorders" (*Comprehensive Textbook of Psychiatry,* Freedman, Kaplan and Sadock, Eds., Vol. 2, Baltimore: Williams & Wilkins, 1975).

Counselors, even those who do not treat homosexuals in any long-term therapeutic relationship, can learn from such discussions that the last words have yet to be written or uttered on the subject of homosexuality. The difficulty in defining it, again according to the recent discussion by Marmor, is related to the variable motivation beneath homosexual activity. As Clara Thompson has observed, homosexuality "may express fear of the opposite sex, fear of adult responsibility, the need to defy authority, or an attempt to cope with hatred of or competitive attitudes to members of one's own sex; it may represent a flight from reality . . . or it may be a symptom of destructiveness of oneself or others. These do not exhaust the possibilities of its meaning" (*Interpersonal Psychoanalysis: The Selected Papers of Clara M. Thompson,* New York: Basic Books, 1964).

There has also been extensive discussion about the influence of genetic and hormonal variables in the development of homosexuality and there are a number of theories, ranging from the psychoanalytic to the behavioral, about the way homosexuality develops in an individual's life. What can the counselor who works most of the time as a teacher, a member of the clergy, or in some similar role do when even the basic definitions seem to be uncertain and at a time when a continuing debate rages about the question of whether homosexuality is pathological or merely a normal variant of human sexuality? The first task for nonprofessional counselors is to acquaint themselves with the terms of the discussion and to take a position which acknowledges its unsettled quality and which builds then on well-informed common sense. The arguments on both sides are very strong and the discussion has been underscored politically by the development of the Gay Liberation movement.

There are many complex issues here, ranging from whether those who feel they may be homosexual should "come out of the closet," to whether homosexuals can take their place in the ministry of the various churches. Literature on the subject is extensive and is sometimes as polemical as it is supposedly scientific. The task of counselors is not to settle any one of these discussions, but to try to listen carefully to the individuals who come to them for assistance and to provide them with the best responses possible. That may mean not taking sides in the discussion about defining homosexuality or deciding whether psychological treatment works or is even necessary.

Para-professional counselors who want to be helpful in a lasting sense can do so by keeping themselves free of the political aspects of the discussion and by avoiding using or being used by the groups who are out to prove something one way or the other. Counseling is not helped by adopting an advocacy role. Para-professional counselors, however, ordinarily occupy positions that allow them to be molders of opinion as well as translators of difficult public discussions. In no situation is this more true than in a discussion of homosexuality. One of the roles that such counselors must fill is that of helping society process its own feelings and reflections on the subject of homosexuality. It remains a deep and tangled subject and it cries out for those who can maintain an attitude of genuine understanding and who can therefore further the communication between interested parties. It is clear that informed para-professionals can reduce the vindictiveness and punitiveness that sometimes attend these discussions. It is by no means easy for people to maintain a mediatory position when everybody else wants to choose sides and have a fight. Counselors are, however, expected to hold that balance.

Perhaps central to being able to help others is an examination of our own attitudes toward homosexuality. People may come to discuss the subject with us for a wide variety of reasons. They may be troubled by what they perceive to be a conflict of their own or they may wish to find out something because of a situation in which they are personally involved, as with a member of their own family. Even though there has been an increase in openness in discussing homosexuality their strong feelings still exist and most counselors can find an edge of that in themselves that may predispose them to look either too negatively or too positively on either the persons who come to them or the nature of the subject they wish to discuss. A relatively recent study of physicians, for example, revealed that those physician subjects who participated in the study generally thought that they did not allow their negative attitudes toward male homosexual patients to interfere with their work. They felt, however, that other doctors did do this. This evidence of psychological projection at work in this profession may find its own counterpart in other professions as well. Another interesting finding is the existence of a positive relationship between the physician's feeling comfortable in treating homosexual patients and his feeling comfortable in the discussion of sexual problems in general (I. Reed Pauley, M.D. and Steven G. Goldstein, Ph.D., "Physicians' Attitudes in Treating Male Homosexuals," *Medical Aspects of Human Sexuality,* Dec. 1970, p. 27).

What can the para-professional counselor do at the individual level when homosexuality is an aspect of the situation with which he or she must deal? It would be rash and imprudent for most nonprofessional counselors to begin any relationship with the intimation that it offers the possibilities for permanent change in a homosexual's feelings or the eradication of whatever conflicts may be present. This, of course, would also be a rash promise to make in counseling with a heterosexual suffering from sexual dysfunction. Counselors begin with a sense of their limitations but a willingness to offer whatever sensible assistance can arise from their informed effort to be understanding. It is not for amateurs, no matter how concerned they are about their clients, to attempt long-term analytic-like therapy; neither should they try to reproduce some of the behavior modification treatment that has been employed in attempting to change homosexual erotic preferences through conditioning techniques.

Enough of warnings, counselors might complain, because they do meet these people and they cannot be totally indifferent nor merely hand them on to other help. Other help is frequently not available right away and counselors, even acknowledging their limitations, are still capable of responses that will be constructive and helpful. Judgments about the extent of counseling may depend upon the helper's training, self-confidence, and the identity—and therefore the expectations others make—of their main occupation. A person coming to a general physician, for example, with concerns about homosexuality may be looking for medical advice and information, while a homosexual seeking out a member of the clergy may be seeking some moral clarification or information on a church teaching.

Counselors may proceed, however, relying on their good sense and good health and following a first principle: *Don't think you know what the problem is in advance.* Despite the openness of the era, the pull of stereotypes in shaping our attitudes remains strong. We may have dealt with persons with homosexual conflicts in the past and expect that all those who see us in the future will in some way resemble them or have similar difficulties.

The current literature about homosexuality, especially in popular magazines, may provide the terms in which individuals choose to describe their problem or phrase their questions. Some current popular attention may provide the occasion for the homosexual's raising an issue but, although it provides a contemporary vocabulary, it hardly ever plumbs the depths or provides any answers. We cannot relate to people troubled by homosexual feelings on the basis of current superficial literary fashions. Neither can we apply notions out of the past as though they were some immutable dogma about human development; that is just as much a mistake as letting one's attitudes be shaped by popular magazines or newspapers. Not every homosexual, in other words, is going to come with the classic case history of a dominating mother and a weak, passive father. There will be clients like this, of course, but we must always be wary of allowing our expectations to make our clients fit into our theories in advance. We cannot even expect that all persons with questions about homosexuality are coming to us in order to find out how to change themselves. This may be true in a large percentage of cases, but the anxiety they wish urgently to discuss may arise from another more immediate source, such as a question about declaring one's homosexuality publicly or because of some difficulty with family life, friendship, or work.

Closely associated with this notion is the need to be sure of why these persons are coming to see us in the first place. If we are poised ready with the same automatic advice to anyone who seems to be homosexual we may miss the individual and give advice that is inappropriate and ultimately unhelpful. If not all homosexuals are in conflict, if, in fact, as some researchers indicate, not all older homosexuals are lonely and desperate, then they may not welcome nor be helped by advice that sounds to them as condescending more than as a product of an effort to understand them. Their purpose in coming, as suggested above, may be signalled to the paraprofessional counselor in terms of the helper's main professional function. While it is true that the emotional components of the problem would have to be acknowledged and dealt with sensitively, much can be learned by trying to understand right from the start how the clients view the counselor and what function he or she is primarily expected to provide for them. The physician may be questioned about the details of some sexual practice or some medical sexual problems. These are not questions without emotional aspects; but the helper is being seen mainly as a medical specialist. So it is with teachers who may be sought out because they seem to be understanding persons who offer the first opportunity to students to discuss their doubts or fears, or just their generalized concern about their own homosexual feelings or about some homosexual experience in which they have been engaged. The teacher is seen as a teacher, a knowledgable and mature guide.

Members of the clergy must also be particularly careful to make their responses in the context of their major professional identification. It is true that persons with homosexual conflicts sometimes seek out the clergy because they are generally recognized as fulfilling the roles of counselors or comforters, as people with spiritual values who represent a religious tradition. Others perceive them more in the role of spiritual authorities who can offer valid information about the morality of certain activities. Connected with this may be the search for absolution, for some sacramental or quasi-sacramental confession to help the counselees deal with their major presenting problem of guilt. This is a complicated issue because the guilt may proceed from neurotic sources rather than from some accurate judgment about genuine moral failure.

Does the counselor then pursue the emotional strands of guilt? Or is it wiser to focus on the request for absolution—the perceived need of the other —and carry that out simply, with a sensitivity and compassion to the complications of guilt? In other words, members of the clergy have to decide on how they minister religiously in counseling situations with homosexuals. It is probably not by trying to be psychologists who try to go deeper into the emotional material. Pastors serve better as religious figures who can respond to the person's sense of guilt, even when this is distorted or inappropriate, accompanying this with the rituals of forgiveness from the individual's religious tradition. This is not to remain naive but to respond in a humanly informed way in a setting in which forgiveness and the lessening of guilt by a responsible religious figure may be quite important.

If members of the clergy can separate the idea of treating the other from ministering to the other they will carry out their function far more effectively and with greater success in the long run. They will have a better opportunity, for example, to refer the person if additional psychological help seems to be required and they will be able to maintain their own position without confusing their identity or trying to deliver a psychological service that they cannot actually give. In order to do this—that is, maintain a ministerial stance—they need not be cold or mechanical in their responses. They may profit, however, from a certain measure of distance which limits complications while it still offers plenty of opportunity for the expression of human concern and understanding.

Ministering to persons with human problems is not the same as taking them on as psychological clients for long-term help. Much can be accomplished through the sensitive use of the opportunities for religious ministry. These need not be incompatible with help from mental health specialists. Clear professional identification with sacramental ministry, even though it seems a limited function, has distinct advantages because it distinguishes the identities that have so often been seriously confused and allows the minister to work in an uncluttered and powerfully supportive manner. Trying to be all things for all people is a heroic but highly impractical ministerial ideal. Functioning in a religious mode offers the opportunity for education about the nature of guilt and the pastoral interpretation of the efforts of these people to lead good lives. If a religious figure can offer them encouragement to do their best and help them to see that God expects no more than this, and when this is communicated with some sensitive psychological understanding, this is constructive and clearly defined ministry. Carrying out such ministry does not require the counselor to become over-involved in attempting to search out the origins of the person's homosexual conflict nor does it require that they try to provide some ultimate treatment. Neither does it involve them in the politics of sexuality. Such religious counselors neither have to give advice about participation in the Gay Liberation movement nor take a moral stand condemning or condoning homosexual activity.

The ministering attitude allows the counselor to help individuals perceive and take more responsibility for the moral and religious aspects of their lives. Some distance is then built in to such ministry. It is not, however, the distance of indifference as much as the wisely adopted reserve appropriate in carrying out this specific professional function. This also minimizes the potential complications of the transference possibilities that are inherent in any counseling situation. When the religious figure—or the teacher or the lawyer or the doctor, for that matter—understands the transference feelings that may be brought to the counseling situation, they will maintain the perspective that allows them to distinguish these carefully and so avoid becoming entangled in them or misinterpreting them in a highly personal way. In fact, some sensitivity to transference phenomena allows other professionals to maintain their own identity and participation in the counseling much better. They can limit their emotional commitment while still remaining concerned; they can avoid over-involvement without unnecessary rejection of the other person.

Nonprofessional counselors are helpful if they avoid focusing exclusively on the specific problem of homosexuality. While it may be interesting to find out more about this particular problem and while the person coming for help may be absolutely absorbed in the conflict and may have the need to describe it in some detail, counselors should not calibrate their responses to the specific situation. It is far better if, while listening to the person's story, they try to make responses that are more generalized and that reflect the person's overall attitudes toward the self. These attitudes are highly important especially in dealing with homosexuals who find it difficult to like themselves or to accept or forgive themselves for the difficulties which they experience in living. This is particularly true with people who seem to be true homosexuals rather than persons passing through some stage of growth or others who have some doubts about their gender identity because of passing impulses or fantasies. All people who are troubled enough to come to see a counselor about something are telling a story about the way they perceive themselves, of the judgments they pass on their own attitudes and behavior, and they need counselors who can hear this larger story as well as the details of the incident which precipitated their seeking help. These more generalized responses help the client explore not just this specific source of anguish but the whole pattern of their lives. Such an attitude on the part of the counselor can release a good deal of the tension that comes from the intense focus on one situation or one relationship.

It is important for counselors, even when they are not fully trained professionals, to be able to tell the difference between a deeply ingrained pattern of homosexual behavior and some passing incident that proves little at all. This has been discussed often enough, but it bears repetition. When an individual in a position of authority offers some basic good information and some general reassurance to a troubled person, this makes an enormous difference in the troubled person's perception of the self and of the way he or she handles whatever misgivings or doubts they have about their normality. Sometimes this is all that otherwise healthy growing persons need. Para-professionals should not hesitate to give this kind of reassurance and to offer some limited re-education about the facts of human sexual development. They can do this within the context of their own primary identity, especially if they use common sense rather than acting like an amateur psychiatrist. Their primary identity, in other words, remains intact even though they are using information from other disciplines. The fact that it comes from them—in the role of minister or teacher or physician—is significant because they are the persons in whom the client has placed trust and whose words have special power.

It is sometimes helpful to suggest certain changes in behavior that may assist troubled persons to deal more constructively with their doubts. If, for example, a person is troubled by homosexual fantasies or feelings and lives in a totally male world, counselors may be able to help them understand the way this environment affects them even when they do not suspect that this is the cause. There are ways to open up a person's environment without drastically changing their lives. One can encourage greater social participation, travel, and heterosexual contacts without assuming control over an individual's life. A more balanced life is a common sense remedy for many minor and fleeting episodes of homosexual feeling.

Counselors may need to make judgments on these incidents in terms of whether the homosexuality is a central feature or only one feature of the episode. It may be, for example, that the person is suffering from an obsessive-compulsive difficulty and that the homosexual fantasies are merely one symbolic dimension of the difficulty that is not basically homosexual. The kind of referral that will be made will depend on the counselor's ability to accurately translate the sometimes confused language of neurosis. The counselor's sensitive judgment becomes the basis for an informed and helpful kind of referral.

Perhaps the wisest course for nonprofessional counselors, is to avoid making major life decisions, such as those affecting career or marriage, for persons with homosexual problems. These are decisions which should be made in the context of long-term therapy. Nonprofessional counselors may help these people to avoid making mistakes if, for example, they are hesitant about choosing a specific career in which they feel their homosexuality may be a problem. Counselors may give their opinion that some delay until greater insight can be developed would be appropriate. So too, it is with marriage which, despite the enlightenment of the age, is still thought by many to offer the promise of a cure for homosexual feelings. People do not get married to cure themselves of anything and counselors should not hesitate to say this. This is especially true for nonprofessional counselors who are functioning in other roles in which they are expected to have opinions on these matters. This is not the same as trying to supervise a person's life. Such judgments proceed from a compassionate fund of common sense that respects the other while providing a prudent assessment that can save them from even greater problems later on.

References

Beach, F. A. (Ed.) *Sex and Behavior.* New York: Wiley, 1965.

Bieber, I. "Clinical Aspects of Male Homosexuality" in *Sexual Inversion: Multiple Roots of Homosexuality,* Judd Marmor, Ed. New York: Basic Books, 1965.

————, *Homosexuality: A Psychoanalytic Study of Male Homosexuals.* New York: Basic Books, 1962.

Cavanaugh, J. *Counseling the Invert.* Milwaukee: Bruce Publishing Co., 1966.

Coleman, J. C. *Abnormal Psychology in Modern Life.* Glenview, Ill.: Scott Foresman & Co., 1972.

Fisher, P. *The Gay Mystique: The Myth & Reality of Male Homosexuality.* New York: Stein & Day, 1972.

Freud, Anna, *The Ego and the Mechanism of Defense.* Trans. by Cecil Baines. New York: International Universities Press, 1946.

Freedman, A. M., Kaplan, H. I. (Eds.) *Comprehensive Textbook of Psychiatry,* vol. 2. Baltimore: Williams & Wilkins, 1975.

Gagnon, J. & Simon, W. "Homosexuality: The Formulation of a Sociological Perspective," *Journal of Health and Social Behavior.* 8 (1967): 177–85.

Horney, Karen. *The Neurotic Personality of Our Time.* New York: W. W. Norton, 1937.

Karlen, A. *Sexuality and Homosexuality.* New York: W. W. Norton, 1971.

Kinsey, Alfred, Pomeroy, W., Martin, C. *Sexual Behavior in the Human Male.* Philadelphia: W. B. Saunders, 1948.

Marmor, Judd, (Ed.) *Sexual Inversion.* New York: Basic Books, 1965.

Pauley, I. R. and Goldstein, S. G., "Physicians' Attitudes in Treating Male Homosexuals," *Medical Aspects of Human Sexuality.* Dec., 1970.

Ruitenbeek, H. (Ed.) *The Problem of Homosexuality in Modern Society.* New York: E. P. Dutton, 1963.

Schofield, M. *Sociological Aspects of Homosexuality.* Boston: Little, Brown, 1965.

Socarides, C. W. *The Overt Homosexual.* New York: Grune & Stratton, 1968.

Thompson, C. M. *Interpersonal Psychoanalysis: The Selected Papers of Clara M. Thompson.* New York: Basic Books, 1964.

NINETEEN

Transvestism

TRANSVESTISM is a difficult problem; many people wish to look away from it or talk about it only in generalities. Thus it comes frequently to members of the clergy or educators who counsel. The situation may be initially presented by anxious parents or it may be reported by the involved young person—usually male—himself. Counselors need a practical understanding of the psychological dynamics involved in these occurrences in order to be able to respond effectively to both short- and long-term goals. The immediate situation may include practical suggestions about the way the child is treated at home in order to lessen the pressures that may have helped instigate or reinforce this behavior. Longer range goals include recommendations about therapy for the individual and/or the whole family. An understanding of this sexual difficulty also alerts counselors to their role in educating people to an understanding of the psychological conditions needed for healthy family life. This is especially important for clergy and teachers who must address themselves to social problems in a broader context by virtue of their work.

It is also clear that a sensitive intervention may be crucial for the future happiness and adjustment of the individual involved. Timing is particularly important because, if a person can get therapeutic assistance at the right moment, it makes the difference between shame and self-understanding, between a life plagued with guilt and one still capable of joy.

Counselors need, first of all, to be aware of their own feelings about this problem. It is entirely possible that we can become overly curious or sometimes punitive for reasons that we ourselves do not fully understand. We need to clear up our ambivalent feelings in order to be successful in the steady effort to understand the complicated language that is spoken in difficult situations of this sort. It demands as much sensitivity as we can muster to see the symbolic significance of such behavior in the individual's life.

The individual must be seen in relationship to the family setting which, according to many observers, determines the nature and course of cross-dressing and similar problems. Counselors must be ready and able to sense the attitudes of the family members who may be dynamically involved in the origin and reinforcement of cross-dressing behavior. If such family members are part of the problem they must be included in the concern and the responses of the counselor. They cannot be left out because successful help for the individual involved may well depend on the capacity of the rest of the family to change themselves and their style of relating to him or her.

It is not the most surprising thing in the world to find very young boys trying on the clothes of the opposite sex, especially in homes in which girls seem to get preferential treatment. Over-reaction to this kind of experimental behavior obviously is not needed. Common sense tells us, however, that if such behavior persists it needs a cautious and even-handed investigation by persons not ready to find the worst.

Generally speaking, however, such experimental behavior is reported in small children as a temporary phenomenon. And healthy people know how to deal with it without making themselves or the child too upset. A sensitivity to anything that seems protracted or unusual in this behavior is, however, important because much of the cross-dressing and related behavior reported at adult levels is clearly rooted in early life experience. Adults report frequently that their problem with such behavior began as early as two years of age. Counselors can be very reassuring by discussing the problem with the concerned parents, by helping them clarify their own feelings about the situation, and by encouraging them to respond in a balanced and understanding manner when the activity appears to be transient and not suggestive of any serious pathology.

The research of psychiatrists James Spensley and James T. Barber of the University of California Medical School at Davis underscores the significance of cross-dressing when it is observed in adolescent boys (*Medical Aspects of Human Sexuality*, June, 1973, p. 136 ff.). On the basis of their experience, Drs. Spensley and Barber feel that such behavior in adolescents "should be clearly evaluated since cross-dressing is not a part of the normal adolescent identity struggle." They also suggest that the entire family be evaluated as well because they are convinced that cross-dressing behavior is "initiated, encouraged, and sustained directly and indirectly by other members of the family."

Spensley and Barber do not perceive this difficulty as having one explanation or one, single, dynamic meaning. Interviewing the whole family together provides some insight into its members' expectations about male or female behavior in their children and helps the counselor to make prudent judgments about the individual boy who is involved with cross-dressing or, as it is also called, transvestism. Spensley and Barber believe, however, that many mistakes are made by categorizing all this behavior under the notion of transvestism, a term which has certain implications about the presence of homosexuality which are not verified in each situation. They offer five classifications for discerning counselors to employ in their thinking and in the development of judgments about referral and the nature of the contemplated treatment.

Spensley and Barber speak first of the importance of observing the family interaction connected with each of these types. They feel that each type has distinctive features related to the style of the family dynamics and that, although there is some overlap, the nature of the family is extremely relevant to understanding the particular difficulty in question. In speaking of the transvestite population they have studied, Spensley and Barber describe family factors which they felt were significant in the shaping of the cross-dressing behavior. The mother proved to be a dominant figure while the father is reported as distant and passive.

The mother is related in a close and then a hostile fashion to the young man in one of the examples which they cite. In this particular instance the boy's cross-dressing started when the mother began caring for her sister's two daughters during the day. The boy engaged in vandalism of the houses along his paper route which he knew were empty. He would dress in girls' clothes and tear the house up, finally destroying the clothes he had worn during this activity. He tried to tell his parents about this problem but the family, according to Drs. Spensley and Barber, found excuses to ignore his symbolic efforts to inform them of his problem.

Although anti-social actions are not ordinarily associated with transvestism, the researchers felt that the other familiar factors were and that two-thirds of the cases they studied fell into this classification. The family dynamics pivoted on the nature of the mother's relationship toward the son who was clearly in a less preferred status than his own sister or the infant female cousins in his mother's care. The mother was hostile toward masculinity in general and toward her son's efforts to achieve masculinity in particular. The father's failure to play a supportive role or to provide a figure of identification is also significant. It was the feeling of the psychiatrists that masturbation was not the primary gratification sought through this cross-dressing behavior; it was more an effort to become like the girls who in his family experience were the desired and preferred children.

This is obviously a complicated scenario, and often the family denies or attempts to minimize its significance. People have enormous talents to avoid the obvious in health and behavior when there is emotional involvement in the situation. Even after an incident such as cross-dressing becomes public, family members may be highly defensive about identifying the dynamics that contributed to the situation in the first place. Counselors cannot use direct interpretation of these intra-familial factors with any more success than mere reassurance. The latter response obviously plays into the hands of parents who would like to minimize the problem but it might also ruin the young person's chances of receiving needed therapeutic help.

In the case of fetishism the individual uses female underclothing in pursuit of sexual satisfaction principally through masturbation. Although female underclothing is frequently used as a fetish object, a wide variety of clothing and other objects may also be used.

In the clinical examples cited by Spensley and Barber there is evidence of a seductive quality in the mother's relationship to the boy involved. His defensive response was an increased hostility that included aggressive sexuality. It is the interpretation of these researchers that boys who employ fetishes for sexual purposes do not wish to appear as girls. They are, in fact, already strongly favored by their mothers and so are quite different from those in category one. Their sexual behavior is a reaction to the seductive nature of the mother's relationship to them. And mothers can transmit seductive impulses without any overt word or gesture. The attitude, even when unmeasurable, is extraordinarily powerful in shaping the psychological atmosphere of the home. The son's response is highly symbolic even though he has no direct insight into it. His acting-out sexual behavior constitutes a hostile form of defense against the mother's overwhelming sexual approach.

This kind of response is highly specific and should not be confused with any of the other classifications. Indeed, hurried interpretations are clearly out of line in any of these circumstances. Some efforts to modify the nature of the relationship between mother and son would obviously remove the need for this kind of unconscious response on his part but this would involve a shift in the mother as a prelude to a change in family dynamics. "Telling" people our sophisticated interpretation does not work well in an emotionally loaded situation in which one can safely predict that there will be resistance to such an understanding of the dynamics. What are counselors to do beyond exercising patience while trying to avoid mistakes and yet convey understanding? They may have to settle for minimal gains. To achieve and maintain these is highly important even if only a few steps are made toward seeing the symbolic, dynamic meaning of the fetishist behavior and its relationship to family dynamics. A little progress is a lot of progress here. If counselors can help people to avoid defensive disgust or anger at the child, they have accomplished a good deal. This opens the way for acceptance not only of the child but of themselves and of their own relationship to the explanatory dynamics. Disposing people for the long therapeutic road ahead is a significant and indispensable contribution.

Transsexual cross-dressing differs from the two previous examples in that the young boy involved clearly wishes to be a girl, not just be dressing like one, but by becoming one as much as possible. These boys exhibit extremely effeminate behavior with very self-dramatizing gestures and mannerisms and a highly volatile emotional life.

There are also individuals who may believe themselves to be women trapped inside of male bodies. Such persons often request transsexual operations in an effort to harmonize their feelings of femininity with their overall sense of themselves. A life history of such persons generally shows a very early onset of these feelings and cross-dressing behavior; sometimes these patients will have been dressed and treated as a girl for an extensive period during their earliest years. This is a complicated psychological entity and, should counselors suspect that a person with whom they are dealing falls into this category, a referral for more intensive evaluation is in order. Counselors also have the role of helping the involved family deal with the situation without panicking or being overcome with shame or guilt. Assisting persons to understand the reality of the problem and helping them to see it in the perspective of overall family dynamics constitutes a vital service to all concerned. This is particularly true for those, like clergy and educators, who may have the role of bridging the incident through counseling that leads to more intensive therapy.

Spensley and Barber use this term to describe a "pattern of multiple immature elements of sexual expression. In other patterns conflict was channeled into cross-dressing, with distinct dynamic motivations. Here . . . there is no channeling of sexual expression but rather a lack of internal and external controls resulting in the emergence of many immature sexual behaviors." These latter include voyeurism, exhibitionism, pedophilia and cross-dressing. In these situations one regularly observes faulty family controls. Typically the involved families do not offer a setting in which the young person can develop a disciplined sense of self and so the individual is left with little power to control internal urges that may become overwhelming.

The researchers characterize the mother in such families as frequently passive but seductive and find that the boy relates to the mother in a "passive and infantile" fashion. Such sons frequently feel quite helpless and inadequate in the face of life and, although they feel guilty about the scrapes into which they get themselves, they have difficulty in developing insight into their behavior. Such young men may, for example, get into sexual encounters with younger children. Such behavior is inappropriate and impulsive; they cannot seem to restrain themselves or use prudential caution. There are many manifestations of this category, however, and to read this behavior carefully and understand it against the background of the family's interrelationships constitutes a prime challenge for the counselor. To be able to distinguish these varied, uncontrolled sexual incidents from other categories in which cross-dressing may be involved is an indispensable first step in moving toward sensible therapeutic intervention.

Although cross-dressing is associated in the popular mind with homosexuality, psychiatrists Spensley and Barber feel that this is a dangerous and unfortunate generalization. It never helps to cry "pervert" and it is a mistake immediately to identify cross-dressing with homosexuality in early adolescence. In fact, this association does not seem to be very common. Adolescents who are homosexuals may dress in women's clothing but the symbolic significance is not the same as it is in the situations previously described. Young homosexuals dress in women's clothing to attract males for overtly homosexual activity. The problem may on the surface resemble the other cited classifications but a sensitivity to the possibilities of differences—and their relationship to differing family backgrounds—is a major responsibility of counselors who are consulted in these circumstances.

In conclusion, Spensley and Barber feel that counselors should understand that problems with cross-dressing symptoms are by no means rare and that lumping them all together is both unwise and unfair. They suggest that "most families directly and indirectly encourage cross-dressing which serves defensive functions for both the individual and the family." This refers to the meaning of cross-dressing in adolescents who are symbolically describing their family situation through indulging in it.

What can counselors do? It is obvious that in most of these situations counselors who are involved full time in some other profession cannot take on the lengthy forms of therapy that may be needed to unscramble family relationships or to help the individuals explore their own conflicts. Knowledge of the various possibilities is, in a very real sense, power in this situation. Such understanding augments the power of judgment while it also prevents counselors from making mistakes or, in moments of clouded emotion, from reinforcing families in their own mistaken or prejudiced attitudes toward the difficulty. There are few areas more sensitive and the fact that a counselor is able to approach it with openness rather than with some preconceived notion that it must be covered up or smoothed over is an enormous help in itself.

There are also some very practical things that can be done to help parents avoid the difficulties they may generate, for example, by excessive treatment of a child as though he or she were a member of the opposite sex. It is not funny nor is it cute to dress a boy in girl's clothing for an extended period of time. Sometimes we can find excuses for this or pretend that it does not make any difference; these may be evidences of the defenses against reality at work in sensitive areas. Counselors who are close to a family may be able to help parents drop this behavior and realign their relationships so that the child has a better chance of developing into himself rather than into a troubled and symptom-laden adolescent.

This discussion has centered on the problems of cross-dressing in younger people. This is not to ignore the presence of continued problems of this kind in adults as much as it is an effort to classify and understand the issues in their developmental settings. Adults with persistent difficulties with cross-dressing may reveal their core dynamics in their life histories through which some appreciation of their earlier experiences can be achieved. They also need an approach that does not condemn as much as it tries to understand while arranging for long-term referral. Counselors who are not full-time workers in psychotherapy should offer support but not attempt to handle the long-range treatment themselves.

While some specific problems will be discussed with suggestions for practical operational responses, it will be helpful not to review some of the points made by psychoanalyst Robert Stoller in his analysis of what he terms "perverse" sexual activity (*Perversion: The Erotic Form of Hatred*, New York: Pantheon, 1975). Stoller makes an effort to break free of jargonish psychological language and to present material that can help counselors identify some of the characteristics associated with personal disturbances that may require long-term intensive treatment. In other words, there seem to be psychological signals that reveal a "perverse" quality, as Stoller defines it, that cannot be written off according to a popular slogan as though it were of no human consequence. This is not to pass a moral judgment on such behavior but to help counselors—who live, after all, in a world in which sex has been highly politicized—to keep matters in perspective.

Stoller defines perversion as "the erotic form of hatred," styling it "a fantasy, usually acted out but occasionally restricted to a daydream (either self-produced or packaged by others, that is, pornography)." He sees this habitual, preferred aberration as "primarily motivated by hostility . . . a state in which one wishes to harm an object." This is differentiated from aggression which, Stoller feels, "implies only forcefulness." The hostility in perversion takes form, according to Stoller, "in a fantasy of revenge hidden in the actions that make up the perversion and serves to convert childhood trauma into adult triumph." Stoller views risk-taking (mostly simulated) as necessary to the creation of the excitement which is such a powerful aspect of the motivation for perverse behavior. The behavior we see and puzzle about or react to with shock constitutes a miniature scenario that makes psychological sense if we could look deeply enough into the personality and life history of the individual involved. The clue to sense is the presence of hostility and this, Stoller believes, can be observed in many activities in which it does not, on first inspection, appear to be present.

He mentions promiscuity as behavior that needs careful analysis, especially in the exaggerated syndrome of the Don Juan character who "reveals his hatred of women innocently and unwittingly to the audience he must gather to vouch for his performance" (p.57). The dehumanization is clear and, as Stoller observes, "it is the difference of what the act means to us that measures whether it is perverse or not, not what anatomical parts are used on whom or what." The theme is clear in sadism and masochism, tastes which have recently been given strong emphasis in pornography. It can also be observed, Stoller says, in something like fetishism where "the desire to harm is only silent, hidden."

The anger of the individual is translated into the special language of perversion, as defined by Stoller. It is this hostility which counselors may frequently sense in the conflicting sexual behavior about which they are called to consult or advise. Sensitive persons will be able to detect it, aware that it is transplanted from previous psychological events into the present situation. Counselors who are able to grasp the psychological implications of the situation will not try to cover it over or defend it as an exercise in popular free choice of sexual object. They will instead be able to assist the persons involved to take the first steps toward self-understanding through a referral to professionals for more intense treatment.

Counselors need neither fear nor moralize in the face of what appear to be twisted psychosexual problems. Nor need they adopt some ill-based position that disregards the possibilities of "perverse" sexual behavior altogether. The road to understanding is a long one but the counselor who can read the signs of the problem can help all those involved—individual and family—to take the first positive steps.

References

Benjamin, H. *The Transsexual Phenomenon.* New York: Julian Press, 1966.

Bieber, I., et al. *Homosexuality: A Psychoanalytic Study of Male Homosexuals.* New York: Basic Books, 1962.

Brown, D. "Transvestism." *The Encyclopedia of Sexual Behavior.* New York: Hawthorn Books, 1961.

Fisher, P. *The Gay Mystique: The Myth and Reality of Male Homosexuality.* New York: Stein & Day, 1972.

Gagnon, J. and Simon, W. (Eds.). *Sexual Deviance.* New York: Harper & Row, 1967.

Green, R. and Money, J. *Transsexual and Sex Reassignment.* Baltimore: The Johns Hopkins Press, 1969.

Karlen, A. *Sexuality and Homosexuality.* New York: W. W. Norton & Co., Inc., 1971. See esp., Chapter 21, "The Erotic Disguise."

Luisada, P. and Peele, R. "The Hysterical Personality in Men." *American Journal of Psychiatry* (1974), 131:518–22.

Marmor, Judd (Ed.). *Sexual Inversion: The Multiple Roots of Homosexuality.* New York: Basic Books, 1965.

Schofield, M. *Sociological Aspects of Homosexuality.* Boston: Little, Brown & Co., 1965.

Stoller, R. *Perversion: The Erotic Form of Hatred.* New York: Pantheon Books, 1975.

————. *Sex and Gender: On the Development of Masculinity and Femininity.* New York: Science House, 1968.

Storr, A. *Sexual Deviation.* Baltimore: Penguin Books, 1964.

Zuger, B. "The Role of Familial Factors and Persistent Effeminate Behavior in Boys." *The American Journal of Psychiatry* (1970), 126:1167.

TWENTY

Child Molesting

INCIDENTS involving molestation—or molestation-like activity—of children are not uncommon. Educators and members of the clergy may find themselves on the edge of or in the middle of such situations several times during the year. They need to understand the nature of the basic problem of child molestation and also understand their own potential role in working with the people affected by an occurrence that can have such multi-leveled effects.

The role for counselors is not that of the punishing authority, the righteously indignant elder, nor the moralizing judge. In a situation that is always clouded with emotion, counselors serve best as sensitive and sensible presences who can put order into the situation while they also respond to the variety of confused feelings that are typically manifested. They may have to deal with the victim, his or her family, and the one accused of the molestation. Counselors may also be in contact with other professionals, including lawyers and law-enforcement officers. The range is quite wide and counselors must be thoroughly prepared with an understanding of the dynamics involved and of the practical options available to deal with this always disturbing event.

The molesters of children are not, as urban folklore has made them, evil, leering predators standing at the school corner studying the parade of innocent children after the last bell of the day sounds. Children are warned, of course, about not taking candy or rides from strangers because the possibility of molestation is never very far from the minds of parents who read the daily papers. The image of the *pedophiliac* as constituting one psychological entity whose offenses spring from a single identifiable set of conflicts has been questioned by psychiatrist David Swanson of the Stritch School of Medicine at Loyola University in Chicago. In a series of articles he has explored, not only the classic pedophiliac, but also other types of persons who become involved in incidents of molestation. He feels that limiting our vision to the classic type may make it more difficult for us to identify other persons who are capable of such activity (*Medical Aspects of Human Sexuality*, Feb., 1971; "Diseases of the Nervous System," *Adult Sexual Abuse of Children*, 1968, 29–677).

In the majority of cases that he has studied, Dr. Swanson has uncovered a criminal psychiatric history that differs from that ordinarily associated with the pedophiliac. Typically, Swanson notes, the molester "had an adult-heterosexual adjustment, although this aspect of their lives was often chaotic as was their behavior generally." Swanson's types include the following:

THE CLASSIC PEDOPHILIAC

Such persons are described by Swanson as having experienced "a consistent and often exclusive interest in children as their sexual object." This attraction is thought to have its roots in the beginning of the pedophiliac's own adolescence. It may be observed in their consistent playing with children younger than themselves, especially in activities that have a sexual overtone or symbolism to them. This may not be noticed or may be shrugged off at the time. However, the masking of this activity with the innocence of childhood evaporates as the person gets older; the age spread between the person and the victim becomes much greater.

The classic pedophiliac is, in a word, more obvious in society and therefore more vulnerable to identification and potential arrest. He must be more careful in his seeking of sexual satisfaction, more covert in his way of approaching and seducing children. The life of the classic pedophiliac gets very complicated and very stressful because he attempts to balance his basic problem with the maintenance of what appears to be a fairly normal life. He ordinarily seeks out children in places of minimal risk, such as parks or organizations in which easily influenced and ill-educated children may be members. His interest may be heterosexual or homosexual and, as Dr. Swanson notes, "productive of guilt or indignant denial."

INADEQUATE SOCIOPATHIC VIOLATOR

Such a person may consciously deny any attraction to children at all. He is discovered because he uses an older female child for sexual satisfaction. Clear in the sociopath are the elements of personality disorder that show up, not only in sexual acting-out, but in other kinds of behavior as well. An obvious strain of dependence and difficulty with self-control runs through these persons; there is something strongly impulsive that may erupt in their seeking sexual gratification from just about anybody. Swanson suggests that this can happen after they experience some kind of rejection or frustration; they may then turn to a daughter or a baby sitter for sexual gratification. Drinking heavily enough to loosen what internal controls there are is common in these situations. Such persons give abundant evidence of immaturity in many other ways and counselors should study the whole pattern of their activity in order to understand them for purposes of diagnosis and therapeutic help.

A counselor would, for example, expect to discover the signs of antisocial behavior in their style of personal relationship. Such individuals have little insight into their behavior and very little subjective experience of guilt. They display irresponsibility in other aspects of their lives; they are neither reliable nor completely responsible in their work or relationships with others. Often enough they have some difficulty with authority or with the law.

Of such personalities are con men and criminals made. Such persons tend to make little of their role in the molestation and they blame others for what happened. One of the things which counselors must be prepared for is the effort of such persons to manipulate or "con" them about their innocence. Their best efforts go into the manipulation of others. These people are not, in the long run, very appealing and counselors must guard against being excessively irritated and therefore punitive in dealing with them.

The Brain Damaged

A person who suffers some accident affecting the central nervous system may have resultant problems in many areas of personal functioning, including the making of adequate social judgments. Such may be the case in a retarded, immature young person suffering from arteriosclerotic illness. These people may feel more at ease with companions who seem to have a comparable mentality and so they seek out or play with young children. They also suffer a special kind of social isolation because of their condition. This unfortunate situation disposes them all the more to inappropriate sexual activity with immature persons. These persons will admit what they have done in molestation-like activities with younger children, but will not really perceive its meaning.

The Situational Offender

This individual has previously led a seemingly normal heterosexual life yet, in the wake of some stressful situation, becomes attracted to an adolescent girl. Such a person may be the victim of intense loneliness or some painful frustration at work and may not have the emotional resources for such problems. His stress may come from a situation of separation or divorce and, once again, he is poorly equipped to handle this pressure. Schizoid tendencies seem to be present in such persons as well as some evidence that the person molested participates somehow in the situation. In some cases the younger girl, who may be a relative or a close friend, is frequently well-developed physically and not at all naive. Such girls have some sense that the man under stress, uncertain and impulsive, can be enticed into sexual contact rather easily. An evaluation of the interplay of the man and girl in such circumstances is appropriate.

There is a popular notion that molesters of children cannot be treated very effectively. This notion hangs on, however, especially concerning the classic pedophiliac who has deep psychological conflicts but who is not necessarily interested in being treated for them. Getting these people into treatment makes everyone breathe a sigh of relief. Unfortunately, "being in treatment" does not guarantee that these persons will maintain control. A careful evaluation is therefore needed in order to determine the person's capacity for cooperation in therapy before any final decision about treatment is made. The counselor can be very helpful in assisting those other persons involved to understand the nature of the problem of the pedophiliac and the wisdom in a thorough evaluation of the situation. It is not easy to take this mediating role, especially in the face of outrage that may be very understandable on the part of parents whose children have been molested. The educative role of the counselor in this regard may be highly significant, however, in working the situation through to a relatively satisfactory conclusion.

With the inadequate sociopathic violator, counselors are faced with the same difficulties they experience with anti-social personalities. The basic problem springs from the difficulties built into establishing any kind of relationship with these people and the consequent problems of sustaining a truly therapeutic relationship with them. They use their customary strategies of manipulation in order to get sympathetic treatment. It may be that, regrettable though it seems, such persons will need, as Dr. Swanson notes, "confinement and supervision" because they "do not significantly respond to psychiatric treatment." Here again the counselor must recognize the limitations involved in trying to treat these people and must, as is the case with all anti-social personalities, be on guard against being manipulated excessively. Counselors can, with a little insight and common sense, prevent other people from being taken in by what may seem a guileless and winning presentation on the part of these people.

Brain damaged people constitute another situation altogether. They are not perverts or terrible people and the counselor may serve a very important function in helping relatives to understand and accept them. Rejection, for the brain damaged person, only intensifies what may already be an extremely painful experience of social isolation. Older people ordinarily do very well with better supervision; this is the best way to help them avoid situations that could involve them in molesting of children. Younger people may need closer supervision and some effort to provide them with other satisfactions which will give a better balance to their lives. They may, for example, need intensive vocational preparation or training so that they can assume a life role that will build their self-esteem through providing healthy gratification.

A person under severe stress who becomes involved in a situational experience of seeking sexual satisfaction with a child is, of all these categories, the person about whom the counselor can be most optimistic. Because the problem is precipitated by stress and because such individuals otherwise possess fairly good adjustive powers, a course of psychotherapy can be very helpful, especially when they are themselves anxious for treatment. Obviously, these people must be perceived in the context of their own difficult lives and those associated with the incident must be helped to understand how situational stresses can trigger behavior that is inconsistent with what has been known about the person previously.

Psychiatrist C. Raymond Kiefer of the Department of Mental Health in Indianapolis suggests some practical viewpoints that may be of help to professional persons who find themselves involved in such an incident (*Medical Aspects of Human Sexuality,* Dec., 1973). He emphasizes the need for counselors to recognize their role as managers in a difficult situation. Even if they are not going to be therapists for long-term treatment they can do much to respond to the immediate emergency through their calm and understanding approach and their sensitivity to the wide variety of feelings that can be experienced by all those involved. This calm and self-possessed presence can reduce the possibility of panic and increase the opportunity for constructive good judgment and positive steps in relieving the situation.

Kiefer suggests that counselors who are called on in this emergency should tell both the victim and the family exactly what they are going to do. That means that counselors should discuss their plans to contact persons involved and whether they will see them separately or together, and what feedback they may be able to give.

Counselors as managers must strive to get the facts out as clearly as possible. The counselor may be one of the first to know about the situation, and an adequate and accurate description of the event is essential if it is to be worked through successfully. Dr. Kiefer suggests that the counselor might see the parent and child together, for example, but try to separate their reactions so that they do not contaminate each other by what they are saying. The counselor may wish to see the child briefly alone in order to get the child's undistorted initial perceptions of what happened. Here the counselor should be alert to the child's greatest fear and concern about the incident.

Here, also, an awareness of subtle reactions and nonverbal cues is important. In the same way counselors should be alerted to the greatest concern of the parents and as clearly as possible, sort out, in the midst of a highly emotional situation, fact from rumor or impression. It is always possible in such emotionally loaded circumstances for misunderstandings to occur. It is also possible, for example, that the reactions of the parents or others may seem out of proportion or inappropriate to the event. The counselor should note these and be prepared to explore them in order to develop an overall understanding of the situation.

The counselor's sense of self-possession can reduce the general anxiety considerably while it also works toward getting the story in an unembellished and accurate form. The child may need a good deal of reassurance. Counselors should not artificially hold back from touching them or otherwise spontaneously comforting them if this is what they feel instinctively to be the right human thing to do. When a child is molested, people—even those that want to help the child—stay at a distance, afraid somehow that they may be themselves accused of molestation. Or they may be hesitant to respond emotionally to a child in need merely because of the tension of the circumstances in general.

Kiefer feels that the child often plays some part in encouraging the situation of sexual molestation. This is a very delicate area and is obviously an interpretation not to be made quickly in private or public. However, Kiefer states unequivocally that "repeated sexual involvement with the same person says clearly that at some level the child wanted the relationship to continue." Some way of sensitively gaining enough information about the incident and about the circumstances that led up to it may be vital if the interests of all who are concerned—child, family, and molester—are to be respected. The counselor may be the only person capable of seeing the entire situation in this perspective.

Counselors may be expected to be sources of emotional support. It is unlikely that people who do their counseling only in connection with another occupation will ever take on the extended psychological treatment of child molesters. This is the task for professionals who practice therapy on a full-time basis. Part-time counselors must then be acquainted with the available resources in their community. They should know, among others, a gynecologist and a child psychiatrist whose services may be important at the time of the molestation incident. Counselors should have a working relationship with these people and be able to discuss the overall situation with them. They should be ready to give supportive follow-up to the family and to other persons involved in the incident while maintaining the kind of neutrality that enables them to serve the interests of all the parties concerned.

Lastly, children should be made aware of the dangers of sexual molestation. Unfortunately, this is often done in the most general way with little regard for the child's relative capacity to understand or for changing needs for information during the developmental years. Healthy people with common sense will not make many mistakes in this area, although even what they may presume or sometimes exaggerate out of proportion is worth noting. Obviously an over-emotional approach that merely makes a child distrustful of a world suddenly ominous around him or her is not at all helpful. Parents, or those who substitute for them, should try to convey basic and simple information appropriate to the child's age without introducing unnecessary elements of fear or mystery.

Psychiatrist Jack Westman of the University of Wisconsin at Madison suggests that information about molestation should be presented as "one aspect of a general sex and hazard education" that needs "increasing ... specificity at progressive points during childhood" (*Medical Aspects of Human Sexuality,* August, 1975). Building on some clear and open level of communication between parent and child, Westman warns of the dangers involved if sexual molestation is the only subject connected with sex that is discussed with the child. This would unnecessarily distort the child's outlook from the beginning.

Sexual molestation should be discussed in line with the general dangers of living with which children must become gradually acquainted. These include dangers involved in taking unknown pills or medicines as well as accepting favors, rides, or undue attention from strangers. The school years, according to Westman, constitute the time in which youngsters become aware involved in taking unknown pills or medicines as well as accepting favors, rides, or undue attention from strangers. The school years, according to Westman, constitute the time in which youngsters become aware "that some people are capable of violent or strange behavior." Children can be helped to understand that "some adults have problems with their sexual behavior." This helps children to see it as a problem of the adult and provides them with a policy of "avoiding or leaving strange adults who attempt to approach or befriend them."

Because children achieve greater independence during adolescence it is appropriate to provide them with more detailed information about the way in which sex molesters may approach them. As Westman notes: "Blanket prohibition during this age is much less effective than an open discussion of the realistic risks accompanying hitchhiking or extended trips away from home."

Children should also be encouraged to report any "unusual occurrences with other people to their parents for discussion." This may offer the opportunity for young persons to understand their own sexuality and the possibility of its being used by others. Westman observes that children can only profit from "understanding that there are exceptions to the general desirability of relating to adults with courtesy and respect." They should learn that it is perfectly all right to avoid "a strange adult who has no legitimate reason for relating to the child." Parents or counselors can also prudently use a news account of an incident of sexual molestation to provide additional information about the subject.

References

Bell, A. P. and Hall, C. S. *The Personality of a Child Molester: An Analysis of Dreams.* Chicago: Aldine, 1971.

Ellis, A. and Abarbanel, A. (Eds.). *The Encyclopedia of Sexual Behavior.* New York: Hawthorn Books, 1961. See esp., A. Ellis, "The Psychology of Sex Offenders" and R. V. Sherwin, "Laws on Sex Crimes" both in Vol. II.

Falk, G. J. "The Truth About Sex Offenders." *Sexology* (1965), 32:271–73.

Gagnon, J. H. and Simon, W. *Sexual Deviance.* New York: Harper & Row, 1965.

Gebhard, P. H., et al., *Sex Offenders: An Analysis of Types.* New York: Harper & Row, 1965.

Karpman, B. *The Sexual Offender and His Offenses: Etiology, Pathology, Psychodynamics and Treatment.* New York: Ace Books, 1962.

Kopp, S. B. "The Character Structure of Sex Offenders." *American Journal of Psychotherapy* (1962), 16:64–70.

Oliver, B.J., Jr. "What the Rapist Is Like." *Sexology* (1965), 31:849–51.

Ploscowe, M. *Sex and the Law.* New York: Ace Books, 1962.

Radinowicz, L. (Ed.). *Sexual Offenses.* London: Macmillan, 1957.

Segarin, E. and MacNamara, D. (Eds.). *Problems of Sex Behavior.* New York: T. Y. Crowell, 1968. See esp., P. Gebhard, et al., "Child Molestation."

TWENTY-ONE

The Sexually Deprived

PERSONS deprived, for whatever reason, of the opportunity for sexual expression must also be understood by counselors. The sexually deprived may experience a certain kind of alienation in a culture that exalts sexual expression in the manner of contemporary Western culture. There is not a great deal of research on the problems of the sexually deprived but such people by no means constitute a small or unimportant segment of the population. They include people who are deprived of sexual experience because of environmental restriction. People in prison are generally denied any normal opportunity for sexual expression. So too are people suffering from certain illnesses as well as those who have sustained certain injuries or have undergone certain surgical operations.

As mentioned earlier, there are also changes in the general circumstances of life that affect a person's opportunity or even interest in sexual expression. The main cause of such problems is the death of a spouse or divorce. There are hidden causes, however, of sexual deprivation which may well come to the attention of counselors. These include, for example, the wife of a man who is impotent or the husband of a woman who rejects sexual relations. There is de facto sexual deprivation for those who, for high ideals and religious motivation, choose celibacy as their lifestyle. This represents a varied group of individuals and no generalization can cover all of them at one time. It is clear, however, that counselors, especially members of the clergy and educators, may come in contact with one or more of these groups in the course of their ordinary work.

Such literature as exists about the sexual deprivation of prisoners tends to stress their efforts to adjust to this problem; perhaps the most common way is through homosexual practices. It seems clear that not all homosexual activity in prison is carried on by men or women who are homosexual. As

A. J. Bloch has noted ("Social Pressures of Confinement Toward Sexual Deviation," *Journal of Social Therapy*, 1955), some prisoners involve themselves in homosexual practices on a "symbiotic basis" in order to relieve "each other's tensions." Such sex is generally lacking in any of the elements that are present in a significant interpersonal exchange. It remains, according to Bloch, impersonal, almost totally physical, and without homosexual ideation.

It is also possible for prisoners to have deeper involvements in homoerotic experiences and a whole subcultural language has come to describe the possibilities of this kind of activity in the confinement of prison. Counselors working with prisoners should not be quick to brand prisoners' sexual behavior with any name until they are certain about the interplay of forces which cause it. It would be inappropriate, for example, to respond to a person forced into situational homosexuality in the same way as one would respond to a person whose whole life has been marked with homosexual feelings and homosexual experiences.

Counselors must also realize that they may have a limited capacity to effect environmental changes in the lives of those who are detained in jails or homes of correction. The question of whether a counselor should also become a social reformer in order to change the nature of our penal institutions is one for each counselor to consider carefully. Counseling itself should not, however, become politicized no matter how zealous or involved counselors who get a close-up look at prisoners may become for movements to change penal institutions, set up conjugal rights visits for prisoners and their wives, etc. There is no doubt that the nature of institutionalization needs to be understood and remedied and that well-informed counselors may constitute a positive force in developing a better penal system. It is also true, however, that counselors may compromise their effectiveness with individual prisoners or find that they are confused in their own perception of their role in working with these people when they are at one moment a counselor and at another a crusader. Counselors, first and foremost, must respond to the total person in the context of his or her life, responding to their perceptions and conflicts as sensitively as possible.

This area is made even more difficult because many prisoners are antisocial personalities and they may well charm their counselors as easily as they robbed and cheated as confidence men on the outside. Counselors can only inspect the nature of their individual relationships with prisoners in order to judge whether they are being manipulated or whether they are, in fact, on solid ground in developing a helpful relationship no matter how restrictive the environment in which it occurs. The sexual experience of prisoners is only one aspect of counseling that may take place within a correctional institution. It is very important, however, because of the strong feelings that surround sexuality under lengthy confinement. Incredible complexities in homosexual triangles, etc., can occur in a prison setting. These frequently contribute to violence and were rated as second only to acute psychosis as a reason for prison violence in a study of thirty-six incidents by the United States Medical Center for Federal Prisoners. Counseling the sexually deprived in prison requires great strength of personality.

When individuals suffer a severe accident that impairs sexual functioning the threat to their self-confidence and self-esteem may be pervasive and destructive. The person's whole gender identity may well be affected by a sudden loss of sexual capacity. Paraplegics and quadraplegics may suffer a deep sense of sexual inadequacy and frustration. It is unfortunate that some counselors or therapists who work with these people tend to rule out sexuality as an important factor in their lives. Even though such patients may not be capable of sexual performance, they can still have strong sexual interests.

Dr. John Money of the Johns Hopkins Institute has explored the cognitive eroticism experienced by such patients quite thoroughly (*Medical Aspects of Human Sexuality,* January, 1970). Sex as a force in the mind is underestimated by those who focus too exclusively on sexual organs as a source of stimulation and sexual expression. The meaning of a sudden deprivation of sexual functioning is strongly affected by the patient's previous self-perceptions and his or her attitudes toward sexuality and its role in their estimation of themselves as masculine or feminine.

Perhaps most important for counselors who work with the handicapped to realize is that sex can remain an important aspect in the lives of those crippled by accidents. Many studies have shown that, despite the crippling nature of the difficulties, many patients are capable of sexual activity. The problem lies in the fact that this has not been recognized widely and, therefore, institutional provisions have not been made for the sexual lives of crippled persons. Other people have a way of thinking that such patients can and should do without a sexual life even if they are capable of one. This is not due to malice but to some kind of cultural conditioning. It reflects a strange and sometimes unconscious way in which outsiders tend to look at these individuals as less than full persons.

In recent years increased efforts have been made to respond to the sexual needs of these patients, especially at rehabilitation institutes in which provision has been made for some privacy during visits from spouses and, on a more ordinary level, for better socialization between male and female patients at times of recreation. There is nothing wrong, after all, with paraplegics being able to go to a movie and hold hands with a member of the opposite sex. This can be a very sustaining and important kind of activity as they struggle to reintegrate a new sense of themselves.

The counselor's role in this setting is, again, not necessarily to reform the institution. Counselors can, however, remain sensitive to the sexual needs of these deprived persons and help them to understand the psychological consequences of their injuries. Working with the factors that build their self-esteem, including their sense of their own sexuality, becomes the province of those skilled in understanding the emotional overtones of life.

This is true for many other illnesses besides those in which severe spinal cord injuries are experienced. There are many situations in which the individual's capacity for sexual functioning is vital in adjusting to the limitations imposed by illness. This is an area in which there is much rumor, myth and downright misinformation. Not all serious illnesses, including heart attacks, necessitate the curtailing of sexual activity. Some people do decrease sexual activity drastically because they are frightened by their illness and are suddenly aware of the fragility of their bodies, something they may never have questioned before. It is not that they are physically incapable of a continued sex life; it is, rather, that they are emotionally inhibited from doing so. Abstinence from sex after a heart attack, for example, is a decision that is certainly not always dictated by the physical findings. It is not a recommendation quickly urged on anyone because such a suggestion may severely damage an individual's self-esteem. All these things must be worked out in terms of the person's total self-perception as he or she reintegrates a modified view of themselves prior to re-entering life after serious illness.

Persons who are divorced or widowed lose the sex life they had developed with their spouse. Most people do not feel free suddenly to make another sexual arrangement outside of marriage, despite the apparently permissive character of American society. Counselors must remember that the loss of sex life is only one dimension of the loss that is sustained by the newly divorced and the newly widowed. Everything about life is changed. There are severe alterations in a person's perception of and capacity for interpersonal relationships.

Much of this takes place on the unconscious level and is revealed only in symptoms of anxiety or depression. Those who grieve must go through what Freud described as "the work of mourning" in order to re-establish a sense of themselves and to be able to re-enter life. Mourning is a process that cannot be interrupted and grieving people must carry it out for themselves. Counselors confronted with those who are suddenly sexually deprived may sometimes find that these clients also suffer from unexpected and slightly bizarre sexual fantasies or urges. These are not unusual in this context and, like other aspects of their sexual functioning, are obviously intertwined with their loss and their efforts to adjust to it.

Other complaints that are related to the deprivation of sexual experience include a numbness or an absence of sexual feelings. Sometimes a widow will have a decreased sense of femininity associated with lowered self-esteem. Others, as has been noted, may be disturbed by their sexual impulses or by what they might class as "temptations" to sexual activity. This can be a very difficult period for these people and the support and understanding of counselors can be crucial in assisting them to get through it successfully.

During a period of sudden sexual deprivation these people may experience a resurgence of sexual conflicts they thought had been buried in their earlier years. It is possible that these conflicts can be handled through the development of a seemingly nonrelated set of symptoms, as, for example, an obsessive's dealing with a conflict about sex through developing ritualized handwashing behavior. The counselor needs a firm grounding in the wide range of feelings and their symbolic expression that is commonplace in the lives of persons suddenly deprived of sexual activity. The behavior of such persons reflects experiences that must be interpreted in terms of their unique life histories.

It is possible during these times for people to do things which would have been uncharacteristic of them at previous stages in their lives. They may get into peculiar relationships with people with whom they would have had very little contact before. Much of this must be seen in terms of symbolic significance of the deprived person's search for closeness or for repairing the overall personal loss that has been suffered.

Celibacy has long been an option for those who choose, chiefly out of religious principles, to dedicate their lives in a special way to the service of humanity and the worship of God. There is no indication that people who choose celibacy suffer any greater difficulties than any other human beings deprived of sexual activity. Indeed, because many of the difficulties are anticipated, and because there is a development of support systems and other ways to reinforce the celibate ideal, many people are able to maintain this choice rather effectively throughout their lives.

This is particularly true if they are able to convey their personalities well in close personal relationships and in work which enables them to express their generative concerns through their service in teaching, ministry, or nursing. There are people who choose celibacy as a way of life that fits their dedication in more secular careers as well; these are lives which are either so time consuming or which involve so much travel that the establishment and maintenance of a home life would be difficult or impossible. Others have celibacy as the only choice left because of circumstances that are not usually foreseen. Some people have had the care of aged parents or of ill siblings and have given up the opportunity for marriage in view of responding to these needs.

If the sexual difficulties of celibacy are no greater than those of the average population they are no less either. The same challenges exist to be open and honest and not self-deceptive in understanding and dealing with sexual impulses. The role of sublimation, a notion still strongly debated by many experts, comes into play. Sublimation is generally thought to be that unconscious mechanism through which the energies that would go into sexual activity are translated into other forms of behavior, such as artistic creativity. Many dispute this contention but it does seem clear that certain forms of expression, since they involve the personality so totally, may well provide an outlet for sexual energies at the same time.

When counselors are dealing with people who, for one reason or another, have not been able to marry, they sometimes suggest activities that would, in effect, offer opportunities for the presumed sublimation of their sexual energies. This can make good sense, especially if the counselor is willing to listen carefully to the person before giving too many suggestions. Counselors should be sure that whatever activities they suggest match the individual's personality characteristics and do not, in any way, tend to challenge or diminish their overall gender identity or self-esteem. It is not wise, for example, for a counselor to suggest to a man a sublimation activity that the client perceives as feminine. More important, however, is a counselor's willingness to see what the deprivation situation means to those who experience it. This is an area in which an imposition of our own experiences and values—or even our expectations—can blur the communication badly.

Counselors should not be surprised to find that celibates, even those whose lives are marked with religious dedication, may experience sexual conflicts. These may be related to previous experiences in their lives and are frequently indicative of unconscious processes that have been tripped off by situational stresses. These people need reassurance and a sensitivity to the fact that they may perceive any change in their sexual reactivity as a challenge to their own religious dedication. Counselors must be able to respond to the anxiety and guilt that sexual conflict may engender and assist these persons to accept themselves totally in a more compassionate and understanding fashion. The sexual difficulties of celibates are almost always related to other aspects of their personality functioning.

There are other situations in which sexual deprivation is present. These include long-term hospitalization and temporary states in marriage such as those times just before and after the birth of a child. Sexual deprivation may characterize the life of the military man or any other person in whose life travel is a necessity. Occasionally such persons may come to counselors for assistance. Generally they want to talk out their tensions or explore the feelings that have been troubling them.

Here again, as in all these circumstances, the counselor's first commitment is to the person's overall life, to that complex of values and experiences out of which he or she has fashioned a unique, individual presence and existence. Counselors must be alert to the discovery of the meaning that sexual experience or its lack has for the person. This becomes the area to be explored in some depth.

Occasionally counselors find persons who are relieved because they have finally entered a period of sexual deprivation. Sex has been a burden or a duty for them, something about which they have previously experienced conflict. They are glad to be rid of it as an obligation. Here too, the counselor must be ready to explore with individuals this unique reaction even though it is not one that might be expected and is not one that seems to match current cultural preferences.

Counselors dealing with one member of a married couple are well advised to bring the other person into the counseling as soon as possible. They are always involved in the sexual problem at some level. They will also be involved in the counselee's efforts to adapt better to whatever the problem of sexual deprivation may be. Joint counseling is an ideal situation toward which the counselor should move. Seeing only one person in a marriage where there is some problem with sexual deprivation complicates rather than alleviates the situation.

References

Bell, Robert R. and Gordon, Michael. *The Social Dimension of Human Sexuality.* Boston: Little, Brown & Co., 1972.

Bieber, Irving. *Homosexuality.* New York: Basic Books, 1962.

Bloch, A. J. "Social Pressures of Confinement Toward Sexual Deviation." *Journal of Social Therapy* (1955).

Bonhoeffer, Dietrich. *Letters and Papers from Prison.* New York: Macmillan Co., 1953.

Dengrave, E. "Sexual Responses to Disease Processes." *Journal of Sex Research,* 4 (Nov., 1968), pp. 257–64.

Harlow, Harry F. and Margaret K. Harlow. "Social Deprivation in Monkeys." *Human Development* (M. L. Haimowitz and Natalie Haimowitz, Eds.). New York: Thomas Crowell, 1966.

———. "The Effect of Rearing Conditions on Behavior." *Sex Research: New Developments* (S. Money, Ed.). New York: Holt, Rinehart & Winston, 1965.

Kroger, W. S. "Comprehensive Approach to Ecclesiogenic Neuroses." *Journal of Sex Research,* 5 (Feb., 1969), pp. 2–11.

Money, J. "Phantom Orgasm in the Dreams of Paraplegic Men and Women." *Arch. of Gen. Psychiatry* (1960), 3:373–82.

Pearlman, Carl K. "Traumatic Causes of Impotence." *Medical Aspects of Human Sexuality* (June, 1975).

Platt, R. "Reflections on Aging and Death." *Lancet* (1963), 1:1–16.

Rubin, I. "Sex Over 65." *Advances in Sex Research* (H. Beigel, Ed.). New York: Harper and Row, 1963.

————. *Sexual Life After Sixty.* New York: Basic Books, 1965.

TWENTY-TWO

The Seductive Client

THIS is not a simple subject. First of all, it is easy to misunderstand, especially because of the emphasis on male counselors and their vulnerability to the hysterical acting-out of female clients. The fact is, however, that, from the viewpoint of the helper, this is the clinical reality. The hysterical personality does occur in males, but not in quite the same way and not with the frequency with which it occurs in females.

It is easy enough to sound the alarm and warn counselors, telling them to maintain an impersonal distance from all clients who might even remotely threaten them sexually. But this would tend to avoid rather than inspect the problem in depth. It is a wise and ancient counsel, but such a warning may not help much in counseling which, unlike surgery, cannot be performed in an antiseptic amphitheater with only a small portion of the person exposed to the scalpel. Counseling is an intensely personal business and it is impossible to rule out beforehand the possibilities of sexual experience in general and of seductive clients in particular.

Counselors, by the nature of their trade, meet and must react to the whole complex of dynamics that are present in a relationship. They cannot look away from things that are embarrassing or anxiety provoking. Helpers have to take things as they come, sensing always their own contribution to the relationship, as they try to present a new alternative to the client's habitual style of relating to others. Therapy does not consist in allowing clients to recreate with the therapist exactly what they do with everybody else. Ideally it offers an environment in which clients can see what they are doing to others and to themselves through their interpersonal style. Therapy offers, among other things, the opportunity to learn new and better ways of relating. If sex or seduction is part of what a client brings into counseling, then counselors deal with this, not as a surface phenomenon, but as something that needs to be faced and thoroughly understood.

Seductive patients generally come with complaints about their marriages or their sex lives. They may come with other presenting problems and then introduce a sexual element into them. This may be the case, for example, with sexual teases or with women experiencing hysterical conflicts. Doctors, teachers and members of the clergy are the most vulnerable to persons who act out their sexual conflicts seductively because they are generally considered figures of trust. Dealing with seductive patients is something of an occupational hazard for them. However, this fact should not cause members of these professions to deal with the seductive client in a hurried or perfunctory way. It is also true that the experience of seduction in counseling may be a bilateral phenomenon in which the needs or psychological conflicts of the counselor may also be involved.

The presenting complaints of potentially seductive patients may closely resemble those of other clients. Not everyone who comes complaining of a difficulty in marriage or sex is necessarily going to be seductive. These patients can be detected in the tone and pattern of their presentation. In order to understand them, counselors must catch and identify correctly the distinctive style in which they establish a relationship. This makes demands on the knowledge, sensitivity and self-awareness of all counselors who may work with these persons. They need knowledge because there is an organized body of information about seductive patients and the specific problems of such relationships. Counselors need *sensitivity* in order to be able to pick up the real communication behind the words and gestures of these clients. They need *self-awareness* in order to understand and deal with their own reactions to the possibility of seduction.

Some observers have made distinctions between the *sexual tease* and the *hysteric.* Psychiatrist James Matthis of the Medical College of Richmond, Virginia, for example, admits the difficulty in distinguishing between these two types but feels that it must be done. The sexual tease, he feels, is the woman who employs words, gestures, mannerisms "and/or physical adornment to incite sexual desire in a male, and who simultaneously communicates the possibility of fulfilling that desire even when that is not her conscious intent" (*Medical Aspects of Human Sexuality,* December, 1970).

Dr. Matthis feels there is a difference between this and the seductive pseudo-sexuality of the hysterical client who is ordinarily quite infantile in her sexuality. Although she may dress provocatively and dramatize herself, the hysteric is looking for someone to care for her like a father rather than someone to love her. "Overt actions are a product of her unconscious desires to be loved as a little girl—not as a woman. . . . The childish part of her usually controls the day and she becomes a helpless victim of her own seductiveness."

The sexual tease, on the other hand, is not deceived by her own unconscious motivations. She is not a little child and she may quite consciously use her sexuality in order to obtain her objective. It can at times, as Matthis points out, be a totally conscious mechanism "for obtaining material ends, or it may be the result of emotional needs of which she is less aware and therefore unable to control."

There is an element of consciousness in the sexual playfulness of the tease. The *manipulative tease,* for example, is quite aware of what she is doing when she employs her sexuality—or perhaps more accurately, her sexiness —to get what she wants. She always runs the danger of going just beyond the teasing stage, however, and having someone demand that she produce the sexual activities she hints at. Observers like Matthis have noted that our culture has reinforced the use of sexuality in order to achieve other nonsexual objectives. This is clear in a great deal of contemporary advertising and is closely related to the way American culture associates sexual attractiveness with personal success.

The *hostile tease* is very different from the manipulative tease. Her objective is quite different. She is out to hurt somebody and she employs her seductiveness to achieve this end. The aim is the put-down of another by leading him on with a superficial sexuality that creates excitement and intensifies the discomfort of her victim. Counselors may find that both the manipulative and the hostile tease bring their style into the counseling situation. The hostile tease may be out to defeat the counselor, to castrate and overwhelm the male counselor as she does other men. The hostility is unmistakable.

Matthis also describes the *competitive tease* who uses her sexuality on a man only when she feels that she is competing for him with some other woman. Such clients seem interested only in men who already belong to somebody else. Competition is a strong motive for such teases and if it is not present they are no longer interested in the counselor. This may be very deflating to some counselors' egos, but it is nonetheless true.

Matthis further speaks of the *self-assuring tease* who, of all these categories, is closest to normal. They know what they are doing or can recognize it after a little reflection. It is not uncommon for persons to use their sexuality in order to gain the attention of others as a reinforcement for their sense of themselves. However, when the client uses this in an overt manner, investing so much self-esteem into making a good appearance, it suggests areas of concern beneath the surface of sexuality that need deep exploration.

The *dependent tease,* according to Matthis, reveals a basic immaturity of personality and an "insatiable need to be dependent on the male." She somewhat resembles the hostile tease because she feels the world owes her a living and because she may become quite angry if her husband or boy friend fails her in any way. Male friends always fail the dependent tease, of course, because these women can never truly be satisfied by anybody else.

These persons, who in varying ways are conscious of what they are doing with their sexuality, present a challenge to the counselor. The counselor may establish a relationship even in the face of seduction, dependence and hostility. The familiar challenge is to get beneath what seems to be the outer activity and find the person hiding behind these sexual maneuvers. The temptation may be to become defensive or to strike back with hostility when we are attacked. Some counselors may find the experience of seductiveness an overwhelming one and they will need to be calm and explore their own personalities lest they overdramatize their experience. These occurrences will affect all counselors sooner or later and they should not be considered unusual.

Some counselors may miss them altogether because they are too preoccupied with themselves to catch many of the messages that others give to them. Others may find the experience somewhat enhancing for themselves and play along with it because of the titillation that it provides in an otherwise dull day. The challenge to respond maturely is important because mismanaged relationships in which seduction is a feature can be disruptive to the counselor's life and work and, as psychiatrist Paul Chodoff has noted, "potentially disastrous" as well. He observes that if a professional "finds himself recurrently playing a role in the drama of seduction with patients, this should be sufficient evidence that adequate self-knowledge is lacking and needs to be acquired or renewed" (*Medical Aspects of Human Sexuality,* July, 1973).

It is helpful to remember that the hysterical patient, who presents many superficially seductive features, is living out a fantasy. Counselors who remember this feel much more comfortable in dealing with such clients, more confident of themselves, and can understand events that otherwise might be quite bewildering. As psychiatrists Stanley Lesser and B. Ruth Easer have observed, the major dynamics of the hysteric lie "in defending the child-woman aspect of herself." But this hides from both herself and others an awareness of the degree "of anxiety and resentment with which she responds whenever demands for adult responsibilities are thrust upon her" (*Medical Aspects of Human Sexuality,* May, 1969).

The hysteric is an interesting client. Hysterics are charming but generally helpless. They may be attractive and vivacious and they bring a colorfulness to therapy that is often lacking in the depressed clients. Their very vivacity has a destabilizing effect in all their relationships and so it does in counseling. They want to live out the fantasy of the child-wife and, as Lesser and

Easer write, the husband of the hysteric "must recognize that he has married a childish, inefficient, dependent, cute, and lovable wife." Counselors experience hysterics in quite similar fashion.

They appear very sexy, dress in a provocative manner, and tell interesting if self-centered stories. They sound fascinating, especially to beginning counselors, while older ones realize, after some experience with these women, that the challenge to understand them is not simple or straightforward. Hysterics can be very frustrating because they act with counselors the same way they act with other males; they seem like little girls wanting a father's reassurance and forgiveness. They are not very good at assuming responsibility or enduring boring tasks. Their lives are filled with emotional crises over rather small points which they consistently over-dramatize.

They are highly emotional. Indeed the hysterical style has been called "the emotional way of life." They are individuals of great extremes but they enjoy and are not eager to give up their emotional qualities. Hysterics use their emotions strongly, and somewhat puzzlingly, in their relationships with others.

Hysterics are bereft unless they feel truly loved. They need to be loved but they suffer genuine conflicts with adult closeness and they have real sexual inhibitions. They seek a father more than a lover and they are more comfortable with an exhibitionistic and seductive sexuality, like that of a little girl, than they are with mature sexuality. They have great difficulties with genital sexuality which constitutes one of the reasons they come for counseling in the first place. Hysterics may force their husbands to adopt a fatherly role in which there is affection but very little real demand for sexual behavior or they may treat sexuality in a childish way, revealing again one of the main components of their personality style.

The conflicts with which hysterics come are frequently built on the way they treat their husbands who are led on by their apparent sexiness but denied any actual experience of adult sexuality. The come-on causes their partners to be frustrated and confused as well as irritated. The husbands of hysterics have a difficult time winning in any situation. They experience the sexual invitation and, if they do not respond, they are thought to be rejecting. On the other hand, if they do respond they are thought to be almost criminally interested in sex and the hysteric flees from them. The husband is made to feel that he is some kind of monster and that the difficulties in their relationship are chiefly his fault. So reads the typical scenario in the presenting problems of an hysteric patient.

Such patients may also have many other physical symptoms. Physical illness is generally something found throughout their life histories. Their other complaints may also include frigidity, dyspareunia, and vaginismus.

It is not uncommon for a hysterical woman to express great dissatisfaction with her marital partner. The basic hysteric conflict can confound many of the central experiences of marriage and can cause enormous problems with questions of conception, pregnancy, childbirth and parenthood. The hysterical style shows through all of these situations and all who counsel, from the obstetrician to the visiting clergyman, will be swept into the hysteric's style of relationship. They will all experience it in some way or other.

Hysteria also appears in males, although neither as frequently nor as dramatically as with females. Male hysterics present a different picture, projecting self-confidence and a seemingly cool capacity to manage their own lives without any trouble. This, oddly enough, is another cultural stereotype that has been extensively reinforced and, to some people at least, has become a model on which they have tried to pattern their own behavior. Such men may seem excessively "macho," but this signals their inner lack of confidence rather than any genuine male competence. Their superficial behavior covers up inner fear and anger; they therefore put a great deal of importance on knowing the way to dress, the right wines to order, and the latest in fashions. James Bond obviously exhibited certain hysterical features. Again, these persons may seem promising and engaging subjects for counseling because their inner fragility is masked.

The regular difficulties of female hysterics may also be observed in their male counterparts. They are narcissistic and vain and they need a great deal of immediate attention. They are so absorbed in themselves that they do not keep very good track of time nor, despite their appearance, do they maintain their affairs or their living quarters in good order. One of the problems that may emerge in counseling is the mismatch of an hysterical person with an obsessive, each really complementing the other for what the other lacks rather than for what they truly share. Obsessives provide the good order that hysterics lack and hysterics provide the energy and zest for life that is denied to obsessives. The difficulty, which also appears in their sexual relations, is not something that can be handled by encouragement or by any manipulation of the external factors in their lives. The sexual complaints of such couples must be seen as only the symptoms of deeper psychological estrangements.

It is always easy to give bad advice and a lot of it has been given in dealing with hysterical women who have difficulties with sexuality despite their temptress-like self-presentation. Urging them to become more sexually active, as amateurs sometimes do, is clearly not helpful. That plunges them into the heart of their conflict and does very little to ameliorate their basic problems. Treating the total person is a very real challenge, especially when the client exhibits seductive behavior toward the counselor.

Counselors remember that this seductive behavior is just part of their overall problem and prepare themselves for the typical kinds of behavior that are also associated with the seductive mode. Counselors preserve their own integrity and reach out most helpfully to the seductive patient when they are prepared for a relationship in which, as has been noted before, the person is living a fantasy life.

Counselors should anticipate that such patients will use the defenses of repression extensively. They defend against any reawakening of their sexuality. This can be observed in their lack of true sexual feelings despite their seductive behavior. It can also be seen in their loss of recall for certain events connected with their still unresolved relationship with their parents. Such incidents are first-hand clues of the defense of repression in action. Hysterics indulge in daydreaming and the use of fantasy because through these they can receive the attention which they crave so much. They can settle for a soap opera world because this symbolic gratification does not upset their unconscious problems nearly as much as a real relationship with another person would. Make-believe is not really a very good solution, but it keeps their anxiety under control.

Counselors can expect heavy emotionality in these people and it is in this area that their seductive style will most clearly appear. They lead others on but they refuse to deal with the demands of sexual intimacy—which is so anxiety-provoking—so they close this possibility off immediately. Their behavior is also marked by regression. Their childlike responses are filled with the use of the mechanisms of denial and isolation through which they keep themselves free of having to face the significance of their own behavior. This is the defense that allows them to be seductive in counseling. They do not let themselves see the meaning of what they are actually doing. They are not conscious of what their appearance and mannerisms project to counselors because denial effectively keeps this material unconscious. This is why they can blame other people for their difficulties with a clear conscience.

Counselors should be prepared for good, indeed, fascinating beginnings; hysterics are interesting and counselors will feel that they have made contact right away. Helpers, even the most dedicated, are not above being flattered by lively and attractive persons who may tell them that they are helping a great deal, that never before has anyone been so understanding, etc.

Counselors should also expect and therefore be prepared for the seductive behavior itself. They have to read these maneuvers correctly, seeing the effort at seduction as typical of the hysteric's style and realizing that its implications are well-defended by the hysterics themselves. The seduction will include body language as well as other coquettish mannerisms. Recalling this, counselors will be far more self-possessed and understanding of the kinds of persons with whom they are working.

It is helpful always to keep in mind the fact that seductive behavior, intriguing though it may seem, is not directed specifically to the personality of the counselor. This may be discouraging but it is nonetheless true that the seductive maneuvering of hysterics is part of their presentation of themselves rather than a sign of real interest in or sexual attraction to the counselor.

References

Arieti, S. (Ed.). *American Handbook of Psychiatry.* New York: Basic Books, Inc., 1959. See Chapter 14, D. W. Abse, "Hysteria."

Blinder, M. "The Hysterical Personality." *Psychiatry* (1966), 29:227.

De Martino, M. F. (Ed.). *Sexual Behavior and Personality Characteristics.* New York: Grove Press, 1966.

Easer, B. and Lesser, S. "Hysterical Personality: A Re-evaluation." *Psychoanalytic Quarterly* (1965), 34:390.

Ellis, Albert. *The American Sexual Tragedy.* New York: Twayne Publishers, 1954; New York: Grove Press, 1962.

Hallek, S. "Hysterical Personality Traits." *Archives of General Psychiatry* (1967), 16:750.

Hermes, H. and Kurth, G. (Eds.). *The Handbook of Psychoanalysis.* Cleveland: The World Publishing Co., 1963. See G. Barebain, "Marriage and Career."

Kelman, H. (Ed.). *Feminine Psychology.* New York: W. W. Norton & Co., 1967.

Marmor, J. "Orality in the Hysterical Personality." *The Journal of the American Psychoanalytical Association* (October, 1952), p. 656.

Wisdom, J. O. "Methodological Approach to the Problem of Hysteria." *International Journal of Psychoanalysis* (May/June, 1961), 62:224.

TWENTY-THREE

Bad Situations and Bad News

As has been discussed earlier, human sexuality can be a problem in itself and it can also serve as the medium of expression for other personal conflicts that cannot surface from the unconscious in more direct ways. One of the most important roles of the para-professional counselor centers on decoding the complex language of human beings, especially the extensive and subtle sexual vocabulary, so that a proper and sensitive understanding can be achieved. Even counselors who have had little experience appreciate the delicacy of this work as well as the energies of concentration and attention that must be given to it. Loneliness can masquerade as promiscuity and one of the faces of the ravaged soul of mourning can be in unexplained sexual activity. The schizoid person may pull back from sexual activity to avoid threatening thoughts of cruelty and sadism, choosing to be alone in his uneasy adjustment. Self-esteem is often the unrecognized motive for the kind of sexual behavior that some people hope will enhance their self-image. Actions that seem to be homosexual may reflect something other than that particular sexual orientation; they may be merely a sign of a temporary situational state. The effort to understand, even when final and full under-standing is not achieved, is one of the contributions that counselors can make in the wide variety of sexually oriented problems or consultations with which they may become involved.

This is not to make a detective of the nonprofessional counselor. Taking the role of somebody who knows more than anybody else is distinctly nontherapeutic—slightly paranoid, in fact—when this, combined with an over-intellectualized display, becomes the style of the helper. Such helpers, much in need of help themselves, are blessedly few. It is far different to see nonprofessional counseling as a passage toward human understanding rather than as a collecting of evidence of the guilt or responsibility of the person involved. This point is worth stressing because para-professionals are so often involved in situations where the problem they are consulted about is a distinct crisis to others. People may be outraged, embarrassed, or deeply shamed by the sexual aspects of the situation, as, for example, when it is learned that a distinguished public figure has been involved in a sexual relationship with someone other than his wife. It is even more important to be the voice of understanding when there is a problem because someone is involved in bizarre or unusual sex practices.

These situations arise fairly routinely in almost any community and the pastor, the educator, and the lawyer may be among the first consulted. An intervention marked by patience and a steady effort to read the symptoms accurately is the best service that can be offered. Para-professionals are in a distinctly advantageous position because they are trusted and respected and their influence is ordinarily strongest in and around the actual event or its discovery. They can operate, in other words, at the time when understanding and common sense are at a premium; when they can help set the direction for successful treatment for the individual and sensitive resolution of the emotional reactions of other interested parties.

It is never helpful to disgrace someone who already feels deeply disgraced and ashamed because of his or her behavior. There are ways of managing difficult circumstances so that the troubled person can get help, the occurrence itself can be managed sensibly, and vindictiveness can be minimized. It is amazing to note how many institutions, sometimes those that are religious by nature, offend in dealing with personnel whose conflicts are manifested in sexual acting-out. They are sometimes treated more compassionately in big business or by government bureaucracy. Wherever persons express their own unsolved inner problems through sexual symptoms, the response that is informed, compassionate, and consistent is in order. The para-professional is in an excellent position to promote dealing with the situation in just this fashion. The response is built ultimately on an attitude that, despite the emotional furor that may be unleashed all around, persists in seeking to understand and to help others to understand the roots of the problem, the symbolic nature of the symptoms, and the kind of continuing treatment that may be indicated. This is not the "bleeding heart" stance. It is rather a strong and realistic view which does not deny the situation—nor try, for example, to eliminate its legal consequences—but attempts to develop a perspective that will be useful both in the short and long term.

An example of this is the discovery in some way of sexual acting-out on the part of a respected citizen who has a responsible job. The knowledge of the activity comes through somebody else who has also been involved. What does the nonprofessional counselor do with this knowledge? Suppose the accused individual is a member of the clergy. Some would report this to the person's superior or, perhaps, to colleagues in hopes that they might take appropriate action. The counselor, however, does not move to do either of these things swiftly. An effort to understand demands some initial verification of the charges; it is not at all unusual for these allegations to be made by persons who are themselves in need of assistance. Being aware of this, the nonprofessional should try to develop some sense of the adjustment and motivation of the informer; the latter may well turn out to be the one who needs referral. However, presuming that the information checks out, the next step is to approach the person accused, not in a spirit of confrontation, but with the concerned interest of somebody who understands how complicated life can be and who puts the emphasis on the other person in an effort to apprise them and to understand them at the same time. This approach is not that of the person who condones everything and who is unnecessarily willing to cover up the incident. But neither is it the condemning approach that has been used with general futility for so many generations. If the key person can be approached with human acceptance and understanding, the odds for a favorable and nonsensational resolution of the difficulty are notably increased. This offers the other the opportunity, sometimes the first they have ever had, to explore a conflict that has troubled them for a long time.

This approach also makes it possible for the individual to make a move toward greater help without its being forced on him. It may also make it possible to handle the public aspects of the situation in a truly sensitive way. In such circumstances, the initiative for this mode of dealing with a difficult problem may rest with the para-professional who is consulted or turned to for advice by other principals. Nothing is ever lost by beginning this way. Troubled persons are helped enormously when they are treated humanely and given an opportunity to take responsibility for their further treatment. Once that is accomplished, the other aspects of the situation can be managed with far less stress and far less pain for all concerned. The capacity to approach such problems with directness and concern rather than with vindictiveness or a desire to overlook and sweep them under the rug is a human quality rather than the outcome of many years of highly specialized training. Counselors who can deal with matters this way can hone their sensitivity through counseling understandings and maximize their effectiveness in situations that bring out the blunderer in many others.

Aside from the example of a prominent or responsible figure's involvement in some acting-out, there are many other circumstances in which the intervention of the para-professional can be extremely helpful. Take the plight of the newly widowed and divorced. These persons, at whatever age, have ordinarily sustained severe psychological trauma, the nature and extent of which is not totally clear to them. Dealing with loss they may well begin to behave in ways that had previously been quite uncharacteristic of them. Such behavior may include sexual activity which is motivated not so much by desire as by confusion and personal uncertainty about what the future will holds for them. There is a phase of mourning, for example, that is largely symbolic and that is very difficult to decipher unless one is attuned to unconscious processes. Para-professionals can offer understanding to the bereaved and they can also help other family members to read the behavior with less bewilderment and more comprehension. It is not unusual, for example, for an older widower to deal with his loss by beginning to drink a little more and, at times, through striking up what seems to be an inappropriate relationship with some other woman. The remaining family members, the daughters and sons, perhaps, become upset and, instead of looking compassionately at an old man trying to patch his life together, they get angry and determine to stop him. This causes many hard feelings and does not help the older man whose new sexual interest is a symbolic sign of his attempts to process his loss rather than evidence of some suddenly released licentiousness. The pastor or educator, doctor or lawyer, who can help these onlookers deal with their own feelings and assist them to see the symbolic pattern in the father's behavior may not resolve the situation completely but will certainly make a healing start at it.

There are other situations in which sexual interests that can be accepted and seem unremarkable in everyday life take on an alien and forbidding character. People who suffer some physical loss are frequently treated as though they were somehow totally diminished as persons. That is why some people find themselves speaking loudly to blind people even though it is sight alone that is lost in them. So it is with sexual activity in, for example, the crippled and the aged. Some mechanism of denial makes many of us perceive paraplegics and others, even when they are still young and vigorous, as somehow sexually neutered. This attitude becomes institutionalized in the policies of rehabilitation centers and hospitals. The crippled are infants in the eyes of the administration and any evidence of sexual interest is looked upon with uneasiness if not complete embarrassment. They are sometimes chaperoned as though they had not achieved their majority, and men and women are at times segregated at movies and entertainments. There is little thought given to providing privacy for anything like friendship or the rites of courtship that are still important to these persons. Para-professionals are not expected to be reformers but they can both help to interpret to others the sexual interests of these people and overcome the hesitant and uncomfortable attitudes of those who work with them. A broad-gauge understanding is required to appreciate the frustration that is only multiplied by the unwillingness of some institutions to deal more compassionately with the sexual needs of those they serve.

While we have come a long way in recent years in appreciating the capacities of the elderly for continued sexual activity, this insight has not been made operational in many settings. Nursing homes, for example, resemble rehabilitation hospitals in their reluctance to deal with the straightforward fact of the sexual needs of older persons. Husbands and wives in the same nursing homes may find it difficult to exchange very simple signs of affection, much less find the privacy and quiet for sexual relations. The presence of counselors who can deal with the feelings of all parties when questions about these issues arise is bound to be healing and helpful. It is important, for example, for members of the clergy to develop a compassionate feeling for the sexual activity that is bound to occur wherever humans gather even when they are old or crippled. To view all this as disorder or sin is merely to make matters worse. To be able to view it with a depth of understanding—and to help others to do the same—is a distinct contribution on many levels.

Perhaps the chief requirement of the para-professional is the knowledge and wisdom, based on good information and good sense, not to be shocked by anything that comes into their experience. Difficult as that may seem, there is meaning there, and a willingness to wait and listen as it emerges as a powerful therapeutic asset. Such, for example, is the occurrence of incest which for so long has been taboo even as a subject for discussion. This does not make it an uncommon or impossible situation, and frequently it is the para-professional who stands on the front lines of life to deal with it. Adequate basic knowledge of the subject is indispensable, as is self-possession in the face of a subject that few talk about willingly and that is not well described as a plot device in most novels.

In the study of psychiatrists Elva Poznanski and Peter Blos, Jr., of the University of Michigan, for example, incest, far from being an isolated event from which great psychological consequences flow, is found in "relationships with sexual contact occurring repeatedly over protracted periods of time" (*Medical Aspects of Human Sexuality*, October 1975, p.54). In fact, clinically observed incest becomes "a way of life, and no one in the family superficially expresses guilt—until an outside authority steps in." The authors found the feelings that are expressed are related more to family disruption than to the intra-familial sexual relationship.

They also see incest as involving the whole family rather than just those members overtly involved in a sexual relationship. The nonparticipants are psychologically involved at some level. It is not uncommon for the mother, for example, to give some unconscious approval to father-daughter sexual involvement. The mother does not want to deal with the truth of the matter and refuses to hear it even when the daughter tells her of the relationship. The mother assents in a nonverbal way to the continuation of the situation, frequently leaving the house so that the father and daughter can be alone.

It is clear that this is not a simple problem and that those involved are not likely to respond to simple injunctions to change. As Poznanski and Blos state, "Families in which incest occurs over long periods of time are usually families with severe psychological disturbances outside of the incest, and characteristically there exists either a poor marital relationship or a very skewed one." The fathers who are involved in incest, far from being over-sexed, are poorly developed and generally inadequate persons. It is clear that dealing with a problem of incest requires counselors to be sensitive but not naive about the possibilities of helping the situation by themselves. Long-term psychological assistance that involves the family system is a desirable goal but one which, because of the complications of the family life and the lack of motivation for change, may be difficult to achieve.

Incest does occur in other family combinations. An understanding of how and why these patterns develop demands intensive psychological analysis. Referral is clearly in order although the para-professionals may find that they must deal with many other persons, including law enforcement agents, in these situations.

Incest is only one of the many situations which may have repugnant aspects to them but which, nonetheless, present themselves regularly in the day-to-day work of pastors, lawyers, nurses, and doctors. They deal, as the police often do, with the unretouched reality of existence, with the corruption of better possibilities, with the degradation of what seems most noble about the person. Such challenges are fairly commonplace for nonprofessional counselors. If they anticipate their own reactions, particularly to situations involving unusual sexual problems, they will deal more effectively and constructively with everyone concerned. Not all the crises will be as dramatic as that of an incestuous relationship but they will all be humanly draining.

Perhaps none is more difficult to enter into than the responsibility of breaking bad news to someone. This is especially difficult if the bad news concerns their sexuality; if, for example, surgery that will affect sexual performance is necessary, or if some accident, such as industrial problems that have occurred in recent years, render people impotent. This can have a devastating impact on their sense of themselves and their need for counseling and emotional support may be long-lasting. It is even more difficult when the person involved is young and has had no chance yet at an adult experience of life. The presence, for example, of a sexual disorder in an adolescent, as Carol Nadelson, psychiatrist at Harvard Medical School, notes (*Medical Aspects of Human Sexuality,* February, 1976, p. 47), "raises a number of complex questions" which need careful thought before proceeding further. The impact is determined, according to Nadelson, by a number of factors including the specific nature of the problem as well as its extent and its implications for adult sexual functioning. It is also important to understand the time in the life cycle when the disorder is discovered and the meaning of this problem for everyone involved. Counselors, who may be working with physicians in these circumstances, must measure their own best service carefully. If, for example, the diagnosis of a serious defect is made while the young person is in the midst of adolescence and dealing therefore with the consolidation of sexual identity, the impact can be very much greater than if it is discovered before this when there is some time to anticipate and develop a strategy for dealing with the problem.

The adolescent will have particular problems because he or she is strongly affected by anything that makes them feel other than normal. They may use defenses that deny the defect or its implications; others may try to use intellectual defenses to understand it. If the problem is infertility, some may plan on other ways of achieving gratification, as, for example, in a career that will associate them with children. Nadelson notes, however, that children under sixteen may use less mature mechanisms in their attempts to deal with stress. They may, in other words, regress, and counselors should be prepared for this. It is highly unusual, however, for adolescents not to experience anxiety about such information and this is also a response that counselors must be ready to handle sensitively.

Such a situation, which serves as a model for many other similar life experiences, also involves the feelings of the parents. They too may have complicated feelings that include guilt, anger, depression, and uncertainty about what to do. They may experience great conflict about telling the child or they may put it off, hoping that it can be handled in some less emotionally expensive manner. Their own feelings of adequacy or responsibility are also at stake. Parents need understanding and support and frequently this must come from the para-professional who is close to the home situation. Clergy are frequently very important sources of support as they supplement the work of the physician in communicating the facts about a medical situation.

Not only can the para-professional assist in helping the parents to review and deal with their own emotions, but he or she can also help plan the way in which the bad news will be communicated to the adolescent. Some professionals, defending themselves against the grief they meet every day, believe in getting the news across as simply and clearly as possible. With news that will affect the sexual and reproductive life of an adolescent some additional consideration should be given to the manner and the timing of the information. This includes some appraisal of the adolescent's level of maturity and his or her capacity to accept and understand what is being said.

There may be other support systems that need to be drawn upon at a difficult time like this so that the young person does not feel isolated or abandoned. There are ways of breaking bad news that can build on the assets of the individual, on their other capacities and resources. It is also possible to stress what is capable of being described in a positive way. As Nadelson notes, it is better to speak of an eighty percent chance of success than a twenty percent chance of failure. Much depends on the counselor's ability to sense all the dimensions of the situation, all the needs of all those involved, including the parents and the physician, and to see that these are responded to in some way. It is also obviously important to build in a next step for the person receiving the bad news. That may consist in a further opportunity for counseling in order to explore their self-image and the effect of this information on it.

Some anticipation of the emotional results of unpleasant news is very constructive in these extremely difficult situations. Any situation that involves communicating information about sexual functioning has staggering implications for the self-esteem of those involved. Bad news cannot be made to go away, but the healthy resources of the affected persons can be tapped if some sensitive and humane planning is employed. This is frequently the responsibility—at least as a coordinator of all those involved—of nonprofessional counselors. Their good sense and human understanding may be two of the most vital if least celebrated community resources in the world today.

TWENTY-FOUR

When To Refer

MOST counselors want to be genuinely helpful. They do not want to take on responsibilities that go beyond their training or native capacity to assist, but neither do they wish to perceive all those who come to see them as immediately in need of being sent to somebody else. Above all, they do not want to convey an attitude of rejection that may only increase the anxiety of the already troubled. Where does a counselor draw the line, or on what principle can the decision to refer be made? How, one may ask, can referrals be made so that they are constructive experiences even though they are episodes that are by their nature brief and bridge-like?

Members of the clergy, educators, and even physicians face this situation frequently. They must ask the questions about their competence in every relationship; with a little experience they develop a trustworthy sense of when and how to refer. This attitude holds, whether the presenting problem is sexual or of some other nature. Two very broad principles have at times been invoked for nonmedical para-professional counselors. If the person seeking aid can be kept in relationship—as a parishioner for the member of the clergy, as a client for the lawyer, or as a student for the educator— then it is likely that these nonprofessional helpers can proceed without making a referral. When, however, the persons seeking assistance are transformed, in the counselor's perceptions, into a different role, that of the patient, then a line has been crossed in the relationship and a referral is in order. As long as para-professionals can remain in their own primary role and, as persons who are well informed psychologically, respond without leaving that role or changing their identity, the moment for referral has not yet come. When they find that they are transforming their own role, when they are becoming psychologists rather than pastors or teachers, for example, then they should identify that change as the time for recommending other professional help.

The second general principle is based on a similar common sense insight. Pastors deal with human suffering and ignorance. The same may be said in different ways of lawyers, educators, and others whose role involves them in the human condition in a distinctive way. Psychologists, psychiatrists, and other specially trained persons deal with psychopathology and, while nobody would deny that this is a profound form of human suffering, it is also specialized enough to demand the intervention of the experts. General physicians without extensive psychological training can approximate these principles in their own way. When those with whom they deal need a kind of treatment that goes beyond that which they ordinarily offer, then the general physician should also make a referral. Good intentions and well-meant advice are no substitute.

Can we pursue these general notions further? The skill and subtlety required in a good referral are related to the sensitivity of the professionals making the referral. Their refined ability to read the language of symptoms correctly, their sense of the transference evidence—that edited version of the client's general style that comes out toward the counselor—enables them to make a tentative diagnosis early in the relationship. The sooner they can sense the root nature of the dynamics associated with the presenting sexual problem, the more effectively and smoothly they can make the referral. This takes experience and, at times, the consultation of someone else, but it does provide the informed understanding of the other that is required. Such diagnosis should not be thought of immediately as a way of pigeon-holing the client; accurate and sensitive diagnosis is a respectful and essential form of authentic human understanding, an extension of the kind of treatment that regards others with the highest concern.

Psychiatrist Daniel H. Labby of the University of Oregon provides some further thoughts on the question of referral. (*Medical Aspects of Human Sexuality,* Dec. 1975, p.79, 80). Noting that the chief presenting symptom in sexual difficulties is anxiety, he suggests an evaluation of this as basic to the decision to refer or not. Is the anxiety an understandable reaction to the unexpected development of a sexual problem in the client's life? Or is it a symptom of a more basic but unrecognized conflict? Labby suggests that "when anxiety mixed with depression not only disturbs sexual functioning but seriously interferes with close personal relationships, or when sexual dysfunction is a symptom of an ongoing depressive state, or the genitals and sex function are being used for acting out the symbolic expression of emotional conflict, primary psychiatric evaluation" is in order. The clinical sophistication required to make this judgment is not enormous; most committed para-professionals can do this much without additional consultation. They can use this decision as the basis for a sound referral.

H. A. Otto has also provided some points of reference for counselors who want to come to sensible decisions about referrals ("Evaluating the Patient's Problem for Counselor or Referral," *Counseling in Marital and Sexual Problems,* Baltimore: Williams and Wilkins, 1965). The nonprofessional can find anchor points, first of all, in identifying the individual's own perceptions of his problems and of the counseling situation. If the person tells of his problems in a disordered and incomplete manner, if there is a confused flavor to the story, and if he or she insists that only their interpretation of events can be the correct one, the counselor has evidence in which to make a judgment for referral. The client's whole set toward the counselor provides valuable clues about the degree of disturbance present.

Secondly, inquiry should be made about the previous history of the individual and his or her family. If there have been problems, what are the individual's perceptions of them? Does the client use denial or withdrawal in some attempt to disown the crisis? Has the person used alcohol or drugs, or acted out in some other way to handle problems?

Para-professional counselors should note carefully the way such clients view themselves. Is their self-concept marked by lack of self-esteem and feelings of unworthiness, guilt, or depressive feelings? The presence of these indicates that more serious problems may be present and that referral for further evaluation or assistance is in order. Connected with this is some sense of whether this is a long-term difficulty, or an aspect of some other chronic personality problem. The nature of the person's motivation for assistance is also relevant here. When individuals have used defense mechanisms to escape dealing with a problem, when they blame it all on someone else, then counselors have good grounds for exploring the possible depths of the underlying difficulty.

In addition to evaluating the clues provided by the way in which the client relates to the counselor, the latter should also note carefully any history of "breakdowns" or "nervous" exhaustion or problems at previous times. Have there been, for example, suicide attempts? All such incidents suggest that the counselor should actively consider a referral for more intensive treatment.

What should para-professionals do when such persons refuse the notion of a referral? This is sometimes a problem in remote regions, as in foreign countries, where help is not easily available. Should the counselor, whether in actuality the local pastor, teacher, or magistrate, attempt some deeper treatment anyway? This would seem to be unwise. Para-professionals should not depart from their primary professional identification even in extreme circumstances. They serve themselves and others best by not attempting to do more than they comfortably can in these situations. The desire to help, which is sometimes the *need* to help, is not enough. Few mistakes can occur if counselors remain within their own role. They may be able to offer supportive encouragement and use the religious or other resources of their profession to be of assistance, but they should not go further.

Suppose, para-professionals may argue, that the person cannot afford further help? There are very few localities in contemporary America in which some form of psychological help is not available at moderate cost. Counselors should acquaint themselves with the available resources in their own areas so that they have the facts at the time of making a referral. Often clients do not realize that they can have at least a portion of their further treatment paid for through some medical plan of which they are members. Those who find that their chief work regularly involves them in this kind of counseling may be able to establish at least a working relationship with physicians, psychologists, psychiatrists and social workers to whom referrals can be regularly made.

Special questions may arise about continuing sex therapy; sex clinics have been established by a number of unqualified persons and, although efforts to establish some accrediting system for sexual dysfunction centers are under way, counselors must still rely on their own judgment in evaluating the agencies and professionals to whom they refer their clients. At a conference held in St. Louis in January, 1976, qualified sex therapists gathered to define some of the burgeoning ethical issues related to this developing profession. Dr. William Masters estimated that 3500 to 5000 offices were "now offering what they call sex therapy but that probably fewer than 100 centers used professional techniques and properly trained professional therapists" (*The New York Times,* January 25, 1976). Dr. Helen Singer Kaplan suggested at the conference that the best guide in choosing a competent therapist "was to pick one associated with a university or hospital-based sex therapy program." Also significant was the suggestion of psychiatrist Judd Marmor who felt that sex therapists be well trained in psychotherapy since "great harm can be done if the therapist fails to recognize and deal effectively with the emotional conflicts involved in sexual dysfunction."

Competent professionals have credentials and have no reluctance about having them examined. These evidences of professional preparation and accomplishment remain the best guarantee that can be sought about the worthiness of a referral source. Para-professional counselors have ethical obligations to check out all those agencies and individuals to whom they may refer clients.

Another issue about which counselors should be well-informed is rape, a serious and emotionally complicated question that has received a great deal of attention in recent years. In Susan Brownmiller's book, *Against Our Will*, she describes rape as a consistently hostile act of aggression on the part of men. Rape is also, of course, the subject of much discussion in feminist publications. Counselors cannot afford to be ignorant of the way in which society deals with the issue if they are called upon in any way in connection with an actual or attempted rape. This is not an unusual experience for clergy and educators who need a grasp on the psychological factors which may be involved. They may not treat the victim directly (although they may on an emergency basis) but they may find themselves at the center of the occurrence, mediators between family, physicians and even the police.

In dealing with a rape victim, the sensitivity of the para-professional is a highly important variable. As in many other situations, the police may play an extremely significant role in dealing with the initial psychological trauma of rape. Special training has been given to police in many large cities to help them carry out their responsibilities more sensitively and effectively. The same is true for nurses and others who may be working directly with the victim. Other para-professionals may function chiefly in second stage responsibilities, as with family members, schoolmates, or other members of the community.

They should recall that in an emergency, when emotions run high, they serve best by maintaining their own calm and self-possession. Counselors may have to assume triage officer responsibilities in emergencies, putting order into the situation, deciding priorities, and keeping the problem as contained and manageable as possible. While their counseling skills may be very useful in assisting those who are emotionally disturbed by the occurrence, their best service may lie in remaining the calm center of the disruption. This will enable them to help people avoid extreme or regrettable reactions. It also makes it possible to establish the facts of the situation more readily and accurately. This is particularly helpful in the case of children who may be so upset by whatever occurred that they cannot explain it to adults, who, in turn, may leap to conclusions that are not justified and not helpful for themselves or for the offended child. Some sensible management of the emotional upset is essential before such a child can be questioned or medically examined.

These situations can be quite complicated and, although the old notion that anyone who gets raped has invited it is no longer an unquestioned part of our folklore, the reciprocal dynamics of rape situations do need to be examined. In writing of this difficulty with children, Edwin Roth, M.D., notes that "Most of the children have not been raped. One can determine this best by properly interviewing the patient. . . . Proper interviewing is accomplished by respecting the patient, obtaining her confidence, talking privately with her, and taking the time to listen to her story." Roth feels that this should be done with children before the medical examination which may be unnecessary and emotionally harmful to the child. Through his experiences he has discovered that many children in these situations "have serious emotional disturbances, with symptoms such as precocious sexual activity, poor school performance, behavioral problems at home and so forth" (*Medical Aspects of Human Sexuality,* August, 1972, pp. 89, 90). Sensitive understanding at this time may lead to a better referral, one that may include some treatment on an extended basis not only for the child but also for other members of the family.

Para-professional counselors can assist in all phases of these situations. They may be particularly helpful in encouraging followup treatment for the emotional scars that are bound to afflict all those affected by the rape experience. Family members may need to talk through their reactions and it is obvious that continued psychological counseling for the victim is essential. All too often others may advise that the victim just "try to forget" the incident. The victim, however, needs to work through the psychological trauma and this takes time and the help of a skilled therapist. Para-professionals may have to deal with the resistance of family members or the hesitancy of the victim; that is essential front line intervention.

Para-professionals may also play a role in educating the rest of the community about the facts connected with rape as well as in developing some positive preventive measures. The police, for example, advocate a few simple rules that can be extremely helpful in protecting women from the possibility of rape. These include such obvious precautions as not traveling the streets alone at night, not accepting rides from strangers, good home security, and the use of only initials on mailboxes, apartment listings, and in telephone directories. Common sense, indeed, but sometimes helpfully reinforced by clergy, teachers, and others who are outside the family and whose cautions cannot be easily dismissed as "unnecessary worrying."

Although the subject of rape is discussed chiefly in regard to women, it is a fact that men may be raped too. The assault is ordinarily homosexual in nature and can be just as emotionally scarring for a man as the experience would be for a woman. Counselors must be aware of the possibility and use the same sensitive but common sense approach that they would use in a situation involving a female.

At times it falls upon the para-professional to deal with surprising and deeply disturbing situations that are complicated by sexual dimensions that are not understood by others who may be quite close to the situation. It may be a member of the clergy, for example, who is presented with what may seem grisly or upsetting details about occurrences that are already deeply tragic in and of themselves. One example may suffice for other similar problems because the demands on the para-professional in all these situations may be the same, that is, to help others understand rather than merely be horrified by the circumstances.

Take, for example, the relatively rare but not completely unusual situation in which a person commits suicide accidentally in pursuit of what psychiatrists term "life-threatening erotic behavior." It helps if counselors are acquainted with the phenomenon and its dynamics. Psychiatrists Robert Litman and Charles Swearingen contend that "overt sexual masochism is more widespread and can be more dangerous than current psychiatric literature would indicate" ("Bondage and Suicide," *Medical Aspects of Human Sexuality,* November 1973, p. 164 ff.). They describe a well-developed subculture of bondage, "in essence the practice for erotic pleasure of being humiliated, endangered, and enslaved; and of being physically bound, restrained, and rendered helpless to a degree that life is threatened."

The discovery of the suicide usually reveals materials that indicate that the person has been engaged in auto-erotic activity while simulating a hanging-like experience. It is generally an accident that the person is actually killed because this is behavior which they have engaged in before (evidenced by the presence of pornographic materials and fetish objects such as pieces of female clothing or chains and leather belts). There is, in fact, a flourishing market for literature and pictures featuring themes and scenes of bondage. Some social commentators have observed a growing preoccupation with and romanticization of this kind of erotic stimulation in our culture. It has, in some publications and entertainments, been romanticized; it is a main theme in the work of the famous Japanese novelist, Yukio Mishima, who committed ritual suicide in 1970.

In their study of nine men who engaged in this kind of behavior, Litman and Swearingen detected certain common psychological characteristics. These included a "death orientation." The subjects eroticized the "situation of helplessness, weakness, and threat to life which was then overcome in survival, and eventual triumph." They also gave evidence of what the authors described as the "Bondage Syndrome," an effort, as they saw it, "to overcome loneliness, boredom, depression, and isolation" and which had as a prominent feature a narcissism which kept these men self-contained and absorbed even when they were involved in this activity with various partners.

Robert J. Stoller (*Perversion,* New York: Pantheon, 1975) offers a theory about this and other "perversions." He sees pornography, the perverse subject's key daydream, as psychodynamically about the same as the perversion. The pornography of their choice reflects in a highly nuanced way their taste in erotic activities. Stoller feels that there is enormous anger expressed through erotic "perversions." While it is difficult to understand how persons develop these conflicts, it is clear that they are in some way or other trying to manage their lives; by testing death erotically, they are trying to triumph over it. As Avery Weisman has noted, "Out of fragments of acts, sensations, organs, meanings, and fantasies, they put together a way of life which condenses conflict into deviant sexual behavior. . . . They simulate what is shunned and idealize what is inaccessible. . . . What is commonly thought of as degradation or depravity may be for them an inverted image of fulfilling reality" ("Self-Destruction and Sexual Perversion," *Essays in Self-Destruction,* E.S. Schneidmann, New York: Science House, 1967, p. 265).

Counselors need to deepen their awareness of these and similarly bizarre occurrences and attempt to bring some understanding of the complicated dynamics that may be involved when such things occur. They must also recognize the fact that such a conflict, should it be presented to them by a troubled person, indicates a need for intensive psychological help. Para-professional counselors cannot be over-horrified nor over-curious when they become involved in these or similar circumstances. Their chief work may be with the survivors of the suicide who may need emotional support and understanding to come to terms with such an event. Para-professionals may be the first ones consulted when, for example, parents discover their child indulging in this or similar activity. The counselor's capacity to handle their anxiety and work toward extending some help to the young person in question may be key elements that make the difference between happiness and tragedy in all their lives. Counselors need to examine and, at times, question the claims that such practices are merely evidence of a different but equally acceptable life style. Timely intervention and response may make the difference between a person's having a chance at a happy life and living in an isolated and conflicted manner. Common sense blended with human sensitivity and compassion are powerful assets in dealing with the bewildering array of distorted sexual behaviors that come to the attention of counselors. A sense of what is healthy is vital because there is so much contemporary rationalization of pathologically deviant behavior. This need not cause counselors to become judgmental moralizers, but it will help them to maintain their balance and their capacity to be of genuine help to all concerned.

References

Brownmiller, Susan. *Against Our Will: Men, Women & Rape.* New York: Simon & Schuster, 1975.

Labby, Daniel H. "The Question of Referral," *Medical Aspects of Human Sexuality.* Dec. 1975, pp. 79–80.

Litman, R. and Swearingen, C. " 'Bondage' and Suicide," *Medical Aspects of Human Sexuality,* Nov. 1973, p. 164ff.

Otto, H. A. "Evaluating the Patient's Problem for Counseling or Referral," *Counseling in Marital and Sexual Problems,* Baltimore: Williams & Wilkins, 1965.

Schneidmann, E. S., *Essays in Self-Destruction.* New York: Science House, 1967. See esp. Weisman, A. "Self-Destruction & Sexual Perversion," p. 265.

Stoller, R. J., *Perversion.* New York: Pantheon, 1975.

TWENTY-FIVE

The Counselor and AIDS

AIDS rose like a medieval specter in the American consciousness during the eighties. From the time that the acquired immunodeficiency syndrome (AIDS) was first detected in 1981 because of the unexpected kind of viral pneumonia found in a small number of gay men in Los Angeles, the always fatal illness has multiplied wildly, generating fear, suffering, confusion, and anger, but enormous compassion as well. Nonprofessional counselors, like almost all Americans, will inevitably find themselves involved with the illness, perhaps directly with an individual suffering from it, almost certainly with someone affected indirectly by it. While nonprofessionals will wisely attempt to refer victims of this disease to experts, especially to the remarkable teams of professionals found in most large hospitals, they still need an understanding of this haunting killer that, like a tornado, slashes a wide path of physical and emotional devastation.

Those who wish to channel their compassion into effective assistance to AIDS victims or to the widening circle of family members, friends, and associates who will be affected by it, need accurate understandings of the disease. AIDS is the most serious of a complex of illnesses termed the *human immunodeficiency virus* infection, or HIV. Studies that used the serological test for antibodies to HIV developed in 1985 for blood screening demonstrated that HIV can be observed in various guises ranging from the person who, without symptoms or complaints, is a carrier to the person whose symptoms meet the technical definition of the always fatal variant of AIDS itself.

The latter term is reserved for those persons with this gravest, deadly form of immune deficiency and the clinical manifestations of some opportunistic infector, such as pneumonia, or growth, such as Kaposi's sarcoma. Not everyone with HIV, therefore, suffers from AIDS in this manner. That distinction is important for helpers to appreciate, not only because of the differing challenges of responding to persons in these categories, but because, as a serious social complication, cases meeting the above medical definition of AIDS must, in most jurisdictions, be reported to local or state health authorities. The technical diagnosis and the responsibility to report this illness belong to medical professionals; other counselors, such as members of the clergy, teachers, and concerned friends and colleagues, will, however, find themselves dealing with the emotional aura that throbs brightly and painfully around such decisions.

Nonprofessional helpers can play a significant role at a number of points in offering education and sensible support to those persons touched in various ways by the ever-twitching dragon's tail of this malady. This is not an illness, however, in which counselors can automatically employ the kind of responses that work in situations in which the basic problem is, for example, the identification and exploration of feelings. As Dr. Francisco Fernandez has written in a primer on the subject for the American Psychiatric Association, "in any case where HIV infection may be possible, any symptoms of a psychiatric nature must be considered organic until proven otherwise." The basic medical complications must, therefore, be understood as powerfully damaging to the central nervous system, resulting in dementia and other morbid states to which the nonprofessional cannot directly respond by fashioning responses directed solely to feeling states.

Manifold emotional reactions do flower, however, on the stalk of this illness, perhaps more than from any other condition of sickness. In regard to these, healthy, self-knowledgeable helpers can be of genuine assistance. Thus, the reactions to a diagnosis of HIV, much as with the diagnosis of any terminal condition, include human experiences of fear and anxiety with which understanding helpers can deal directly and effectively. Death rises suddenly in the still young eyes of these patients, shaking loose a scroll of predictable, agonizing symptoms. The afflicted immediately understand that the path before them may lead to disfigurement through Kapsoi's sarcoma as well as racking fevers, increasing fatigue, and the possibility of increasing rejection and isolation as they grow weaker. They are also faced with disclosing to their parents or loved ones the true nature of their illness, a stressful and uncertain prospect.

It is not unusual, therefore, for patients to express themselves in angry, desperate ways, as the massive weight of the sickness settles on them. The nonprofessional can support them in these trials by identifying and buttressing their healthiest defenses; he or she can also offer them education on the subject in the rumor-filled universe of their suffering and provide the commonsense psychological benefits of just being with them when there is not much else that can be done.

BACK TO BASICS

Before discussing the nature of nonprofessional interventions in detail, some basic principles of working with these sorely afflicted persons must be reviewed. These are not only essential clinical insights based on therapeutic experience but they are the instinctive reactions of people of good sense. The unfettered, unself-conscious human response offered by the untrained counselor is usually the best therapeutic response as well. In other words, nonprofessionals should recognize their own strong points and reinforce them in themselves just as they attempt to identify and brace them up in the patients with whom they work.

Most sensible persons, unexpectedly involved in a critical situation, do not attempt to usurp the roles of trained professionals. Untrained counselors respect the strictly medical reality of the illness and defer, where that is appropriate, to the well-trained and highly experienced teams of doctors and nurses with primary responsibility for the patient. They recognize that individuals who intervene by changing the sick person's medication or by the introduction of some nontraditional form of therapy, such as a special diet, may, for all their good intentions, do more harm than good. While medicine is just beginning to understand the nature of the immune system, and while untested alternative therapies may have some merit, the commonsense rule is to stay within the limits of one's own background and training when dealing with HIV or any other major illness. That obvious restriction, however, leaves plenty of room for nonprofessionals to be of assistance by being themselves.

Desperately sick people do want to talk, when they have the energy to do so, and they need listeners. The surrounding cluster of family and friends often want to talk as well, especially during the long, uniquely enervating hours of waiting in hallways and parlors that go with hospital visiting. This is obviously one of the principal areas in which amateur counselors can work effectively. Even here, however, they must put their basic human capacity simply to understand the woes of others before any attempt to explore their origins or, in any sense, to "treat" them by psychological means.

Counselors without extensive training should, without exception, work with other persons on the *conscious* level of functioning. They may have ideas, even correct ones, about the deep motivation of the patient but they should keep these to themselves and deal with the world of the sick as the latter structure it in the present tense. Nonprofessionals do not, then, attempt to explore unconscious material, nor do they engage in strategies that may, even without their advertance, break through the surface of the ill person's psyche. This is the fundamental commonsense principle of being truly helpful to all people in distress. It is extremely important to follow this in dealing with those stricken with any manifestation of HIV and in dealing with surrounding company of relatives or friends. This is not a restrictive covenant placed on the intervention of nonprofessionals; it embodies rather a prudent and sound sense of direction about the level on which such helpers can function most constructively.

The teacher, the neighbor, the member of the clergy—or any of the many others, such as lawyers and undertakers—who may become involved with an AIDS patient or member of his or her family, contribute enormously by remaining on this conscious plane. That is where the struggling individual can deal with problems in terms of current realities rather than remote causes. It is perfectly acceptable, indeed essential, that in any *supportive* treatment this focus be maintained. Commonsense helpers are never called upon to do *uncovering* or *reconstructive* therapy. There is hardly time for the well-trained to do this in a terminal illness and, in any case, it would work against the reasonable goals of really helping individuals manage their way through an illness that is already overwhelming.

On the conscious level, however, enormous good can be accomplished. The main objective is, as has been noted, to champion those resources of personality, imagination, and spirituality that are found, to some degree, even in the most gravely ill of us. Even when these can only be evoked in a muted and minor key, they can be the decisive strengths by which human beings not only manage but transcend the ravages of mortal illness. The first line of functioning for helpers stretches through this territory. The skill demanded of those who man this line is to identify the available strengths of the suffering person, to reinforce them and bring them into play.

Wise nonprofessionals do not tamper with the defenses of the HIV

patient. Whatever they are—even if they include elements of rationalization or distortion at times—they ordinarily represent the best
the individual can do at the moment. Confronting techniques are,
therefore, not to be employed by the nonprofessional in dealing with
people who, battered by chronic disease, have enormous difficulty in
just inhabiting their own personality in any vital or resonant manner.
We do not blow on the candle that is just guttering out because we
despise its feeble and uncertain light. We shield it from the wind,
allowing it to burn as truly and as long as it can. That is precisely what
we do when we relate to desperately sick persons when we nurse what
little strength they have in order to help them to live fully even a sharply
diminished existence.

Helpers must monitor their own reactions and functioning in order to
observe this first principle. If they become too intense, they may disturb
the patient's unconscious, damaging whatever compromise adjustment
they may have fashioned. Helpers who become too inquisitive or moralistic may also dislodge levels of unconscious reactions with which they
cannot cope, thus aggravating the condition of the suffering person.
Supporting conscious defenses of the AIDS patient, even when these
do not seem ideal to the helper, is enormously beneficial. Many nonprofessionals have a healthy sense of their own limitations; they thereby
draw on their own health in responding to persons in distress. This
healthy sense of using wisely one's best reserves—and not trying to do
the work of the psychiatrist or clinical psychologist—is the hallmark of
commonsense helpers at their best.

The need to understand one's most effective function in relationship
to the professional teams already in place in most major health-care
centers is a further corollary of this commonsense approach. The
intermingling of physical and emotional reaction and causation is highly
complex, and the nonprofessional must take cues from the specialists
who have a more subtle and informed understanding of how these
operate in each individual case. This is of particular importance in an
illness in which, as noted, the infection of the central nervous system
may give rise to symptoms that may seem totally emotional in nature.

COMMON PSYCHOLOGICAL REACTIONS TO HIV

Aware of the above cautions, helpers will still recognize in HIV
patients psychological reactions that are also observed in other patients
with terminal illnesses. Perhaps the most common—and, it might be
said, the most human—is *denial.* When we are suddenly faced with a

crushing piece of news, even the healthiest among us employs the mechanism of denial, if only to gain time and space in which to begin to regroup ourselves psychologically and admit the truth of the event—a catastrophe, the death of a loved one, a significant loss of any kind—into our consciousness. "I don't believe it," we say, or, "It can't be." Gradually, we are able to accept the truth but, under the first impact, we ward off the shock by some measure of denial. Just as we can expect and accept such a reaction in ourselves, so we should expect and accept it in patients who have been given a diagnosis of an HIV-related illness.

We cannot survive without denial, so the helpful counselor will allow patients this necessary and essential defense by which they can look away from the cold shadow of threat long enough to ward off panic. Denial also allows individuals to express an insurrectionary reaction, a rejection, often bitter, of the medical verdict that so suddenly deprives them of their independence and their future. The ability to differentiate this reaction from a dangerous variant of it is indispensable to the counselor. At times, some individuals employ denial not to reorganize interiorly and to adjust to the illness but to mask its reality and to cover their hostile and destructive impulses. Such massive denial is always primitive and dangerous.

Such persons may, for example, recklessly engage in sexual activity with many partners without regard to the consequences for themselves, others, or, eventually, the public in general. They seem bent on revenge, on infecting the world that has deprived them of their own health and is soon to take their lives. Such patients reject any therapeutic assistance. Their rebuffs to those who wish to help them are not difficult to identify even by nonprofessionals. When such potentially destructive impacted embitteredness is encountered, the nonprofessional should not try to temper the anger or to cajole such patients into more rational behavior. The helper should immediately refer the person to a professional or advise a team member of this behavior. Because of possible neurological as well as characterological complications, these patients need immediate and careful evaluation by professionals with the resources needed to manage them.

Perhaps one of the most difficult groups to work with is composed of individuals who have tested positively for HIV but who have not as yet contracted the illness. These persons are faced with a painful and anxiety-provoking reality. They carry the HIV, but in their minds they do not know when or if they will be stricken with AIDS itself. The disease has been tracked only since 1981 and, every year, more of these persons do come down with the illness. Still, the medical evidence, while seeming to suggest a certain inevitability about AIDS following HIV positive testing, has not proved this. Such persons live, therefore, under a shadow and need the kind of understanding support that nonprofessional counselors can provide successfully. It may be that such individuals will confide their anxiety about their condition first to a member of the clergy, a general practitioner, or a respected teacher or coach. These first-line counselors are in an excellent position to assist them psychologically and spiritually and to refer them for professional help when, in their judgment, the time has come for it.

OTHER REACTIONS

Counselors working with AIDS patients may be the first ones to notice the small signals of profound neurological changes under way that need professional medical evaluation and treatment. For example, when patients describe periods of forgetfulness, report or evince difficulties in concentration, or a loss of interest, these are often regarded as understandable incidental psychological reactions to the massive burden of the illness. These mild symptoms should alert nonprofessionals to the possibility that these reactions foreshadow deeper central nervous system disorders such as the *AIDS dementia complex,* that group of irreversible organic disorders that destroy brain function.

Delirium, with features such as insomnia and restlessness, is frequently encountered in hospitalized HIV patients. At times this is misread as a depression or some other purely psychological problem. Nonprofessionals who pick up signs of these problems should again refer the patient for a thorough medical examination. Such prompt referral makes accurate diagnosis possible and, in many cases in which the physical cause is responsive to therapy, a timely and helpful treatment.

While nonprofessionals remain alert to these possibilities, they may more often encounter the truly psychological complications of this illness group. These include *demoralization* and *despondency,* desolating feelings that lay waste to the psyche. In turn, the damaged spirit of the patient, evidenced by a negative self-image, affects the entire world of the afflicted individual, straining social and work relationships until they are no longer manageable. This further isolates the individual, compounding the already severely compromised level of his or her psychological functioning.

Following the tradition of Elizabeth Kubler-Ross, some have described the reactions of the HIV patient as one of adjustment that can be charted out in rough stages. These include the initial crisis, with the reactions of denial, anxiety, anger, and sadness, and is marked by efforts to strike some bargain in regard to health and sickness. The second stage sees denial yielding to a mixture of other emotions, including guilt, anger, and self-pity. This period, marked by a sharp decrease in self-worth, may find the patient estranged from his family and friends. A return to drug use and dangerous sex practices may occur at this time.

In stage three, according to this schema, the patient begins to accept himself or herself as a person compromised by the nature of the illness. He or she may begin to appreciate the unique character and quality of each passing day. In the next stage the person actively prepares for death. This may be marked by a fear of complete dependency on friends or strangers. It is not uncommon for patients, during the darkest moments of this death-sentence illness, to contemplate suicide. None-- theless, those who work with the dying also see evidence of the life force continuing to assert itself in the individual's efforts to hold on to existence.

People who have worked with gravely stricken individuals under- stand that these stages seldom occur in pure form. They may be scrambled, combined with other undescribed intervals, or they may be reversed or, like a new river, cut an unexpected and unpredicted path through the landscape. Sensible counselors understand that they can- not force persons to go through these steps in some orderly fashion. Any attempt, out of naïveté or unmerited confidence in one's therapeutic abilities, may prove disastrous to the individual as he or she tries to come to terms both with life and death. Their heroism may at times be difficult to identify, their fight to right themselves before dying may at times be hard to discern. But these elements, along with fear, uncertainty, and anxiety, will be present and need to be reinforced by the helper. The person who would be of real assistance to the patient must respect the patient's unique journey and understand that he or she will die, not as the textbook or the expert suggests, but as best he or she can. This pilgrimage through a final illness is made, like the rest of life, humanly, imperfectly, and not without nobility.

Perhaps only those who have experienced a chronic illness, even a nonfatal one, can begin to appreciate the internal world of a person bereft of health and hope, and of the frustrating daily struggle to try to reclaim some semblance of oneself from the seemingly scattered and ruined fabric of one's personality. This, however, is what the chronically afflicted HIV patient experiences with an illness that, bad enough in itself, also carries the seeds of social disapproval and ostracism at the same time. Nonprofessionals can respond in this very area, for what they can bring, in place of medical expertise, is the gift of compassionate understanding. Nothing deepens the isolation of the chronically ill more than the pressure, sometimes generated even by well-meaning friends and relatives, for them to be "normal" again. This distinctive void can be entered, if not filled, by nonprofessionals who can sensitively grasp at least some of the feelings of such demoralized patients. Indeed, it is precisely the point at which they can safely, confidently, and therapeutically enter the cramped and darkening world of the patient.

EDUCATION AND PREVENTION

Helpers without professional training can not only learn much about HIV but can, often in crucial intervals, serve well as teachers about this complex of illnesses both to patients and their families and friends. Perhaps no illness has suffered from politicization as much as AIDS. Counselors cannot operate effectively as sources of strength if they involve themselves as ideologues or advocates for any markedly partisan viewpoint, such as the notion that AIDS is a divine punishment or, on the other hand, that promiscuous sexual activity is a guaranteed right. What they must stand up for consistently is the suffering patients in as humane a way as possible as they battle this always fatal attack on their often young lives. If they are well-informed on the subject, they can provide educational information that not only clears the air but that, with many patients, may prove beneficial in their dealings with their illness.

Education is also necessary if counselors are asked to play any significant role in the prevention of HIV disease. Behavior change is an important component in lessening the spread of this illness, which is still found, almost exclusively, among homosexual males, intravenous drug users, bisexuals, and persons of Haitian nationality. The risk of contracting AIDS is minimal among monagamous partners and its spread among heterosexuals, unless they have multiple partners or use contaminated needles in the use of drugs, has not increased dramatically, although at one point there were ominous predictions in this regard. Indeed, persons who do not engage in high-risk sexual or drug-taking behavior are not at great risk. This is an important fact in educating persons about the dangers of AIDS.

Studies have shown that dangerous sexual and other practices can be modified by programs of education that result in behavioral changes on the part of those individuals who might otherwise place themselves at risk. Knowledge about AIDS is the most important motivating factor in assisting people in changing their behavior patterns. This cannot be merely theoretical but must be applied in the particular world of the individual. A recurrent "optimistic bias" has been identified in many persons who engage, for example, in dangerous sexual behavior. Even if they are educated about the nature of AIDS and its transmission, they believe that they know how to control their sexual lives already, that they will make prudent choices of partners, and that they will be spared the consequences of infection. Educators must be able to pierce this rationalized defense if long-term permanent modification of their activity is to occur.

While science continues to search for a cure for AIDS, expectations that this will be discovered soon—so that AIDS will be transformed, somewhat like diabetes, into a manageable chronic illness—must be examined realistically. It has been found that persons at risk who choose to believe that a cure will be developed before they are infected do not modify their sexual activity but, instead, increase their sexual partners and continue to engage in high-risk sexual practices. While peer support for change has proven effective, the complexities of network relationships in the gay community are not fully understood. What educators and counselors wish to assist persons with is the internalization of their convictions about their control of their behavior.

Impulse control, supported by resources of a social and religious nature, has, not surprisingly, proven effective in reducing the risk of infection. It is significant that nonprofessionals, while not capable of giving detailed instruction on the medical aspects of prevention, do often represent the stable traditions of work, family affiliation, and religious conviction that can be the source of effective motivation in assisting persons at risk to understand and to make changes of a positive nature in their way of life.

Commonsense helpers may also be able to help persons avoid the kinds of rationalizations that are ultimately self-defeating. One of these is the role of the *innocent victim* that, underscored emotionally, politically, and sometimes even in the popular arts, is a serious misconception. While the nonprofessionals will ordinarily attempt to refer resistant individuals for specialized help, their direct common sense is often effective in helping people to assess their lives and their life-styles realistically. Again, this is best achieved through approaches that do not make the other person more defensive but, because they are characterized by compassionate understanding, allow them to see more clearly into themselves.

References

Counselors will find many articles and reports on articles about AIDS in the daily media. These should be seen in the context of scientific research which proceeds by small increments of knowledge. Scientific articles add, as professional readers understand, to our knowledge but seldom revolutionize understandings in and of themselves. They must be appreciated in relationship to the mass of related research that is going on at the same time. It is helpful to be conversant with the *AIDS Update* supplied every year by the Center for Disease Control in Atlanta. While much of its content is technical, there are fine articles in the *AIDS Primer* published by the American Psychiatric Association as part of their AIDS Education Project under the title HIV, ARC, AIDS.

Helpful reflections on AIDS in relationship to the history of plagues are found in the Spring 1988 issue of *The American Scholar*. Susan Sontag brilliantly meditates on the political dimensions of the subject in *AIDS and Its Metaphors* in *The New York Review of Books,* October 27, 1988. Nonprofessional counselors will benefit from reading philosophical and historical pieces almost as much as from reading more technical presentations on this subject.

AIDS Primer. AIDS Education Project. Washington, D.C.: American Psychiatric Association.

Cavenaugh, S., Clark, D., and Gibbons, R. "Core Symptoms of Depression in Medical and Psychiatric Patients," *Journal of Nervous and Mental Disease* (1983), 171: 705.

Cohen-Cole, S. A. and Stoudemire, A. "Major Depression and Physical Illness: Special Considerations in Diagnosis and Biologic Treatment," in Oken, D. (ed.), *Consultation Liaison Psychiatry, The Psychiatric Clinics of North America.* Philadelphia: W. B. Saunders Company, 1987.

Curran, J. W. "The Epidemiology and Prevention of AIDS," *Annals of Internal Medicine* (1985), 103:657–62.

de Haes, J.C.J.M., Van Knippenberg, F.C.E. "The Quality of Life of Cancer Patients: A Review of the Literature." *Social Science and Medicine* (1985), 20:809.

Emmons, C., Joseph, J., Kessler, R., et al. "Psychosocial Predictors of Reported Behavior Change in Homosexual Men at Risk for AIDS." *Health Education Quarterly* (1986), 13:331–45.

Fauci, A. S., Macher, A. M., Longo, D.L., et al. 1984. "Acquired Immunodeficiency Syndrome: Epidemiologic, Clinical, Immunologic and Therapeutic Considerations." *Annals of Internal Medicine* (1984), 100:92.

Group for the Advancement of Psychiatry. The Sexual Practice History. Washington, D.C.: GPO, 1984.

Holland, J.C.B. and Tross, S. "Psychological and Neuropsychiatric Sequellae of the Acquired Immune Difficiency Syndrome, and Related Disorders," *Annals of Internal Medicine,* (1985) 103:760–64.

Joseph, J.G., Montgomery, S.B., Emmons, C.A., et al. "Perceived Risk of AIDS: Assessing the Behavioral and Psychological Consequences in a Cohort of Gay Men," *Journal of Applied Social Psychology* (1987).

Klerman, G.L. "Depression in the Medically Ill," *The Psychiatric Clinics of North America* 1981, 4:301–18.

Lester, Bonnie. *Women and AIDS: A Practical Guide for Those Who Help Others.* New York: Continuum, 1989.

Morris, J. N., Suisa, S., Sherwood, S., et al. "Last Days: A Study of the Quality of Life of Terminally Ill Cancer Patients, *Journal of Chronic Diseases* 1986, 39:47.

Ostrow, D.G. "Issues and Analysis: Psychiatric Implications of AIDS. *Masters Psychiatry* (1985), 1:21–23.

———. "A Psychiatric Overview of AIDS." *International Journal of Neuroscience* (1986), 29:1–13.

———, Joseph, J., Monjan, A., et al. "Psychosocial Aspects of AIDS Risk," *Psychopharmacology Bulletin* (1986), 22:678–83.

———, Joseph, J., Monjan, A., and Phair, J. "Psychological Correlates of AIDS Risk and HTLV-111 Exposure," *Proceedings Annual Meeting American College Neuropsycho-pharmacology* (1985), 9.

Selik, R. M., Haverkos, H. W., and Curran, J. W. "Acquired Immune Deficiency Syndrome (AIDS) Trends in the United States, 1978–1982," *American Journal of Medicine* (1984), 76:493.

Spikes, J. and Holland, J. C. B. "The Physicians Response to the Dying Patient," in Strain, J. J. and Grossman, S., *Psychological Care of the Medically Ill: A Primer in Liaison Psychiatry.* New York: Appleton-Century-Crofts, 1975, pp. 138–48.

Additional General Bibliography

Burgess, A. W. and Holmstrom, L. L. "Rape Trauma Syndrome," *American Journal of Psychiatry* (1974), 131:981.

Brownmiller, S.: *Against Our Will: Men, Women and Rape.* Simon & Schuster, New York, 1975.

Farber, M. *Human Sexuality.* New York: Macmillan Publishing Co., 1985.

Frank, E. "Frequency of Sexual Dysfunction in 'Normal' Couples," *New England Journal of Medicine* (1978), 299:111.

Furlow, W. L., ed. "Male Sexual Dysfunction," *Urologic Clinics of North America* (1981), 8:1.

Harlow, H. F. "The Nature of Love." *American Psychologist* (1958), 13:673.

Herman, J., and Hirschman, L. "Families at Risk for Father–Daughter Incest," *American Journal of Psychiatry* (1981), 138:967.

Henderson, D.J. "Incest," in Sadock, B. J., Kaplan, H. I., and Freedman, A. M., eds., *The Sexual Experience*. Baltimore: Williams and Wilkins, 1976, p. 415.

Kinsey, A. C., Pomeroy, W. B., Martin, C. F., and Gebbard, P. H. *Sexual Behavior in the Human Female*. Philadelphia: W. B. Saunders, 1953.

Kirkpatrick, M. *Women's Sexual Development*. New York: Plenum, 1980.

Marmor, J., ed. *Homosexual Behavior*. New York: Basic Books, 1980.

Masters, W. H., and Johnson, V. E. *Human Sexual Response*. Boston: Little, Brown & Co., 1966.

Mooney, J., Ehrhardt, A. A. *Man and Woman/Boy and Girl*. Baltimore: Johns Hopkins University Press, 1972.

Sadock, B. J., Kaplan, H. I., and Freedman, A. M., eds. *The Sexual Experience*. Baltimore: Williams & Wilkins, 1976.

Sherfey, M. J. *The Nature and Evolution of Female Sexuality*. New York: Random House, 1972.

Stewart, B. D., Hughes, C., Frank, E., Andersen, B., Kendall, K., and West, D. "The Aftermath of Rape: Profiles of Immediate and Delayed Treatment Seekers," *Journal of Nervous and Mental Disease* (1987), 175:90.

Stoller, R. J. *Sex and Gender*. New York: Science House, 1968.